Advance Praise for *Why Nations Rise*

"Manjari Chatterjee Miller tells a sophisticated story about why some rising powers like China become great powers, while others like India do not. She maintains that how a state thinks about its role in the world matters as much as its material capabilities. This book is essential reading for anyone interested in understanding the dynamics of the emerging multipolar international system."
—**John J. Mearsheimer**, R. Wendell Harrison Distinguished Service Professor of Political Science, University of Chicago

"In *Why Nations Rise*, Miller explores how rising powers become great ones. Armed with a provocative argument and comparative case studies, this book makes the case for the critical role of the narratives that states hold about what it means to be a great power and the proactive steps they take to become one. Anyone interested in power transitions should read this book."
—**M. Taylor Fravel**, Arthur and Ruth Sloan Professor of Political Science, Director, Security Studies Program, Massachusetts Institute of Technology

"Manjari Miller's comparison of national narratives throughout history provides unique context for the contrast of Chinese great power ambitions and Indian reticence. For scholars the inclusion of national narratives in the determination of state power is a significant contribution. For policymakers the lesson is clear: the 'India card' that matters most in the larger geopolitical equilibrium of Asia is for India to succeed on its own terms."
—**Michael J. Green**, Senior Vice President for Asia and Japan Chair, Center for Strategic and International Studies

Why Nations Rise

Narratives and the Path to Great Power

MANJARI CHATTERJEE MILLER

OXFORD
UNIVERSITY PRESS

OXFORD
UNIVERSITY PRESS

Oxford University Press is a department of the University of Oxford. It furthers
the University's objective of excellence in research, scholarship, and education
by publishing worldwide. Oxford is a registered trade mark of Oxford University
Press in the UK and certain other countries.

Published in the United States of America by Oxford University Press
198 Madison Avenue, New York, NY 10016, United States of America.

© Oxford University Press 2021

Library of Congress Cataloging-in-Publication Data
Names: Miller, Manjari Chatterjee, 1976– author.
Title: Why nations rise : narratives and the path to great power /
by Manjari Chatterjee Miller.
Description: New York, NY : Oxford University Press, 2021. |
Includes bibliographical references and index. |
Contents: Why nations rise...or remain reticent—
The active rise of the United States—The reticence
of the Netherlands—Meiji Japan and Cold War Japan : a vignette of
rise and reticence—The active rise of China—The reticence of India—
Thoughts on power transitions, past and future.
Identifiers: LCCN 2020037918 (print) | LCCN 2020037919 (ebook) |
ISBN 9780190639938 (hardback) | ISBN 9780197558935 (paperback) |
ISBN 9780190639969 (oso) | ISBN 9780190639952 (epub) | ISBN 9780190639945 (updf)
Subjects: LCSH: Great powers—History. | World politics—19th century. |
World politics—20th century. | World politics—21st century.
Classification: LCC JZ1310 .M55 2021 (print) |
LCC JZ1310 (ebook) | DDC 327.1/12—dc23
LC record available at https://lccn.loc.gov/2020037918
LC ebook record available at https://lccn.loc.gov/2020037919

DOI: 10.1093/oso/9780190639938.001.0001

1 3 5 7 9 8 6 4 2

Paperback printed by LSC Communications, United States of America
Hardback printed by Bridgeport National Bindery, Inc., United States of America

For Jeff, my best friend and biggest cheerleader. I love you.

CONTENTS

ACKNOWLEDGMENTS

"Writing a book is lonely. No one writes a book alone." These words were written by the children's author Kelly Barnhill in a book that my ten-year-old daughter insisted I read. It was a great story but it is this sentence, written in Barnhill's acknowledgments, that resonated most with me as I finished my own manuscript. The research for this book took me nearly a decade. There were days I was lonely as I holed myself up to write and think. There were days I was obsessive when I couldn't get the arguments to fall into clear patterns. There were days I was joyous as I discovered new nuggets of information. There were also days I nearly gave up. But I didn't. Because I had help—from people generous with their time, their knowledge, their patience, and their love. Here they are, in no particular order:

- Renata Keller, Chris Dietrich, and Justin Hart for helping me discover American history.
- Kanti Bajpai, Thomas Christensen, Erez Manela, Steven Miller, Rajesh Basrur, Jia Qingguo, and Rohan Mukherjee for inviting me to air my thoughts at various stages of the manuscript. Michael Laffan, Paul Kennedy, and Charles Maier for their time, and fascinating conversations. Paul, thank you for the word "reticent!"
- Dick Samuels for encouraging me to study Japan and providing many suggestions of how to start. Mike Green and Dave Leheny for listening and providing further input.
- Michal Ben-Josef Hirsch for directing me to an obscure paper with one extremely interesting line about the Netherlands which sparked my research. Henk te Velde for helping me discover the Netherlands, and introducing me to many colleagues, including my fantastic research assistant Corné Smit. Corné for your patient work and translations. The many Dutch academics who

generously shared their time and knowledge particularly, Ben Schoenmaker, Maartje Jense, James Kennedy, and Vincent Kuitenbrouwer.

- Stacie Goddard, Thomas Berger, Henk te Velde, Kate Sullivan de Estrada, Josh Shifrinson, Andrew May, and Jorge Heine among others for an incredibly important and useful book conference which refined my thinking. Kate for also being an amazing friend and gnome-maker-in-arms.
- My posse of fabulous female colleagues at Pardee—Kaija, Shamiran, Jay, R1 (Rachel Nolan), R2 (Rachel Brulé), and Noora—for helping me with wine zooms, crazy group chats, and all-round support which enabled me to finish the book in the middle of a pandemic. Goats all the way ladies!
- Kevin Gallagher for being a rock star mentor, listening, and forwarding me pertinent articles.
- Think tankers and academics in Beijing, Nanjing, and Shanghai for talking with me and helping me understand. Indian academics and government officials, particularly IFS officers, for sparing time for me in their busy schedules, and for their candidness. Chen Ting and Rishika Chauhan for helping me gather data.
- David Barboza for encouraging me to write a book that would bridge the academia-policy gap. Katie Bacon for forcing me to explain my writing—even when I didn't want to.
- Dave McBride for helping me work with OUP.
- The Smith Richardson Foundation for making the research for this book possible.
- My two children, Neer and Namya, for making me feel like the luckiest mom on the planet. (Look kids, mommy *did* get the book done!)
- My husband Jeff, for everything. Because that's what he is to me.

Why Nations Rise . . . or
Remain Reticent

What are rising powers? Why do some countries become rising powers, but not others? What does it mean for a country to rise? Today one can find a thriving industry of newspapers, articles, and books on China and India, the two countries that are regularly referred to as "rising powers." Yet when I recently asked a noted British journalist who had just published a book on India what he thought a rising power was—and why India was one—he seemed taken aback. He paused for a minute before offering that it was "probably" a country with some mix of influence and power—both economic and military.[1] But when I tried to pin him down on how much power and what kind of influence, he couldn't clarify. It seemed, as he acknowledged during the conversation, that one just simply *knew* when a country was rising. To be fair to him, these questions only occurred to me many years after I first began studying China and India. To show why, I'll explain my early experience of studying these two countries.

Back then, in the early 2000s, most people I told about my research could not fathom my interest. Indians were baffled that I wasn't concentrating my energies solely on India, my country of birth, and even more puzzled why, if anyone were to pick another country to study at all, it would not be Japan or the United States—clearly more important countries. Chinese friends and acquaintances were surprised because they were unaccustomed to an Indian studying Mandarin or taking an interest in modern China, and some politely indicated that they were not flattered by any comparison between the two. And Americans seemed bewildered on two fronts: that I was studying the two countries and that I was comparing them to each other; what, after all, did the two have in common?

But by 2012, when I was on the cusp of finishing a book about both countries and their curiously similar response to the historical legacy of colonialism (*Wronged by Empire*), people's attitudes toward my research had changed

Why Nations Rise. Manjari Chatterjee Miller, Oxford University Press (2021). © Oxford University Press.
DOI: 10.1093/oso/9780190639938.003.0001

radically. Far from bewilderment and questions, I now began to receive hearty congratulations from Americans, Indians, and Chinese, who commended my study of a "hot" topic. And indeed comparing the two had, by this time, become fashionable: not only were both countries now being studied, contrasted, and compared in the West, but they were also being studied, contrasted, and compared as *rising powers*. Moreover, they were treated as a special category of actors—the United States and the world feared China's rise, while wondering how to use India's rise to counter the coming *Pax Sinica*.

Yet I had this nagging suspicion that, despite the attention to *both* as rising powers, they were different—China was embracing its rise in a way that India was not. Recently, I looked back through my notes and documents to understand exactly when I came to this idea that China and India were very different kinds of rising powers. I eventually found a short outline from 2009. It consisted of notes for a précis I had been invited to present at a conference titled "Rising States and Global Order" at the Princeton Institute of International and Regional Studies (PIIRS) at Princeton University. The outline had some very preliminary thoughts based on peripheral data I had gathered in the course of conducting fieldwork for *Wronged by Empire*. In it, I had written, "India's current ideological chaos (which nearly shut down the nuclear deal) makes for striking contrast with China. Unlike India, China is acutely conscious of its international position, and has made a strategic effort to formulate and reformulate a 'grand ideology' that outlines its international image. Although India *says* it is a rising power it is [*sic*] yet to *believe* it." My commentator at that conference was the political scientist John Mearsheimer. He asked me, if what I was implying was correct, what could this tell us about rising powers and their international strategy or behavior? In other words, why did this difference between China and India, if it existed, matter? I did not have an answer for him at that conference, but I'm still grateful for his question, because it sent me on the intellectual journey that led to this book.

In 2013, having finished my first book, and now bombarded with references to the rise of China and India, I acted on my nagging thoughts. I began scanning Chinese and Indian newspapers. Narratives of China as a rising power were also reflected in Chinese newspapers which, like Western newspapers, were full of articles and op-eds with references to China's rise, and what it meant for China to rise. These narratives discussed what kind of great power China would become, how it should respond to its changing environment, what its relationship with the status quo power, the United States, should be like, and whether China's rise would be contested. In short, they were chock-full of stories about the story of China's rise. On the other hand, when I turned to read Indian newspapers I found no such stories. There were very few narratives that asked or answered these questions.

I was deeply puzzled by this. The world now habitually referred to both as rising powers; therefore, shouldn't they both also think of *themselves* as rising powers? After all, I knew from my past research that it was not that Indians did *not* think of themselves as a great country and a great civilization. But, I also noticed, India consistently faced complaints that it didn't *act* as a great power.[2] Instead, it was always "emerging but never arriving."[3]

I took a trip to India that summer to explore a little more and to ask government officials what they thought of India as a rising power. My interviews—some conducted at the highest levels of Indian foreign-policy decision-making—amazed me. Indian officials I spoke with were deeply uncomfortable with the label "rising power," and seemed to engage in little strategizing about how to respond to India's changing environment or to deal with the consequences of its rise. In short, I found that although India was rapidly increasing in both military and economic strength, Indian officials did not seem to have consistent and concrete narratives about what that could mean, how India could use its rise for leverage, or what kind of great power India could become. Moreover, I found foreign policy officials in *other* countries deeply frustrated by India's behavior on the international stage. Although dubbed a rising power, India seemed to have a reputation of not living up to the role.[4] Meanwhile, China's behavior alarmed these same officials, who were convinced of the coming China threat and the challenge it posed to the liberal order.

These differences raised a whole host of questions. Was China unique, I wondered? Was it, in fact, unusual for rising powers to both believe and behave as if they were rising? Was India's path actually the normal road for a rising power? And what did it really mean to behave like a rising power or to have narratives about that rise? Contemporary sources in both academia and the media were of limited help. "Rising power" was an oft-used term, but no one could really identify exactly which country today was indisputably a rising power, and why. Only one fact was agreed upon: some amount of increasing military and economic power was indeed important. This made sense; how, after all, could a country be a rising power if the component of "power" was missing? But beyond that, there was little agreement. Particularly confusing, the very element that identified them as rising powers—increasing military and economic power relative to the established great power of the day—was also used to identify their *behavior* as rising powers. Thus, a country *was* a rising power if we observed that it had increasing economic and military power, and it *behaved* as a rising power if it increased its economic and military power, resulting in an unhelpful tautology.

So I decided to look to history to see if with the benefit of hindsight I could better understand our expectations of China and India, and in doing so, clarify what we mean by and should expect of rising powers. There are deep divisions among international relations scholars, but even the most argumentative of them would agree that rising powers are a category of actors that can tip the world toward war or toward peace. What could we learn from historical cases of countries that possessed this quality and others that we associate with rising powers today? What patterns could we find? Also, and crucially, how did we come to think of a rising power as a special, and often dangerous, kind of actor in international relations? While this thought has long historical roots—thousands of years ago, Thucydides's *History of the Peloponnesian War* declared, "it was the rise of Athens, and the fear this instilled in Sparta that made war inevitable"—it also has modern theoretical roots. To understand the rising powers of China and India—and why we think of them as rising powers—grasping this theoretical foundation (and its problems) is essential.

What Do We Know of Rising Powers?

The phrase "rising power" is, today, a ubiquitous term. It is used indiscriminately by academics, policymakers, and the media to describe not just China and India, but countries as disparate as South Africa,[5] Turkey,[6] Brazil,[7] Iran,[8] and Russia.[9] Despite the popularity of the concept, however, research on understanding rising powers as a category of actors is sparse: why we perceive some countries but not others to be rising is unclear, and sometimes contradictory.

Briefly, the theory of power transitions—termed "one of the most successful structural theories in world politics"[10]—treats these countries as a distinct and special category of game-changing actors in the world. Power transition theorists argue that "the differential growth in the power of various states in the system causes a fundamental redistribution of power in the system."[11] They believe that in any international system—that is, a world composed of great, middle, and small powers—there eventually rises a challenger country. The challenger, or rising power, is dissatisfied with how "goods" are distributed in this system. ("Goods," in this case, mean the acquisition of power along with the rules and regulations, both formal and informal, that govern our international order.) According to power transition theorists, a challenger country seeks not just to overturn how power is distributed, but also to create and impose its own rules instead of those that were imposed by the reigning great power. Thus, the rise of this challenger, more often than not, results in conflict and even war with the established great power. This is called a "recurring pattern" in world politics.[12] This school of thought seeks to answer meta-questions about war and peace, conflict and cooperation, stability and instability in the international system.[13] Power transition theorists rarely take the time to examine the particularities of specific rising powers, their specific trajectories, and their propensity for conflict.[14]

A more in-depth scrutiny of rising powers and their behavior has been undertaken, although implicitly, by historians—the classic example of this is Paul Kennedy's *The Rise and Fall of the Great Powers*—as well as political scientists who seek to understand great powers and great power behavior.[15] Finally, there have been many books focused either on a single country that also happens to be a rising power, usually China or India,[16] or on comparisons of the rises of India and China to assess the strengths and weaknesses of each and the obstacles faced by them as they gain power.[17]

This work on rising powers has relied on two fundamental assumptions about countries that are rising.

The first is that rising powers can be identified and compared primarily by measuring their relative material capabilities.[18] According to this assumption, countries rise because their economic and military power relative to that of the status quo power (the great power of the day) increases sufficiently to pose a challenge to the latter. Power transition theorists emphasize that since it is the relative power of the challenger vis-à-vis the defender that determines the likelihood of war, increasing economic and military power is, therefore, the most important indication of a state emerging as a rising power. Sometimes, a rising power is also assumed to be a country that is increasing, or aspiring to increase, its "soft" co-optive power.[19] Accordingly, discussions of rising powers will often include soft-power measures such as influence in global affairs[20] and visibility.[21] On this premise, scholars have dissected, for example, whether or not China and India have been successful in wielding soft power and how this advances or stymies each country's rise.[22]

The second assumption is that a rising power is a country that is likely revisionist; that is, it is unwilling to accept a position of subordinate power in the way "goods are distributed in the international system"[23] and will therefore eventually challenge the existing international order—and the great powers who maintain it. War is likely when a power transition occurs, not just because a rising power gains approximate power parity with the great power defender, but also because a rising power is also a country that is dissatisfied with the status quo. Thus, the challenger or rising power is expected to increase its hard and soft power relative to the status quo power, and almost by definition to engage in revisionism, often expressed as expansionism, as it rises.

Why Is What We Know about Rising Powers Problematic?

As it turns out, using these assumptions to identify when or why a state is rising is less useful in the real world than the theoretical one—for a variety of reasons. Let's start by looking at relative material capabilities as a measure of which state is a bona fide rising power. Some accounts today focus only on India and China as rising powers, while others focus on the BRICs (Brazil, Russia, India, China) as a group. The BRICs acronym was created in 2001 by an analyst at Goldman Sachs.[24] In doing so, Goldman Sachs, in effect, concocted a group of rising powers, and differentiated them from other states simply on the basis of their rapid economic growth and their exclusion from the governance structures of the world economy.[25] But Brazil's status as a rising power can be questioned, as can Russia's. Brazil is not a nuclear weapons state, an arguably necessary precondition to be called a rising power today. Russia could reasonably be termed a declining rather than a rising power. The newer iteration of BRICS now includes South Africa. Yet, apart from its myriad other problems, South Africa was one of only eleven countries that actually saw a drop in its life expectancy between 1990 and 2013.[26] Moreover, South Africa voluntarily relinquished its nuclear weapons program, weakening the claim that it could be termed a rising power. Even China's rise, predicated on its military power relative to the United States, has been debated. China's power as a proportion of US power is increasing, but the absolute advantage in capabilities continues to be in favor of the United States.[27] While a recent RAND report suggests that although China has improved its capabilities in many areas, it continues to trail the United States in both military hardware and operational skills.[28]

Neither is it clear that a rising power is always a country that is inevitably going to challenge the status quo power. A rising power is often dubbed expansionist. Expansionism, typically understood as military and geographic encroachment[29] (and less typically as the "expansion of political interests"[30]) is seen as both the natural outgrowth of the rising power's increase in material power[31] and as negative behavior—reinforcing the general conviction that rising powers engage in revisionism. This is problematic for many reasons. The concept of expansionism as applied to rising powers is both narrow (military assertiveness and geographic conquest) and muddy (an "expansion of political interests" could also apply to the foreign policy behavior of many states in general, rather than to rising powers as a special category of actors). This concept does not allow us to capture the distinctiveness that should mark the behavior of a special category of actors, and it also does not allow us to distinguish *between* rising powers. And expecting expansionism because a rising power is increasing its capabilities does not tell us when it will expand, why it will do so, or why, if ever, it would refrain.

China, for example, has been shown to be both conformist as well as revisionist, depending on the issue area.[32] Moreover, since both China and India are considered to be rising powers, they should have similar reputations for dissatisfaction with the current international system. But they do not. By and large, India is seen as a benign rising power, one whose rise is, unlike China's, conforming to the existing international order.[33] Yet just as China can be conformist as well as revisionist, so can India, and they often do not overlap in what areas of the international order they accept or reject—China has changed its stance on climate change, embracing the Paris Agreement, and has made conciliatory noises on the norm of Responsibility to Protect (R2P), to cite two examples, while India is a reluctant signatory to the Paris Agreement, and utterly rejects R2P. When rising powers have been acknowledged to engage in "supportive" as well as "predatory" behavior in terms of the international order, this has been predicated on the waxing or waning capabilities of the status quo power—that is, the rising power engages in behavior designed to strengthen rather than weaken the global position of the current great power.[34] This provides a useful reading of the rising power's strategy toward managing a great power, but does not speak to the general behavior of rising powers in the world order or why they rise.

Finally, equating a country's status as a rising power with the possession of material resources, i.e., military and economic power, ignores the social-relational aspect of a country's status.[35] If a state is seen to be rising, it is not *just* the increasing capabilities in of themselves that bestow that status. It is the *recognition* of those capabilities by external actors as a symbol of the state's rising power status. One way to understand this in context is to compare military expenditures as a percentage of gross domestic product (GDP) for states. We can see from these expenditures that it is not simply the expenditure per se that matters; it is also which countries are being compared. For example, in 2015, India's total military expenditure as a percentage of its GDP was 2.4% (a decrease from 3.6% in 1988). China's was a comparable 2.0% in 2015. In the same year, Mali's military expenditure was 2.4% (an increase from 2.2% in 1988), while Ecuador's was 2.5% (an increase from 1.5% in 1988).[36] Yet the latter countries are obviously not recognized as rising powers. For those who would argue this point and suggest that it is not percentage increases or decreases but rather the sum total of capabilities that matter, consider this: as of 2016, Germany ranks in the top ten countries globally for military strength,[37] yet it is rarely termed a rising power.

Either applying or adding the concept of "soft power" is also problematic. Soft power is an ambiguous, unmeasurable concept, and there is no agreement on what constitutes "influence" and how much of it a state needs to possess to be called a rising power. By some measures of soft power, Brazil could be said to punch above its weight in international regimes. Brazil enjoys a prominent position in the World Trade Organization (WTO) because of its skills of coalition building, "insider activism," and ability to manipulate the informal norms of the WTO, rather than because of its "commercial power."[38] Should this qualify it as a rising power, even though its military and economic power is not comparable to that of Russia, China, or India, let alone the status quo power, the United States?

China lacks soft power, and is acutely conscious of this lack.[39] Yet we accord it the status of a rising power.

Thus, power, either hard or soft, is an incomplete measure of a rising power. We are left, then, with "no commonly accepted definition of what an emerging or rising power is," and "no consistent indicators of what a rising state looks like."[40] What we can deduce from this established discussion on rising powers is that *while power is a necessary condition for a country to rise, and to be perceived as a rising power, it is certainly not sufficient.* So what *is* a rising power, and what does it mean for some countries, but not others, to rise?

Rethinking Rising Powers: Why Nations Rise (or Stay Reticent)

What *Is* a Rising Power?

There is a crucial fact that is assumed but left unstated when we talk of rising powers—*a rising power is a state that is rising to become, in the near future, a great power.* After all, the material capabilities of many countries are constantly increasing relative to others. Not all of these countries are dubbed rising powers, although they may indeed be rising within a regional or even international context. The term "rising power" is very specifically intended to capture a special category of actors—those who are in the near future expecting to join the ranks of the great powers and eventually determine, as great powers do, the structure, major processes, and general direction of the international system.[41] Moreover, "rising power" is a modern term; a century ago, English-language newspapers referred not to "rising powers" but to countries that were becoming great powers.[42]

Consequently, we can say that rising powers are countries that *should* be rising to become great powers. And to understand them, we can first establish our expectations of a great power. Fortunately, the international relations literature is prolific on the question of how we can recognize a great power. The most commonly accepted definition of a great power utilizes military capabilities alone. A great power is one that holds at least 5[43] to 10 percent of global military power.[44] The Correlates of War project, which is the data set most widely used to identify major powers, includes power capabilities measured in terms of total population, urban population, iron and steel production, fuel consumption, military personnel, and military expenditures.[45] Yet because capabilities alone can result in mis-measurement of great powers,[46] academics have added both the element of behavioral choice and external recognition to the definition of a great power. Thus, in addition to possessing unusually high relative capabilities, a great power's interests are global rather than regional,[47] and it is recognized both formally and informally by other states as a great power.[48] But even within the category of great powers there are tiered differences. Some countries are major powers, others are greater powers, and still others are superpowers. These differences can be attributed not only to the distribution of material capabilities, relative to other powers in the system,[49] but, because "statistics and military budgets aren't everything," also to their behavior in terms of projection of interests and reputation.[50] Not every major power will become a greater power, and nor will every greater power become a superpower. There are tiers of great powers.

Thus, we can logically juxtapose two important elements from the great power literature in order to construct an understanding of rising powers. A rising power, or a country that is rising to become a great power, should increase its relative military and economic power, begin to globalize its interests, and begin to gain recognition as a great power-to-be. There can be differences *among* rising powers; these differences can be attributed not just to capabilities, but also to the powers' behavior; that is, some countries rise *enough* to be on the path to great power, while others may rise, but only in a material sense.

Increasing relative military and economic power is observable. But how do we perceive a rising power globalizing its interests and gaining recognition? When a rising power perceives its interests to be globalizing, it attempts to acquire global authority. That is, when a rising power perceives its self-defined national interests to be increasing in scope (expanding beyond the regional or local) and depth (in complexity and breadth of affected issues), we can observe it taking on more global authority and responsibility suited to its changing interests. But the notion of "authority and responsibility" is not one that is defined by the rising power. *Rather, it is set by the established great power norms of the day*. In any given time period, global society has an example of great power behavior in the status quo power(s) of the day, as well as in norms and institutions (or international order) established by that great power. Early 19th-century Russia gives us an example of a rising power that did not meet the great power norms of the day. Russia had the material capabilities to be recognized as a great power. However, its illiberal system of governance and resulting modus operandi in international politics marked it as glaringly different from the "first-class powers."[51] As such, European states continued to harbor doubts about its entry into the ranks of the great powers. In order to gain this recognition, Russia attempted to adopt European great power behaviors—"having ambassadors plenipotentiary, being a guarantor power, participating in conferences, gaining a *droit de regard* . . . that were explicitly associated with great powers" of the time.[52]

Thus, a country that is rising to be a great power attempts to take on authority, and actively tries to shape its role in the international system *in the fashion of the current great powers*. This suggests, crucially, that a rising power is *not revisionist* (at least initially). It is, instead, accommodational. It has to *accept* and conform to the current international order before it can reject it.[53]

The acquisition of global authority is intricately linked to the rising power's quest for recognition. Only when a rising power conforms to great power norms will it be able to shape *recognition*—both internally and externally—of it as a country that is on the path to become a great power. Thus, a rising power also actively attempts to shape both domestic and international perceptions of its position as a great power-to-be. External recognition, a key feature of great powers, is an element that is bestowed by international society, contingent on both established capabilities and proven global interests. Without these two, external recognition would presumably be nonexistent. In effect, we know a great power when we see one. But not only is external recognition, as we have seen, more ambiguous (predicated on material capabilities) and risky (assumptions of revisionism) for rising powers, in effect necessitating a response,[54] but we can also posit that *internal* recognition is just as important as *external* recognition for these countries to gain domestic support as their international position changes.

But here is the nub: just as there are differences between great powers, there are differences between rising powers. If a country seeks to increase its relative material power without attempting either to acquire global authority or to court both external and internal recognition of itself as a great power in the making, *it is unlikely to become a great power*. Countries that engage in all of these behaviors are *active* rising powers—they are actively rising to become great powers. Countries that engage only in increasing their material power are *reticent* powers—they will not rise to become great powers unless they engage in the other two behaviors.

Thus, a country rising to be a great power—an active power—not only begins to acquire relative military and economic power, but also begins to actively acquire global authority by acting in accordance with great power norms, and, simultaneously, begins to actively court internal and external recognition as a great power-to-be. It is consequently an accommodational power.

Active powers may eventually become *activist* powers, that is, what we think of as revisionist powers, but they need to *first* acknowledge, show themselves to play by, and master the rules *before* they can gainsay them. And reticent powers need not stay reticent. If they eventually acquire the other two behaviors, they will become active powers. And activist powers are not born of military and economic power, they are made. As we will see in this book, some countries may indeed have the material strength to both globalize authority and shape recognition, according to the great power norms of the day, but may still not display the will to do so. Reticent powers do not suddenly embark on the path to become active powers.

So we come to a very important question: why do some countries actively rise while others remain reticent? Because rising to become a great power is a *process*. This process encompasses not simply material might—that is, the requisite military and economic power—or geopolitics or opportunity, but also a particular type of narratives, narratives about how to become a great power according to the prevalent norms. These narratives are as integral as material power to the process of active rising. Countries that undergo this process are both active and accommodational. Countries that do not complete this process stay reticent. To understand where these narratives come from and why they matter for rising powers, we need to look at a concept that I call "idea advocacy."

Idea Advocacy: A Marketplace of Narratives

As we will eventually see through cases in this book, rising to become a great power is a process—active powers develop, in addition to their material power, "idea advocacy" or narratives about *how* to become a great power. A reticent power does not, and may even reject such notions. These narratives—or the lack thereof—are a key difference in the behavior between active and reticent powers.

Idea advocacy can be understood as the generation of new ideas and recombination of existing ideas by the elites in a rising power to form new narratives about the country's appropriate behavior as a great power-to-be. These new narratives, in conjunction with a rising power's increasing capabilities, drive the power to acquire global authority and shape recognition of its rise. The philosopher Max Weber once said of great powers, "At a minimum, in order to be a great power, a power has to think of itself in terms of being great, of having an historical task."[55] A country rising to *become* a great power has to think of itself as a great power-to-be, has to display awareness that its position in international politics is changing, and yes, has to set itself a historical task.

The concept of idea advocacy itself is deeply rooted in international relations, and can be traced to a theoretical concept called "idea entrepreneurship." To understand the concept, we need to break apart the phrase and understand each component separately.

In international relations, ideas can be beliefs that are held and expressed by individuals and groups or beliefs that are embraced by institutions, influencing their attitudes and behaviors.[56] Ideas can also be beliefs about correct standards of behavior that are held by international society at large.[57] A set of beliefs (I will use ideas and beliefs interchangeably) can influence how a country behaves on the world stage by serving as "road maps" or "world views." These "maps" help a country make sense of the world and guide it in forming policy,[58] and can be expressed as important narratives. International relations experts continue to debate whether the material goals, or interests, of a state are distinct from its beliefs, or whether the beliefs themselves constitute the interests. One school of thought suggests that since foreign policy actors often have incomplete information and the absence of certainty about the consequence of their actions, they can rely on ideas to help choose strategies to further their goals.[59] In this mode of thinking, ideas impact *which* foreign policy interests are prioritized by actors. But there are others who argue that "interests cannot be separated from ideas about interests."[60] In other words, ideas can be causal, but can also be the foundation of interests in a variety of ways. This does not mean, however, that ideas themselves are simply static entities that affect the choices of actors. Ideas can change and can be affected not just by the political and economic conditions in which they operate, but even by the strategies and goals of the actors—a "feedback" effect as it were.[61] In fact, it is the very dynamic nature of ideas that can enable actors to conceptualize and reconceptualize the world.[62]

Entrepreneurship—broadly, the creation of a new or innovative venture by risk takers who achieve their goals in a new environment and destroy the status quo[63]—has rarely been studied in the context of the foreign policy or security of countries.[64] Instead theorists, particularly international political economists and institutionalists, have drawn connections between ideas and entrepreneurship to show how they can influence a country to institute reform. They have offered the concept of "political/ideational entrepreneurs" or agents who either institutionalize new ideas or recombine existing ideas to influence the political leadership.[65] Such agents are a source of innovation in that they put forward new or creative ideas, and seek to build support for those ideas.[66] There is a consensus that these idea entrepreneurs tend to be elites, i.e., those who can shape the political debate by framing issues, outlining problems, and ultimately influencing political agendas.[67] Foreign policy ideas are also often associated with elite individuals who emerge from formal and informal epistemic communities or bodies of experts or "knowledge regimes" and individual leadership.[68] The direction of entrepreneurial ideas can be top-down, where policymakers construct and communicate ideas and then mediate the public debates that ensue from these ideas, or bottom-up, where the interactions of activists and experts can produce ideas that are selected by policymakers.[69] Either way, a virtual marketplace of ideas[70] becomes crucial for policymaking. This is because as actors think about, discuss, and exchange their ideas about political action, countries learn from their rich discourse.[71] Particularly, this exchange of ideas leads them to interpret the available information, reinvent ideologies and identities, and even construct new institutions.[72]

We can take away from such theories three important elements: beliefs matter for the behavior of countries in the world; beliefs about world behavior predominantly come from entrepreneurial elites in the country; and beliefs are pluralistic and dynamic.

If we think back to power transition theories and the assumptions made about rising powers, we can see why idea advocacy expressed as narratives about how to become a great power would be particularly important. The root of power transition theories, as we have seen, is the dissatisfaction of rising powers with the distribution of goods in the international system. Crucially, though, this dissatisfaction has more to do with the *domestic beliefs* of the rising power about the distribution of goods in the international system than the distribution of goods itself. That is, it is not necessarily how the goods are actually distributed but rather how the rising power *believes* they are distributed that matters for power transitions, and possible future conflict with the status quo power. Thus, just as international society feels the need to "manage" a rising power and assess its satisfaction/dissatisfaction, a rising power manages its own rise through its beliefs about its changing status (including how to undertake "long-range planning" and form "a coherent strategic program"[73]). Rising powers, who are by definition in a precarious position in the international system—often seen as revisionist and as potential threats—are compelled to define their national and international priorities, and manage external and internal perceptions about them. External perceptions matter because great powers closely observe rising powers, and particularly their "legitimation strategies" (or explanations of their aims and motives), to assess threat.[74] And internal perceptions matter because rising powers need to satisfy domestic audiences.[75]

Narratives about attaining great power are not the same as grand strategies, although they are related to them.[76] Grand strategies are important for great powers[77] as they help them assess the limits of their capabilities, the prioritization of goals, and the most effective long-term pursuit of their interests. Similarly, actively rising powers or countries that are becoming great powers also develop grand strategies as they seek to change their status and gain power parity with the status quo power;[78] elites in rising powers care deeply about status as a moniker of great power, and develop strategies to attain it.[79] But grand strategies themselves are underpinned by ideas—it is either composed of core ideas[80] or influenced by them,[81] or both.[82] Thus, this is another reason that narratives of elite entrepreneurs about great power are important—they can contribute to the formulation of the grand strategies of a rising power.[83]

What kinds of beliefs about how the active rising power should behave comprise these narratives of elite entrepreneurs? Active powers have narratives that contain three distinct kinds of beliefs about how to attain great power.

First, the beliefs reconcile the material capability of the rising power with the constraints of the international order. In other words, as the material capabilities of a rising power increase, the beliefs focus attention on those goals that are now perceived to be materially attainable within the constraints set by the current order. Second, and related to the first, the beliefs acknowledge the current norms of great power, outline the rising power's acquiring of global authority/responsibility in that context, and outline its relationship with the status quo power(s), and the current international order. In this way, beliefs help the rising power actively shape its role in the international system and act like a great power-to-be in order to expand its influence. The beliefs acknowledge, therefore, what great power currently looks like, what the norms of the international order are, and the rising power's responsibilities in the context of that international order to eventually be recognized as a great power. And finally, the beliefs explain the purpose and goals of a rising power's increasing international involvement, helping to build support for that involvement both domestically and internationally.

The narratives of these beliefs can emanate from a set of elite individuals belonging to a formal or informal expert community or from a single influential leader.[84] Thus, the narratives may be initiated by leader elites and taken up by elites in expert communities, or they may be initiated by expert communities and taken up by individual leaders. It is important to emphasize here that this means that idea advocacy (or the advocacy of beliefs) is a *marketplace of narratives* about great power behavior rather than one single narrative about how to be a great power; that is, there may be differing, sometimes even contradictory, narratives about how to attain great power. But even differing narratives would recognize what the current norm of great power *is*, whether they advocated, modified, or rejected conformance with it. Eventually, as some narratives become more important than others, there may emerge a consensus among the elites about the rising power's behavior.

Reticent powers, on the other hand, do not have idea advocacy or these narratives about how to attain great power. They may, and often do, have beliefs about the world, their foreign policy, and their behavior. But these beliefs are not about *becoming a great power*. Lacking such narratives, these powers, even while increasing their economic and military power, remain reticent about their role on the world stage—they neither acquire global authority, nor do they actively seek to shape either internal or external perceptions about their role as a great power-to-be.

Rising to Become a Great Power: A Story about Stories

Before moving on to specific cases, let's take stock of what we've learned. Active rising powers are countries that increase their military and economic power and also change their behavior on the world stage—they globalize their authority by conforming to great power norms, and try to shape both internal and external recognition of their rise. They do so because they are going through a process of rising that includes not just material indicators but also narratives about great power. Reticent rising powers are countries that may increase their military and economic power but do not globalize their authority or try to shape recognition of the material change in their status. This is because the process of their (material) rise is incomplete—it includes material power, but does not include narratives about great power. Where narratives about becoming a great power come from—and why some countries develop them at all and others do not—is an interesting question which I will discuss briefly in the conclusion of this book. But for the purposes of the story here, which is to show how some countries begin taking on global authority and shaping recognition of their rise while others do not, we can look to history and find some fascinating patterns. What we find is that the elites in some countries at different periods of time had narratives about themselves as great powers-to-be. Because the narratives accompanied rising military and economic power, they were neither wishful thinking nor suicidal; in fact, they were often strategic—they took into account material and geopolitical constraints—and were cognizant of the dangers of overexpansion.[85] They also took into account the current notion of what it meant to be a great power, and conformed to that notion.

But the narratives were not the inevitable consequence of a country's rising military and economic power. Because what we find is that in the same time periods there were other countries *who also had increasing material power*—but they did not develop these narratives. The former—the active rising powers— pushed to acquire global authority and shape recognition of their rise, and this behavior accompanied these narratives. Eventually, these active powers were also activist powers and became great powers. The latter—reticent powers— did not acquire global authority and seemed indifferent to pushing for internal and external recognition of their role. They also had very different narratives about their international role, often even rejecting the current norms of great power. We can turn now to three different time periods, and six very different cases of active and reticent powers to illustrate these patterns. Classic theories of power transitions tell us that rising powers change as they become stronger.[86] This is a story about the process of change, and how material strength needs to be accompanied by narratives. My goal is to tell a story about the stories these countries tell, or fail to tell, about themselves.

Ideas of Great Power in the Late 19th Century

International relations has always been characterized by competition between powerful political entities. The mid- to late 19th century was no different in that respect. It was an era of European great power competition. The United

Kingdom, France, Spain, Austria-Hungary, and Russia all jockeyed for power and influence. Yet it was also an era like no other. The global economy was interconnected on an unprecedented scale, leading to an economic boom in Europe. There now existed a transoceanic and transcontinental trading and financial system that was based in western Europe. This, combined with the spread of free trade, faster transfers of technology, explosive growth in manufacturing, and better modes of transport, created a different kind of international order.[87] Moreover, the Industrial Revolution had led to technological changes which, in turn, powered a new kind of military and naval strength. Not only did European powers have greatly improved firepower (the advent of the breechloader, Gatling guns, Maxims, and light field artillery, for example), but their naval sea power was now extended from domination of the open seas to even inland waters, including major waterways.[88]

But perhaps most importantly, this era was distinct from any other before it because all of this great economic and military power and influence was anchored in place with a different kind of territorial conquest—colonies. Great powers in the 19th century were not just great powers. They were *colonial* great powers. A tiny percentage of the world's countries controlled a huge percentage of the world's territory and population. By 1878, European countries controlled 67 percent of global territory; by 1914, this had risen to 84 percent.[89] In the center of this colonial universe, Britain was the undisputed superpower. In 1830, the United Kingdom accounted for two-thirds of Europe's industrial growth and 9.5 percent of the world's manufacturing. By 1860, it produced 53 percent of the world's iron, and 50 percent of the world's coal and lignite. It consumed 50 percent of the world's raw cotton. Its energy consumption was five times that of either the United States or Prussia/Germany, and 155 times that of Russia. It accounted for one-fifth of the world's commerce and two-fifths of the manufactured goods trade.[90] Britain's jaw-dropping strength was in no small part due to its control over its colonies. Britain ruled over a full quarter of the land on Earth.[91]

It is important to understand that Britain and the other European countries of the time were great powers *because* they held colonies. To be a great power meant owning overseas colonies and having subsequent sway over the lives and deaths of millions of people. Industrialized Europe and the non-industrialized territories they controlled did not just have vast disparities between them in economic and military power. When a European country owned colonies, it also meant the establishment and maintenance of unequal economic relationships, bloody wars with and plunder of native populations, the introduction of diseases that decimated those populations, and the constant use of brutal force to retain the territories. As Theodore Roosevelt put it, colonization was "not merely a political but an ethnic conquest."[92] Thus, such conquest was accompanied by unabashed jingoism, proselytization, and a conviction of ethnic, cultural, and moral superiority—the idea that European civilization was civilization itself. Great power norms meant controlling colonies, and this was the accepted and acceptable idea of the day.

In this competitive world of great power jockeying and colonial acquisition, some countries by the late 19th century were indisputably rising to join the ranks of the great powers. In 1898, Lord Salisbury, the British prime minister, famously remarked that the world was now divided into "living" and "dying" powers.[93] These "living" powers—Japan and the United States, for example— were all rising powers, on the cusp of joining the ranks of the great powers. Not only were they rising in material terms, industrializing and growing their economies, investing in their navies, and modernizing their standing armies, relative to the established great powers of the day,[94] but they were beginning to take on more global authority and responsibility according to the current norms of great power, and to shape recognition of their rise. They were *active* powers. What did it mean to act according to the prevalent norms of great power? Again, great powers in the late 19th century were not simply great powers: they were *colonial* great powers because they had "impulses to emulate the established powers."[95] No wonder, then, that in the late 19th century the United States and Japan not only went to war (the United States with Spain; Japan with China and Russia), but also acquired colonies, and used the ownership of those colonies to shape internal and external recognition of their rise.

Political scientists generally equate rising power behavior of this time with the phrase *expansionism*,[96] missing the point entirely that not only was it a particular *kind* of expansion—colonial expansion, which meant taking on the "responsibility" of colonial territories and acquiring millions of overseas subjects—but it was also accommodational, in that it was perceived as *appropriate* great power behavior. Political scientists also tend to attribute expansionist behavior to opportunity acquired through material power. Some have argued that American expansionism heralded "an activist foreign policy," because the United States had the capacity to do so, and it now had leaders who perceived the opportunity.[97] Others have said that expansionist behavior was inevitable, the defensive consequence of a rising power's need to shore up its security.[98] However, the expansionist behavior at the turn of the 19th century that can be witnessed in countries like the United States and Japan was more complex than that. Both the United States and Japan *chose* to go down the path of colonial great power.

While the United States and Japan were certainly acquiring the capacity to globalize authority in the style of the great power *du jour*, not every country that increased its wealth in the late 19th century (and was provided opportunities to increase authority) *did* so. The case of the Netherlands provides us a different perspective. Post-1870, the Netherlands was becoming one of the richest countries in Europe—it industrialized later than the other European powers, but when it did, its economy boomed. Moreover, the Netherlands, which had acquired its colonies a century or more previously, was a colonial power, considered second only to Great Britain in its mastery of colonies. Indeed, its colonies were so immensely profitable that other countries, including France and even Britain, tried to emulate Dutch administration strategies in order to exploit their own colonies more efficiently. The Netherlands parlayed its wealth into expanding and improving its military and shoring up its defenses, both on land and at sea. But the Netherlands was surprisingly *reticent*. It was a power that was materially rising in important ways, but not an *active* power, as it passed up opportunities to expand its colonies further, bartered away existing colonial territories with little gains, and instead focused on consolidating its holdings in its colony of Indonesia. And while certainly the Netherlands was constrained by geopolitical threats—it feared first France and then Prussia—it was reticent even when compared to small and weaker European countries. In other words, despite having colonies and no small amount of economic wealth and some military power, *and* despite opportunity presenting itself for an active role *within* its geopolitical constraints, it shied away from acquiring authority, and made little push to acquire internal or external recognition of its material achievements.

Why did countries like the United States and Japan take on global authority in the style of great powers of the day, while others like the Netherlands remained puzzlingly reticent even given their capacity? As historians who study these countries have comprehensively recorded, the United States and Japan both had extensive ideas on how to be a great power—they had a plethora of narratives which would, in turn, not only push them to globalize but also shape internal and external recognition of their changing status. And these narratives meant that they tried to become great powers by imitating the established great power ideas of the day. The Netherlands did not have these narratives, and it even denied the label it could plausibly claim—that of colonial power—insisting not only that it was not an imperialist power but that to be an imperialist power was immoral.

The United States as a rising power had what historians have termed "visions of greatness."[99] After 1870, America entered an era of astonishing wealth and prosperity with improvements in productivity and living standards. To recover from the decimation of the Civil War, it also invested heavily in its military and, crucially, in its navy; US officials and naval experts worried that the American navy was no match for the powerful and global European navies, and pushed for naval expansion. And eventually, it would acquire colonies, the symbol of great power in the late 19th century world. Its narratives linked becoming a great power to conceptions of liberty and racial hierarchy.[100] Some narratives advocated that liberty meant national greatness operationalized as territorial expansion. Others believed that becoming a great power meant refraining from colonial ambitions abroad that could "betray" the cause of liberty at home and lead to the country's downfall. Still others promoted the idea that becoming a great power meant conquest and colonization, racial fitness and pride.[101] Presidents such as Grover Cleveland, William McKinley, and, later, Woodrow Wilson personally held strong ideas about anti-imperialism and great power that had to be balanced with elite ideas of becoming a great power in the style of the colonial Western powers of the day.[102]

In Japan's case, the Meiji Restoration showed the country's "determination to acquire the power to be the equal of the Western world, or even to overtake the Western world."[103] The Meiji Restoration was achieved by a section of the established ruling class—young low-ranking samurai—and was triggered by events that compelled Japan to enter the international system.[104] The forcible opening of Japan to the West by Commodore Perry in 1854 foreshadowed an eventual military coup in 1867 by Japanese rebels that would sweep away the Tokugawa *shogunate* ruling Japan, and "restore" the young Emperor Meiji to the throne. The Japanese elite that eventually took control demolished the samurai warrior class, and wanted to convert the existing feudal society into a modern centralized states. These elites became "obsessed with the goal of overtaking the West and doing whatever was necessary, even risking Japan's very cultural identity, to achieve that goal."[105] Forced modernization, which spurred the economic and military revitalization of Japan, was accompanied by certain narratives that were "not only necessary to expansion" but also influenced the way it was carried out.[106] Many of these elite narratives centered on imitating the great powers of the day, Western powers, in order to become a great power; Japanese elites advocated learning Western methods, adopting them, and then besting them. The only way to make Japan a great nation, they argued, was to acquire the "spirit" of the West—its self-reliance, its rationality, its technology.[107] Other narratives advocated going further and wholeheartedly adopting the rules of the existing Western international order and Westernized legal codes,[108] and using those rules to establish domination and bring countries under Japanese colonial protection.[109] These beliefs were countered by others who believed in preserving traditional Japanese values or, at the very most, combining these values with Western ideas.[110]

In each case—though the two countries differed geographically, politically, and culturally—elites were using *idea advocacy* not only to generate new ideas but also to recombine existing ideas to form new narratives about the country's appropriate behavior as a great power-to-be. Many of the divergent beliefs about America's role in the world after the war with Spain, for example, were not organic (that is, without historical roots) and can be traced back to earlier narratives about manifest destiny and racial superiority. But they crystallized into, as we will see, one of the "great debates"[111] in US foreign policy and expansionism.

Interestingly, on the face of it, realist arguments about US expansionism being the result of the search for security or the result of opportunity and capacity seem to make little room for ideas and beliefs that proliferated in the United States at that time. But in actuality they are contingent on the beliefs of US decision-makers *about* US power. Even those who suggest that the United States engaged in expansionism because of strong decision-makers, and that leaders such as McKinley and the role they played have been underestimated, point to the vivid debates that took place in the United States at the time as what swayed him.[112] Similarly, there was a marketplace of narratives in Meiji Japan about the path to great power in the style of the great powers of the day—European great powers. What is striking is that even though Meiji Japan vastly differed from the United States geographically, politically, and culturally, it too had idea advocacy—there was a plethora of elite Japanese beliefs about how to achieve great power.

The Netherlands, on the other hand, did not have such narratives, and neither did it recognize itself as a successful and increasingly rich country. Rather, the Dutch had what has been dubbed a "small state mentality," that of a country whose era of achievement was past. It stayed an almost aggressively passive player in international politics—even compared to countries like Belgium that were similar in size and position—thinking of itself as unheroic, and lacking military spirit. Its elite narratives often focused on being a good country, not a great country. This was a particularly curious notion for many reasons. The Netherlands had once been a great power during what has been called its Golden Age, and in the late 19th century was thought by historians to have entered a second Golden Age, due in no small part to its wealth. And while it was understandable that the Netherlands would not want to engage in behavior that would be risky, fearing as it did encirclement by greater powers, it was curious that the Dutch even refrained from behavior that would be *in keeping* with their already existing status—as we know, the Dutch *already* held colonies, but they not only refused to believe themselves to be an imperialist country but also began voluntarily ceding these colonies.

Ideas of Great Power in the Cold War and Post–Cold War World

As we've seen, the late 19th century was marked by the era of colonial great power, where great powers were those with the economic and military clout to own colonies. But in the 20th century, ideas about what it meant to acquire and hold great power shifted. It was not that great powers no longer had empires or engaged in imperialism. But rather, there were several shifts in world politics that changed the way we think about great power. One of the most important occurred in the Cold War period, as anti-colonial national movements gathered force all over the world. Eventually the forces of decolonization led to a moral normative shift in the international system—that is, the idea of owning a colony became fundamentally wrong.[113] Such moralistic notions were reflected not simply in the discomfort of many in the United States with the idea of an American empire (while some accepted the idea of American imperialism and debated only whether the effects of this were positive or catastrophic for the world, others rejected the idea of an American empire altogether[114]). This discomfort was also felt, at least ostensibly, by the Soviet Union, the other superpower. The Soviet Union claimed to wholly reject the idea of colonialism and to support the decolonized developing countries. Its constitution declared imperialistic wars and colonial slavery to be the characteristics of capitalism. Thus, it was clear after the end of World War II that, in the new bipolar Cold War world, while aspiring to be a great power was acceptable, aspiring to be a great colonial empire was not. But if great power did not mean owning colonies, what did it mean?

The post–World War II world saw the rise of multilateralism—a new order of business for countries, conducted via the mechanism of international institutions. Three decades ago, political scientist Robert Keohane defined multilateralism simply as "the practice of coordinating national policies in groups of three or more states."[115] But multilateralism in the Cold War world was also more than that. It assumed that countries would create and operate institutions that would reduce transaction costs through providing and sharing information. This would in turn enable countries to more easily achieve their goals. For great powers, multilateralism meant not just interdependence but controlling the processes of interdependence.

Even prior to the end of the war, the Atlantic Charter laid out the aims of the United States and the United Kingdom. In signing the Charter, President Franklin D. Roosevelt and Prime Minister Winston Churchill declared a commitment to not just territorial integrity and self-determination, but also to the ideas of free trade and collective security. Though the Charter did not fulfill the specific goals of both leaders, it laid down a foundation that would be used after the war not just by colonial territories through the world to fight for their independence, but also by the United States to create a liberal international order. The Bretton Woods Conference, convened by the United States with British cooperation, expanded on the ideas enshrined in the Charter. Under US leadership, the provisions of the Bretton Woods system laid down the principles of free trade, allowing for the free movement of goods and money, and creating new rules for the postwar international monetary system. Economic cooperation through new institutions was seen as not only the path forward to peace, but also as a boon to US economic interests, as it would provide unimpeded access to the resources and markets of the world.

The rise of the Soviet Union and the deteriorating US-Soviet relations dashed Roosevelt's hopes that the Soviets could be persuaded to join the new economic order. However, multilateralism was the order of the day not only through economic institutions. Rather, there was also multilateralism through the creation of security institutions. In 1949, the North Atlantic Treaty Organization (NATO) was created by the United States, Canada, and eleven Western European nations as a collective security institution to protect against the Soviet Union. The original membership would expand over the Cold War era. In turn, six years later, the Soviet Union and its allies created the Warsaw Pact. Similar to NATO, the Warsaw Pact was built on the assumption of multilateral security cooperation to deter an enemy attack. Multilateral security and economic cooperation were the defining hallmarks of the Cold War world. In the 1990s, when the Cold War ended with the collapse of the Soviet Union, collective security institutions struggled to redefine themselves in the absence of the Soviet threat. But the triumph of the liberal order, represented less by the victory of democracies over non-democracies and more by the flourishing of capitalism,[116] meant that multilateral economic institutions continued to thrive. The United States had won the Cold War, meaning in effect that post–Cold War great power norms meant unparalleled leadership in terms of economic interdependence. In a globalized and increasingly networked world, the country that could have the most connections, set the global agenda, and unlock innovation would be the central player.[117]

In both the Cold War and post–Cold War world, great power meant, as it had before, rapidly increasing military and economic superiority. But instead of the acquisition of colonies, the symbol of great power was the wielding of global influence through different kinds of international institutions—security, economic, and diplomatic. And after the collapse of the Soviet Union, the control of economic and monetary institutions became even more crucial for great power. Some have argued that such great power was also imperialist, even without formal colonial territories. The historian Charles Maiers, for example, has elegantly made the case that the United States should be considered imperial, whether or not we dub it an empire,[118] because it wields power overseas through its institutions.[119] What Maier was implying was that even though the United States no longer had formal colonies, the reach of American great power could be extended to every corner of the globe because of the United States' ability to create and lead international institutions. However, we don't need to determine here whether such reach was indeed imperialistic or non-imperialistic. What we can say is that during the Cold War and post–Cold War eras, acquiring great power was set within the context of rapidly increasing interconnectivity of global economies and politics. And with globalization came the need to manage it. No wonder, then, that the exercise of great power was tied to international institutions. The Cold War oversaw the proliferation of international institutions—from institutions that controlled and set security agendas, like arms-control regimes, mutual defense pacts, and proliferation regimes, to those that controlled global politics and economics, like monetary and financial institutions and political membership organizations. Participation and, more significantly, power in such organizations became key to acquiring, maintaining, and increasing great power status. Thus, recognition of great power during this time was not simply the recognition of a country's capabilities, but also a recognition of its ability to set the global agenda through institutions by *controlling, directing and impacting the processes of globalization and interconnectivity.*

During the Cold War period, the country whose rise again came to be feared was Japan. In 1937, when Japan joined World War II, its economy was less than 4 percent of world manufacturing output. By the 1980s, Japan was the world's second-largest economy, with more than 15 percent of world product.[120] Academics and popular writers ranked it "number one" and "a model to all the world."[121] Japan rapidly transformed from an enemy to an ally of the United States. Yet despite America's considerable investment in Japan in order to gain its help in the fight against communism, it was taken aback by Japan's rapid economic growth. The fact that Japan was now in the first rank of developed countries became a source of American and international anxiety. A proliferation of fiction and nonfiction books and articles in the media began casting Japan as a dangerous challenger to the world. Not only were Japanese elites amassing power at worrying rates, but they were apparently out to dominate the United States through nefarious ways and means. The 1992 bestselling thriller by Michael Crichton, *Rising Sun*, for example, sensationally portrayed the Japanese as out to viciously and systematically destroy American businesses. Crichton's fearmongering fell on receptive ears: a Newsweek/Gallup poll conducted in 1989 showed that most Americans believed that Japan was as much a threat as the Soviet Union.[122]

Yet Japan remained curiously reticent on the world stage. It did not behave like an active power: it did not convert its massive economic wealth into military strength; it was content to remain under the American security umbrella; and it showed no signs of taking on global authority—leadership and responsibility— in economic or diplomatic institutions. One expert declared that Japan "simply had no appetite for world responsibility."[123]

By the 1990s, Japan's economic bubble had burst and the world's eyes turned to two new rising powers on the scene—China and India. The 1990s marked the rapid increase in military and economic power in these two countries, resulting in constant references to their rise. Moreover, during this period, the capabilities of the two countries were comparable (this would change in the 21st century). But they behaved very differently. China's foreign policy behavior changed dramatically in the 1990s, as it transformed its bilateral relations with other countries and established significant multilateral networks. It enmeshed itself, often for the first time, in existing trade, diplomatic, and security regimes. It also spearheaded the creation of new institutions. India, on the other hand, did not. Instead, it frustrated many of its partners by refusing to step up and assume leadership in both multilateral and bilateral settings. It also often refused to support the United States in the post–Cold War order. India was, in a word, reticent.

While China's increasing economic and military power was accompanied by narratives about great power and how to become a great power, similar narratives were missing in both Cold War Japan and post–Cold War India. China *accepted* the norms of great power in the post–Cold War world and tried to play by the rules and seek great power validation. The Chinese elite discussed China's role in the world as a rising power, and debated the merits and demerits of multilateralism as well as the importance of controlling the forces of global interdependence. The decade of the 1990s was when China became an *active power, but one that was also accommodational of the great power norms of the day*. Japan did not take this path, and neither did India. In Japan's case, it had an alternative vision of its role in the world, as that of a "trading state." In India's case, there was a strong continuity of Cold War ideas about nonalignment that stymied it from expanding its role and globalizing its interests. Either way, both powers hung back, while China actively rose.

An Answer to Why Powers Rise or Remain Reticent

International society has always been consumed with the rise of new great powers-to-be. On the one hand, we worry about rising powers because we fear they will upend the international order and the world we live in. On the other, we are not very good at understanding *why* we should fear them or *whether* indeed we should. As for the question that John Mearsheimer asked me more than a decade ago about the difference between China and India and why it matters, I now have an answer. Some countries become active rising powers not simply because they acquire material power, but also because they deliberately acquire global authority and seek recognition, and initially go to great lengths to show that they *accept and accommodate* the existing international order. These countries go on to become great powers. Other countries may count as rising powers in material terms, but because they do not attempt to acquire global authority or seek recognition, they are reticent powers. They will not become great powers unless they become active powers. Rising to become a great power is a *process*—not, all things being equal, a natural and given outcome of increasing material power. Narratives, or idea advocacy, about becoming a great power are key to that process. Active powers have such narratives. Reticent powers, even when they have strengthening material attributes of wealth, military might, or both, do not. And while with the benefit of research hindsight, I was wrong in that long-ago précis to think of beliefs in India as "ideological chaos"—what I found was deep continuity in foreign policy ideas, just not entrepreneurial ideas about attaining great power commensurate with its changing material status—the lack of great power narratives have contributed to India's reticence.

Thus, there are three important conclusions from this book. First, looking to history we can find a significant pattern: rising powers that became great powers had *both* material capabilities *and* narratives about becoming a great power. These powers were *active* rising powers and they were initially *accommodational*. They did not become great powers by destroying the international order. They became great powers by buying into it *before* they openly attempted to remake it. China, even today, attempts to borrow norms established by the United States, and to use those very norms to advocate an end to US dominance.[124] Second, an *activist* rising power, meaning a country that will be revisionist, is not a sudden phenomenon. The rise of a country to become a great power is a process. The United States went from being an *active* power, displaying its accommodation of the international system, to being an *activist* power, rejecting international norms and attempting to remake the international order. While there has been much discussion of why rising powers become *activist*,[125] the fact that rising powers need to be active before they can turn to activism has been missed. Fearing a country simply because of its increasing capabilities does not *prima facie* make sense. Nor does thinking that simply because a country has increasing economic and military strength, it will *want* to remake the international order. Finally, some countries display reticence and remain reluctant to take on global authority in the international system, despite adequate wealth and/or military power. This tells us that, on the one hand, we need to pinpoint the norms in the current order that matter for active powers—such norms can be utilized as a point of convergence for the active power and the established great power of the day. On the other hand, we need to avoid the assumption that increasing military and economic capabilities alone can compel a country to assume more responsibility, and adjust our expectations accordingly.

Why do some countries develop idea advocacy or narratives about becoming a great power? In terms of explaining why some countries begin increasing their military and economic power, we know that there are many established theories, ranging from opportunity to the perception of a threat to individual leaders. Similarly, idea advocacy, too, can be rooted in a range of different causes. The purpose of this book isn't to examine exactly why idea advocacy arises although in the concluding chapter I will briefly consider potential causes for why some of these countries thought like great powers-to-be while others did not.

But first, in the following chapters, I examine two detailed and two mini-cases of active and reticent powers—the United States and the Netherlands in the late 19th century, and Meiji Japan and Cold War Japan. I then turn to China and India in the 1990s post–Cold War world. We see in each case of an active rising power— the 19th-century United States, Meiji Japan, and post–Cold War China—the idea advocacy that accompanied the increasing economic and military power. And in the cases of reticent powers—the 19th-century Netherlands, Cold War Japan, and post–Cold War India—we see material power and many ideas about foreign policy but no idea advocacy. These are not perfect comparisons, nor am I suggesting they should be. These countries are chronologically, politically, geographically, and culturally varied from each other, and I am aware of these differences. My goal is not to leave the impression that all active rising powers are alike, and all reticent powers are alike. Nor do I wish the reader to think I discount the impact of factors such as international environment and geopolitical threats. But each of the cases provides differing examples of opportunities taken and opportunities missed across time and space. Moreover, the cases of active and reticent powers present a puzzle. The United States, Meiji Japan, and post–Cold War China, as we would expect of rising powers, all invested in increasing their economic and military power. But they also engaged in behavior that, contrary to what we expect of rising powers, was surprisingly accommodational of the norms of great power at the time. The Netherlands, Cold War Japan, and India also invested in many ways in increasing their material power. But they passed up not only opportunities that might have increased their influence, but also those that arguably could have further enhanced their economic and military power. The mini-cases of Japan in two time periods are a bridge between the late 19th-century and late 20th-century worlds, and the transition from the Western age of great power to the beginning of what has been called an Asian age of great power. Japan presents an additional curiosity—it was *active* in one time period and *reticent* in another, even when considered a rising power in *both*, suggesting that idea advocacy is not historically inevitable.

Together the cases showcase intricate patterns of similarities and differences. The United States and Meiji Japan *agreed* on how a great power needed to behave in the late 19th century—despite very different regimes and cultures (Western democracy versus Eastern monarchy). What is more, they embraced narratives of accommodation, even when those very narratives could be seen as contrary to core issues of identity. A hundred years later, an authoritarian China would do the same, with narratives that conformed to post–Cold War notions of great power. China's behavior differed from that of 1990s democratic India, despite initially comparable levels of economic development and military investment that led to *both* being dubbed rising powers. Late 19th-century Netherlands and Cold War Japan were both rich countries, with high levels of income comparable to the great powers. While the former undertook military modernization that was primarily defensive, the latter prominently eschewed military development. Both relied on security guarantees provided by more powerful countries—and they both displayed behavior that was highly reticent, even when set in the context of their material capacity and geopolitical constraints. Why? As we will see, some of these societies had idea advocacy about attaining power and tried to adopt and debate great power ideas of the day, while others did not. The next chapters will lay out the fascinating narratives in each country.

The Active Rise of the United States

When we think of the United States today, we think of preponderant, even overwhelming, raw power. This is not surprising. In the post–Cold War era, the United States stands as the world's only superpower—an empire in denial, as Niall Ferguson has alleged,[1] but an empire nonetheless. Pax Americana may not have the population or territory of Pax Britannica or Pax Romana, but for sheer force, technological superiority, and influence, the United States remains unmatched. Even the rise of China, while rapid, has not yet come close to the aggregate power projection capabilities of the United States.[2] But the United States was not always a great power and, despite American conviction of its superior place in the world, it was sometimes overlooked during its early decades by the other powers of the day. The mid-19th century saw the gradual rise of the United States; by the late 19th century, its ascent was recognized by the other great powers. During this time, in addition to displaying its economic might and flaunting its military prowess, the United States also acquired overseas colonies, which, as we've seen, were the 19th-century symbol of great power. This was despite a long-held conviction among American elites that, even with American expansion within the region, the United States was inherently an anti-imperialist, anti-colonial country. Yet, by the end of the 19th century the dominant strain of elite opinion conformed to and even justified the norms of great power that existed at the time (even while there were competing strains). In other words, in many important ways, the behavior of the United States as it rose was accommodational—it accepted the norms of international great power. It was an active power before it became an activist power and imposed a new international order. And at the same time, there was a variety of narratives in the country about what kind of great power the United States would become. Some of these narratives were deeply conflicted as they sought to both reconcile and reject the conception of the United States as a colonial great power. These narratives were particularly prominent and stark in their divisions during the seminal event of the Spanish-American War of 1898 and its aftermath, which we

Why Nations Rise. Manjari Chatterjee Miller, Oxford University Press (2021). © Oxford University Press.
DOI: 10.1093/oso/9780190639938.003.0002

will examine in depth here. Eventually, the United States as an established great power would reject the idea of holding overseas colonies. But as we will see, before it did so, as a rising active power it came to *accept* the idea, even while some of its own citizens resisted it.

America: The Long Rise

Some have argued that the United States was a great power right from its inception; others have pointed out that it was always destined for greatness; while still others believe America was not placed firmly on the path to becoming a great power until toward the end of the 19th century. Each of these claims about when the United States was on the cusp of entering the "great power club" have relied on metrics as disparate as the confident beliefs of the founding fathers, America's bold expansion across the continent, the potential of its economic markets, its geographic isolation, and its willingness to assert control over the Americas. What is clear is that, by the material great power metrics of the day, in the 19th century the United States entered a long period of rise. The world from the mid- to late 19th century was, as we saw in chapter 1, a world of colonial great powers. These countries held sway over the lives and deaths of millions of people around the globe. These countries were also all European nations. Civilization meant European civilization; wealth meant European wealth; colonies were European colonies. In this world where great power was concentrated a continent away, the United States rose slowly. On the one hand, it expanded across the North American continent, becoming an established regional power, but on the other, it had no significant army, virtually no navy, and no overseas colonies. It did, though, have tremendous economic potential, and post-1865, with the end of the Civil War, this potential would be realized even while the country suffered major economic downturns.

For much of the 19th century, recognition of the United States as a great power to be was mixed. The historian Ernest May noted drily that it was not that the other countries were "oblivious to its existence" but rather that they thought of it only occasionally, as possibly a useful "chess piece in the game of world politics," similar to Sweden or the Netherlands. That it could be a major player on its own was not really considered.[3] The slights were both broad and minute. Diplomats rarely compared the United States to, or even thought of it in terms of, the acknowledged great powers of the time—the Russian consulate in the United States had no minister for almost two years; a German envoy in the United States eagerly opted to take a pay cut in order to be posted to Spain; Britain dispatched to the United States an ambassador whose embarrassing peccadilloes necessitated a distant and less significant posting; and when the Ottoman Sultan decided to cut expenses, he closed the embassies in relatively minor countries like Sweden, Belgium, and the United States.[4] A Britisher noted that the true danger from America was "in the Settler. . . . Not in their armies and navies."[5] The diplomatic correspondence of the time forces on one, as another American historian noted, a painful awareness of the "low estimate in which the physical power of the United States was held."[6] But by the end of the 19th century, particularly after the Spanish-American War of 1898, the United States would be established and recognized as an active rising power, one possessing the symbol of great power: overseas colonies. European observers would begin worrying about a world order dominated by the "American moneybags."[7] And the United States itself would think of not just international greatness but of becoming *the* great power of the day; in essence, it would start "measuring itself for Britain's shoes."[8]

The Rise of American Capabilities

Emerging from the Civil War after 1865, the United States' industrial economy, which had been stymied by the conflict, began to again rapidly expand. The American economy was fueled by both steel and oil. While the United States had been and remained a big exporter of both agricultural and mineral products, it also now became an exporter of manufactured goods that it had previously imported. This was particularly evident in iron and steel products, which were "the cutting-edge of late 19th century technology."[9] While prior to the Civil War the United States exported around $6 million worth of iron and steel manufacturing, by 1900 it was exporting approximately $121 million worth of iron and steel goods. In doing so, it threatened to displace European countries that relied on raw materials from the United States in order to export finished goods to America and the rest of the world.[10] During the same time, American oil production increased rapidly. While in 1859 the United States produced approximately 2,000 barrels of oil, by 1869 US production was 4.25 million, and by 1900 it was nearly 60 million barrels.[11]

Around 1870 is considered the early beginning of a golden era of the accumulation of American wealth, and an improvement in living standards and productivity. The United States was reaping the fruits of the British-led Industrial Revolution. By 1870, per capita income in the United States had reached 74 percent of British per capita income.[12] It has been argued that during the 1870s, the rapid growth in American manufactured goods (value added[13] to manufactured goods shot up to 82 percent and even to 112 percent after 1879) and the increasing importance of industrialists and financiers combined to create the seeds of a vast American commercial empire.[14] By 1893, America's trade

exceeded that of every major power except Britain.[15] Per capita income increased
from $531 in the 1870s to $933 in 1898. The United States had always been a
leading agricultural exporter, but now it overtook Britain, France, and Germany
in steel and coal production along with overall manufacturing output. Exports
increased from $281 million to $1.231 billion (putting it at third behind Britain
and Germany), and the United States also accounted for one-third of the world's
industrial production.[16] This explosive growth fueled the creation of unimagi-
nable wealth, the likes of which had hardly been seen before. The business writer
John Steele Gordon points out that the pace of this astonishing accumulation of
national wealth can best be understood by noting the rapid increase in personal
fortunes during the course of the 19th century—John Jacob Astor, who died in
1848, left a fortune of $25 million; Commodore Vanderbilt left $105 million by
the 1870s; Andrew Carnegie sold his business in 1916 for $480 million; and by
that same year, John D. Rockefeller was worth a whopping $2 billion.[17]

But the country's economic growth, as production outpaced consumption,
was also punctuated with major downturns—depressions in 1873, 1882, and
most notably in 1893 led to wide unemployment, decreased demand, and the
disruption of the banking system. Moreover, the two decades preceding 1893
had seen a continuing drop in the price of agricultural goods, which in turn
led to rural political unrest, while the industrial cities saw labor unrest that
splintered along class lines.[18] But despite the severe economic suffering in the
early 1890s, the economy would recover, and between 1897 and 1907 America
would enjoy "a prosperity beyond anything previously experienced"; its exports
and imports doubled, its bank deposits increased to $4.3 billion—a figure larger
than the gross domestic product of 1860—and the amount of money in circula-
tion increased from $1.5 billion to $2.7 billion.[19]

Military growth, though, was a different story. Between 1865 and 1890, the
United States military was slow to recover from the decimation of the Civil War.
The army in 1880 consisted of just 36,000 men. In comparison, Russia, which
had a much smaller economy than that of the US, had an army of 862,000 strong,
while Britain's army, although more modest, still had 248,000 men in 1880.[20]
Importantly, many Americans distrusted government and believed that the military, like all of the civil branches of the public service, was both inefficient and
mostly unnecessary.[21] And even though after the Civil War the US army was successful in its battles with Indian tribes, it suffered "horrifying losses" during those
battles because it was "poorly staffed, poorly equipped, and poorly managed."[22]

The most glaring gap between the United States and the European powers,
however, was in their navies. Reportedly, President Martin van Buren had
declared, well back in the 1830s, that the United States "required no navy at
all, much less a steam navy,"[23] signaling the general lack of interest in a strong
US navy. Meanwhile, throughout the 19th century, European countries were

massively expanding their numbers and sizes of ships and investing in naval ar-
chitecture and technology. Though the Civil War did spur the United States to
build up its navy—the Union navy had around 700 ships with 5,000 guns[24]—
most of it was dismantled after the war. Five years after the Civil War ended, the
navy shrank to trifling proportions—a mere 200 ships mounting 1,300 guns,
with most of the ships not even fit for service. They were made of wood and iron,
and, in a time of advancing technology, were old and obsolete, as were the guns
of the fighting ships.[25] Moreover, nearly half of the US Navy's enlisted personnel
were foreigners. A letter to the editor published in the *New York Times* lamented
that the lack of discipline, organization, and training led to a high rate of dropout
among Americans, who were then replaced with foreigners. "In no other navy
in the world does such a condition of things exist. In no navy except that of the
United States would such a state of affairs be permitted."[26] The American navy
of the time was no match for the powerful navies of Europe that had fanned out
over the globe, helping to both acquire and hold their colonial possessions.

More importantly, both the navy and the army were decentralized and
influenced by localism; due to the military's small size, it was supplemented by
autonomous militia units supplied by the states that would, when necessary, join
the regular force. However, the militia system was chaotic and the soldiers were
badly trained, if they were trained at all, leading to a waste of resources and very
slow response times. Nationally, too, the forces were not well managed, with
no clear lines of command. The army and the navy were each led by separate
bureaus that theoretically reported to the secretary of war and the secretary of
the navy. In practice, however, the chiefs of the two bureaus often maintained
close relationships with congressional committees and bypassed not only the
secretaries of the army and navy but even at times the White House.[27]

But by the 1880s, the United States had begun to acknowledge the need to in-
vest in its military. Although there was no sweeping reform, American attitudes
about the army and navy changed,[28] leading to a number of key organizational
shifts. Military education was reformed to train and professionalize the military; the position of assistant secretary of war (along with assistant secretary
of the navy) was established in 1890; key issues such as coastal fortifications
were moved from the control of Congress into the professional military and executive branch;[29] and the military received a larger share of the federal budget.
These changes are strikingly evident, for example, when comparing the report of President Ulysses S. Grant's secretary of war in 1874 with the report of
President Benjamin Harris's in 1891. In the former, Secretary William Belknap
complained bitterly that Congress had restricted the recruitment of troops to
the severe detriment of the army, and requested an increase in budget and numbers, warning that otherwise there would be "severe consequences."[30] In the
latter, Secretary Redfield Proctor listed the improvements and fortifications that

had been undertaken, including new methods of recruitment, examinations for the promotion of officers, and the establishment of an adequate coastal defense system.[31]

By the late 1880s, influenced by naval reformers such as Alfred Thayer Mahan and Stephen B. Luce, the United States had also begun acknowledging the need for a world class navy. A report to Congress in 1889 by the secretary of the navy, Benjamin Tracy, warned that America, with its 13,000 miles of exposed seacoast, was vulnerable to attack. Tracy pointed out that the European powers and China each had larger numbers of both armored and unarmored ships, and he requested twenty world-class battleships, which would be divided between the Pacific and Atlantic coasts. He also recommended the construction of cruisers, torpedo boats, and vessels for coastal and harbor defense. "If the country is to have a navy at all, it should have one that is sufficient for the complete and ample protection of its coast in time of war. If we are to stop short of this, we might better stop where we are, and abandon all claim to influence and control upon the sea."[32] This report was remarkable in that it marked the beginning of the shift from a passive to an offensive naval strategy. By 1890 Congress had adopted Tracy's recommendations and had permitted the construction of three splendid battleships at the cost of $3 million each. By 1893, the reforms had raised the status of the United States Navy from around seventeenth in the world to seventh.[33] Over the next decade the navy's budget more than doubled, rising from $22 million in 1890 to $56 million.[34]

These gradually increasing capabilities allowed the United States to amass regional power, and take important steps to obtain territories and exert an imperialist influence in the region. By the end of the 19th century, after its victory in the Spanish-American War of 1898, the United States had succeeded in acquiring a bona fide overseas colony, the Philippines.

The Active Path to Great Power

The United States' international role and presence were extremely "minimal" for most of the second half of the 19th century.[35] However, the seeds of its eventual active behavior—globalization of authority, and the shaping of perceptions— were sown during this period, when it began asserting itself as a regional power.

From the very beginning of the 19th century, the United States engaged in nation-building, a process that would continue for the next century. But after the American Civil War ended in 1865, the United States also embarked upon substantial expansion in the region. Conquering the lands of the West was the most important task after the war. But additionally, the United States sought to establish both economic and strategic control of the Western Hemisphere. Thus, it sought to annex islands in the Caribbean and Pacific, unilaterally construct an isthmian canal in Central America, and assert its economic supremacy in Latin America as a whole.[36] For example, in 1867, the United States pulled Hawaii into a reciprocity treaty; in 1868, William H. Seward, the secretary of state, negotiated a treaty with Colombia that gave the United States the sole right to construct a canal; in 1869, President Grant drew up, ultimately unsuccessfully, an annexation treaty to acquire Santo Domingo (now the Dominican Republic); in 1884, another treaty, the Frelinghuysen-Zavala treaty, tried to establish the right of the United States to own and control a canal, this one in Nicaragua.

A few incidents particularly stand out in this period as examples of America's active move toward the beginnings of global influence. In 1895, the United States decided to intervene in a standoff between Venezuela and Great Britain. Tensions between Venezuela and the United Kingdom over the boundary between the former and British Guiana had been simmering for five decades, as the two countries went back and forth over a large disputed territory that was eventually discovered to have substantial gold deposits. Venezuela did not have the capacity to assert its claims, and in 1887 it severed its diplomatic relationship with Great Britain. Meanwhile, Venezuela appealed to the United States to intervene, and in 1895 the United States decided to take the matter up. secretary of state Richard Olney sent a dispatch to the British Prime Minister Salisbury that asserted the right of the United States to intervene in the boundary dispute. The United States stated that if the boundary dispute was not settled by arbitration, it would administer the border itself. The ultimate upshot of this salvo was that the United Kingdom, after much negotiation, accepted that the United States would play a role in resolving the conflict, and in 1896, the two countries agreed on a treaty of arbitration.[37]

Second, the United States gradually moved toward the annexation of Hawaii. In 1875, Secretary of State Hamilton Fish negotiated a reciprocal trade agreement with Hawaii that enmeshed the islands both economically and politically with the United States but "stopped short of formal annexation."[38] But in January 1893, the white planter elite, who had their roots in New England, organized a coup against the native queen, Liliuokalani, hoisting the American flag in Honolulu and declaring Hawaii to be a protectorate of the United States. They hoped that by doing so they would inspire the US government to formally annex the islands. Two weeks later, their hopes seemed to materialize as the United States signed a treaty of annexation with Hawaii. However, the incoming Democratic president, Grover Cleveland, refused to adhere to the treaty, and withdrew. Five years later, in July 1898, Hawaii was formally annexed with a joint resolution by Congress.

Finally, and most crucially, America went to war with Spain in 1898 and defeated it, ending Spain's colonial empire in the Western Hemisphere. Nearly sixty years later, historian Thomas Bailey would declare that "every school boy knows, or would know if he bothered to read his textbook, that the United States did not become a world power until 1898."[39] Although Bailey was being facetious,[40] his statement points to an inescapable fact—the Spanish-American War of 1898 and the subsequent American annexation of the Philippines are considered *the* events that heralded the emergence of the United States as an international power to reckon with[41] and the rise of the American century.

This war occurred after a long history of unrest in Cuba, a Spanish colony. Cuba had already led a ten-year failed struggle for independence from 1868 to 1878. This rebellion was resumed in 1895, and rapidly devolved into a guerrilla war against the Spanish forces, which outnumbered the Cubans in men, artillery, and finances. But as the conflict intensified, marked by massive Spanish brutalities against the Cuban population, the United States decided to intervene. There were two important immediate factors in February 1898 that preceded American intervention. First, a scandalous letter from the Spanish minister in Washington, Enrique Dupuy de Lôme, to a friend fell into the hands of the Cuban rebels, who delivered it to US Secretary of State William R. Day. The letter, headlined in the American press as "The Worst Insult to the United States in its History," contained several unflattering comments about President McKinley and his diplomacy. Second, the USS *Maine*, a battleship sent to Havana to provide naval presence, exploded and sank, killing 266 American sailors. While no investigation then or subsequently has been able to prove who was responsible, the United States detected the hand of Spain. McKinley demanded that Spain grant independence to Cuba; Spain responded by breaking off diplomatic relations; and the United States declared war. The war was a short one, marked by two early successes: in the Atlantic, Admiral William Sampson blockaded Havana; in the Pacific, a fleet of ships that had been sent to the Philippines prior to the *Maine* disaster was now secretly authorized by the assistant secretary of the navy, Theodore Roosevelt, to destroy the Spanish fleet in Manila. By July, the war had ended with a decisive victory for the United States.

The subsequent and historic Treaty of Paris of 1899 ended America's first foreign war in fifty years. It netted the United States the Spanish territories of Puerto Rico, Guam, and the Philippines. The treaty's significance is difficult to overstate. It destroyed the Spanish Empire and set off America's acquisition of overseas territories. Even more momentous was the acquisition of the Philippines, an overseas colony. Transformed into a colonial power, the United States took possession of the country and promptly found itself warring with Filipino rebels fighting for independence. For the first time, the United States had policed the affairs of the Caribbean, and then involved itself in the international politics of the Far East, fighting "men of a different color in an Asian guerrilla war."[42]

An Active and Accommodational Power

In these behaviors, the United States was an *active* power. It not only began to acquire relative military and economic power, it began to acquire global authority,
but it did so by acting in accordance with great power norms. The United States
was *accommodational* in its behavior because it conformed to the great power
norms of the time.[43] Its intervention in Venezuela, its ultimate annexation of
Hawaii, and the Spanish-American War and the acquisition of the Philippines
show the rising United States behaving in keeping with the colonial great power
norms of the day. America showed a willingness to begin asserting "imperial"
authority overseas. Secretary Olney's dispatch during the Venezuelan crisis
demonstrates the assumption of this authority. "Today," he wrote, "the United
States is practically sovereign upon this continent, and its fiat is law."[44] Similarly,
with the steps toward the eventual formal annexation of Hawaii, the United
States was taking steps that were entirely in keeping with the norms of gradually
acquiring a colonial empire.[45]

This behavior was not mere expansionism, a natural outcome of its increasing
material capabilities. In the case of Venezuela, for example, it was the US intervention that prompted the acceleration of the demand for a larger navy (at the
time of the crisis, the United States had just one battleship versus Britain's naval
might[46]), rather than the other way around. The material gains to the United
States from intervention were also not clear at the outset, and eventually the arbitration panel convened to oversee the crisis would issue a judgment that would
in fact favor Great Britain.[47] And throughout the intervention, US actions were
mostly in accordance with the behavior displayed by colonizing great powers.
Olney never discussed American policy with the Venezuelans, even during the
height of the crisis. And even though it was Venezuelan territory that was at stake,
the Venezuelans were themselves completely excluded from the negotiations.[48]
In the arbitration process, the Americans also valued British colonial demands
over the wishes of the Venezuelan government. The British demanded that territories where British subjects had been settled for more than fifty years would
be excluded from arbitration, meaning that Britain could legally claim more of
the disputed territory. The Americans eventually accepted Britain's position,
over the repeated protestations of the Venezuelan government. The news of the
American sellout triggered riots in Venezuela. And when the arbitration commission granted most of the disputed territory to Britain, the United States did
not raise any objections. That America was behaving similarly to other colonial
great powers was recognized by Great Britain, the country that was the exemplar and, arguably, the keeper of such norms. The *Economist* stated, for example,
that in taking these actions the United States was establishing "a kind of protectorate" over the Americas.[49] Although Venezuela had initially been eager for the

United States to intervene, the result was so antithetical to what it considered its interests that just a few short years later Venezuela would support Spain in its war against the United States.

Similarly, categorizing America's intervention in the affairs of Spain in Cuba as the result of security or economic interests alone is problematic. Not only was there an absence of perceived threat, but economic special interests also were not decisive factors.[50] The United States became an empire not only when "its security and vital interests were not at risk,"[51] but also when "imperialism was not a [structural or interests-based] make or break question of national existence."[52] It was also not clear that *not* acquiring an empire would have hurt the United States economically. The research on business interests, how enmeshed they were in colonial expansionism, and whether they believed it would be economically beneficial is mixed, but it is generally accepted that special interests (business, military lobbying, missionaries, etc.) were not decisive factors in the US intervention.[53] While the United States certainly now had the capacity to intervene,[54] there is also mixed evidence as to whether the decision was driven by strong leaders. President McKinley, indecisive and besieged, was himself "neither a jingo nor an enthusiast of expansion"[55] but gave in to the pressure to intervene, probably because of either public opinion and/or fear that he would lose influence in the Republican Party. Unsurprising, therefore, is the popular joke of the time: "Why is McKinley's mind like a bed? Because it has to be made up for him every time he wants to use it."[56] While most historians agree that America's intervention was a particular kind of expansion, a colonial expansion, they assert either that this was unintentional—"a momentary fall from grace," as historian Bemis put it,[57] or that this was absolutely deliberate—a planned exploitative economic imperialism.[58] Whatever the *intent* of American policymakers, a debate that rages to this day,[59] two facts are inescapable—it *was* a different kind of expansion than the United States had engaged in previously, and America emerged from it as a recognized imperial power with an overseas colonial territory. What we can understand from these facts is that rising America was engaging in *active* behavior, playing by the international norms of colonial great powers, not overturning them.

Narratives of Attaining Great Power

During the process of its rise as an active power, the United States was also debating how to become a great power. Some historians assert that the United States has always, right from its inception in 1776, thought of itself as a great power.[60] Indeed, in a letter from 1811, John Quincy Adams made clear to his mother, Abigail, that he thought of America as "a nation . . . Destined by God and nature to be the most populous and most powerful people ever combined under one social compact."[61] But while it has perhaps always had visions of *national* greatness,[62] visions of *international* greatness came later.[63] How the United States would *become* a great power on the world stage, what kind of great power it would be, how it would actively promote its national greatness in world affairs, and how it would eventually reshape the international system had not yet been thought of. And crucially, it struggled with whether it should become a *colonial* great power, and if yes, how this could be reconciled with traditional perceptions of American anti-colonialism.

As we will see, in the mid- to late 19th century, and particularly by the end of the century, as the United States expanded global authority and shaped perceptions of its rise, there were narratives—or idea advocacy—accompanying its increasing material strength that portrayed the necessity of colonialism in attaining great power. Conflicting narratives warned, however, that possessing colonies could lead to destruction of that very goal. Often arguments about America's expansionism and power during this period are contingent on the beliefs of decision-makers *about* US power—what leaders believed they could do given America's military and economic strength—even as they sometimes dismiss the role of beliefs.[64] What we see in the narratives that accompanied the growth of US economic and military power is that America's active behavior was not just about what decision-makers believed they *could* do, but also about what they *should* do, and what kind of great power America should be. These narratives existed during some of the key actions that America undertook in Venezuela and in Hawaii, but they also came out in full force after the seminal Spanish-American War. The war forced the United States to move away from its long held principle of non-intervention[65] and to confront the question of what kind of role the country would now want to play in international politics.[66] Meanwhile, the United States had to grapple with domestic problems spurred by its intervention.

To understand why these later 19th-century narratives were so important, we need to also look to early 19th-century ideas about the role and identity of the United States. Two particularly stand out as crucial to later American identity, as they contained ideas that would impact later narratives about America becoming a great power: the Monroe Doctrine of 1823, and the idea of Manifest Destiny, coined in 1845.

On December 2, 1823, President James Monroe made a speech to the US Congress. Two paragraphs in that speech would come to be known as the Monroe Doctrine. In the context of the United States' relationship with Russia, President Monroe declared,

> The American continents, by the free and independent condition which
> they have resumed and maintain, are henceforth not to be considered

as subjects of future colonization by any European powers. . . . We owe it, therefore, to candor and to the amicable relations existing between the United States and those powers to declare that we should consider any attempt on their part to extend their system to any portion of this hemisphere as dangerous to our peace and safety. With the existing colonies and dependencies of any European power we have not interfered and shall not interfere. But with the governments who have declared independence and maintained it, and whose independence we have, on great consideration and just principles, acknowledged, we could not view any interposition for the purpose of oppressing them, or controlling in any other manner their destiny, by any European power in any other light than as a manifestation of an unfriendly disposition towards the United States.[67]

This stirring speech did not come to embody a powerful *doctrine* until much later.[68] Initially, not only did it fall flat among the American public, but the reaction among European powers was merely to be slightly "irritated" by it, matching with their view of America as a weak rather than a strong country.[69] But it did capture, with the non-colonization clause, a belief cherished by American elites of the time that their country and ethos were viscerally opposed to colonialism. John Quincy Adams, who had a direct hand in Monroe's speech, was a known opponent of colonization, believing that "the whole system of modern colonization was an abuse of government, and it was time that it should come to an end."[70] Although in the following years the Monroe Doctrine would be interpreted and reinterpreted, the principles of anti-colonialism and non-intervention were seen as its foundation.[71] And these principles became an important foundation for later narratives about American colonial expansion abroad.

The second important idea appeared in 1845, when American journalist John Louis O'Sullivan wrote an article in the *Democratic Review* about the annexation of Texas. In this article there was a buried phrase that criticized European interference in America's affairs:

[O]ther nations have undertaken to intrude themselves . . . in a spirit of hostile interference against us, for the avowed object of thwarting our policy and hampering our power, limiting our greatness in checking the fulfillment of our manifest destiny to overspread the continent allotted by Providence for the free development of our yearly multiplying millions.[72]

The use of "manifest destiny" in this article attracted little attention. But a few months later, O'Sullivan used it again in an editorial for the New York

Morning News. This time he stated, with regard to the US claim to the territory
of Oregon: "that claim is by the right of our manifest destiny to overspread and
to possess the whole of the continent which Providence has given us for the
development of the great experiment of liberty and federated self-government
entrusted to us." This editorial had tremendous impact, implying as it did that
there was a "higher law" that governed America's behavior.[73] Many prominent
Americans adopted the concept wholeheartedly, even as they adopted it for
differing ends. Manifest Destiny certainly impacted America's westward expansion to gain markets, enlarge the union, and showcase racial superiority,
but expansionists also had to reconcile its racial and economic aggression with
"the belief in American innocence."[74] As a consequence of this belief, "very few
Americans" viewed the expansion in the West as "an act of colonialism."[75] The
tensions inherent between America's national vision of itself as exceptional,
non-colonial, and destined by a higher authority to expand in the region versus
its interventions and acquisition of overseas colonies, just like the European
powers, were prominently displayed by the later 19th century in the narratives
of the time about how to become a great power.

The narratives of attaining great power that would be displayed prominently
by the end of the 19th century were certainly about increasing economic and
military strength—Mahan, for one, thought great power was impossible
without a command of the seas—but they now also encompassed ideas about
the nature of the United States itself, and what it would become. They were
not organic. Rather, they drew on ideas that had existed in the United States
for many decades—ideas about liberty, democracy, and America's destiny as a
unique country. While some used the Monroe Doctrine and Manifest Destiny
to advocate for colonial great power, others used them to oppose it. But the
narratives also took on newer iterations conforming to the norms of great
power of the time. And they were often controversial and contested. While
some, particularly early on, indeed saw the Monroe Doctrine as advocating
isolationism, others used it to justify internationalism and the links between
the United States and European great powers, even the hated British. Still
others by the late 19th century would invoke it to promote active behavior.[76]
The notion that imperialism and great power were the inseparable norms of
the day was a concept that American elites struggled with—thus the doctrine was often invoked to cloak the influence of colonial great power norms
on late 19th-century American foreign policy.[77] Manifest Destiny pushed the
idea of American exceptionalism, and this was used by some to later argue
that *because* America was exceptional, it was its duty to help make others fit
for self-rule. These struggling narratives could be seen during the crisis in
Venezuela and the US annexation of Hawaii, but they burst into full force after
the Spanish-American War.

A few years prior to the intervention in Venezuela, for example, politicians including Secretary of State James G. Blaine, appointed in 1881, explicitly sought to mimic the British Empire. He wrote a series of notes to the British demanding the modification of an old treaty in Central America so that the United States could fortify and politically control any canal built in the Central American isthmus in the future. "This government will not consent to perpetuate any treaty that impeaches our rightful and long-established claim to priority on the American continent." While making his demand, he argued that the United States was simply doing in its neighboring region what the British had been doing in Egypt with the Suez Canal. The next secretary of state, Frederick Frelinghuysen, continued in the same vein, citing the Monroe Doctrine to justify US behavior.[78] A few years later, Olney used the Monroe Doctrine to justify intervention in Venezuela, declaring European colonialism unacceptable. But even though he eschewed a US "protectorate" in Venezuela and sought to reassure the public that the United States did not "contemplate any interference in the internal affairs of any American state," others, notably Theodore Roosevelt, wrote joyfully that now that the United States had intervened in Venezuela, it should do the same in Cuba.[79]

In the early 1890s when President Cleveland refused to annex Hawaii despite the request of the rebels to do so, his decision could be understood against the backdrop of the conflicting narratives from American expansionists, including those who were vehemently against any kind of imperialistic behavior. Cleveland did not just refuse to annex Hawaii—he authorized, in addition, an investigation into the matter, which concluded that the revolution had been "a shameful affair orchestrated by a small special-interest group." The *New York Times*, for good measure, said annexation would "sully the honor and blacken the name of the United States."[80] But in July 1898, when Hawaii was finally annexed, President William McKinley justified it as "not a change" but "a consummation."[81]

America was rising. It was flexing its economic and military muscles, yes, but it was also fiercely contending how it should rise. Nowhere would this become more obvious than during the Spanish-American War and its aftermath. Different, and sometimes conflicting, narratives—a "crisis of identity," as historian Frank Ninkovich has termed it—would engulf the public space post-1898. These narratives comprised one of the "great debates"[82] in US foreign policy about how America should achieve international greatness. Even opposing sides of the issue firmly believed that America was now becoming a great power. *That* was undisputed. What was disputed was *how* to assume the mantle.

In the 1890s, the depression, clashes in rural and urban areas, and an anxiety about immigration all combined with an awareness that the United States was beginning to amass unprecedented military and economic power. This created a volatile backdrop against which the unrest in Cuba, and stories of the brutal violence against Cuban rebels by Spanish troops, were to play out. American elites were anxious about the values that would make the country great, and were divided on whether that meant preserving the old values, redefining them, or looking abroad for solutions.[83] Non-interventionists argued that potential American involvement in Cuba would have no noticeable effect on stimulating foreign economic expansion, would enmesh the United States in a conflict that could stymie its domestic industry, and would pit it against a European power at a cost to its values. Elites such as Senators Mark Hanna, Nelson W. Aldrich, and Orville H. Platt called for prudence and discretion. However, among many others there was a rising hyper-nationalism—"jingo nonsense," as McKinley contemptuously put it to Carl Schurz, an influential and staunch anti-imperialist.[84] Some of these so-called jingoes, like Roosevelt, fell into the camp of thinking that American values were declining, and saw war as a way to national rejuvenation—in 1897, he declared to an audience at the Naval War College that the "fight well fought, the life honorably lived, the death bravely met . . . count for more in building a high and fine temper in a nation than any possible success in the stock market."[85]

But it was also about the United States acquiring global authority and acting like a great power by assuming responsibility, and eventually acquiring colonies. Cuba's misery and the unfolding humanitarian disaster struck a chord in American public opinion. The fact that the United States had the economic and military heft and *could* do something about Cuba "helped convince [many] they *should* do something . . . it was a question of whether the nation stood for something in world affairs."[86] As Republican Senator Henry Cabot Lodge asked, "What are the duties of the United States in the presence of this war? . . . if that war goes on in Cuba . . . the responsibility is on us; we cannot escape it." Enrique Dupuy de Lôme's insults against McKinley and the sinking of the *Maine* served to further inflame these ideas. Ultimately, with slogans such as "Remember the Maine! To hell with Spain" abounding, the American public supported war, and the newly elected McKinley bowed to public opinion.[87]

These narratives became more contested after the war. With the signing of the Treaty of Paris, the question now became whether the United States should or should not possess a colony—the Philippines. This question framed the heart of what it meant for the United States to attain great power. Should the United States be a colonial great power, in the tradition of the great powers of the day who held and profited from overseas colonies? The narratives around this issue pitted American elites fiercely against each other. Who were these elites? They came from many different backgrounds—to debate whether becoming a great power required America to assume the mantle of colonialism. Although these elites can be broadly divided into two ideational camps—the anti-imperialists and the expansionists—the views, even within each camp, were far from monolithic. Rather, as we will see, there was a plethora of different kinds of beliefs, leading to many different narratives on how the United States should follow the path to great power.

Reacting to the notion that, with the Treaty of Paris, the United States was now an interventionist state with colonial territories, anti-imperialists vehemently objected to America's overseas expansion. Some sought to oppose the Paris treaty itself and its provisions about the Philippines; others opposed the war with the Filipino rebels that followed; and all opposed the very idea of an American colonial administration in the Philippines. "Anti-imperialism became a nationwide movement that captivated headlines and made a significant impact on US foreign policy."[88] "Democrats, Republicans, progressives, conservatives, party stalwarts, independents, businessmen and labor union chiefs"[89] all came together to oppose America becoming a great power. Anti-imperialism generated thus a fascinating unity among American elites from not just different but even contradictory backgrounds—the movement had such widespread support that it cut across many otherwise divisive lines. These highly influential men included former senator Carl Schurz; prominent senators such as George Hoar (Massachusetts), Walter Mason (Massachusetts), Augustus Bacon (Georgia), Edward Carmack (Tennessee), and Donelson Caffery (Louisiana); Congressman Thomas Reed (Maine); three-time Democratic presidential nominee William Jennings Bryan; former president Grover Cleveland and his secretary of state Richard Olney; industrialist Andrew Carnegie, who even then was one of the most famous men in the nation; the philosopher William James; the economist Edward Atkinson; writer Mark Twain; the presidents of Harvard (Charles Eliot), Stanford (David Starr Jordan), and Northwestern (Henry Wade Rogers); the head of the American Federation of Labor, Samuel Gompers; and even prominent clergymen like Bishop Henry Codman Potter. They vocally expressed their opinions through speeches, letters, pamphlets, editorials, and debates on the floor of the House and the Senate.

Why were these men so adamantly opposed to the idea of the United States becoming a colonizing power in the tradition of the European great powers? They had many different, sometimes even contradictory, reasons. As the historian Frank Friedel pointed out, "Their arguments were moral, humanitarian, economic, military and racist."[90] Some of the anti-imperialists argued, for example, that empire was contrary to the very ideal of American liberty[91] and American exceptionalism. George Hoar declared in a letter, "No man . . . will successfully challenge . . . the affirmation that under the constitution of the United States, the acquisition of territory, as of other property, is not a constitutional end, but only a means to a constitutional end . . . and that there is therefore no constitutional warrant for acquiring or holding territory for that purpose."[92] William Jennings Bryan believed that were the United States to become a colonizing power, it would be abandoning a vital principle of democracy—that governments should derive their powers through the consent of the governed.[93] Even though he supported the ratification of the Paris treaty, he did so in the belief that this would be the path for the US Congress to eventually support the freedom of the Philippines. When it became clear that the United States would not only annex the Philippines but subdue it with force, he poignantly asked:

> Shall we keep the Philippines and amend our flag? . . . Shall we add a new star, the blood star, to indicate that we have entered upon a career of conquest? . . . No a thousand times better to haul down the stars and stripes and substitute the flag of an independent republic than to surrender the doctrines that gave glory to "Old Glory."[94]

Others claimed that America needed to be the protector of liberty, not its assailant, one that inflicted bondage on another peoples. William James lamented, "we are cold-bloodedly, wantonly and abominably destroying the soul of people who never did us an atom of harm in their lives . . . [the American republic has become] a hollow, resounding, corrupting, sophisticating torrent of . . . brutal momentum and irrationality."[95] Many Republicans who joined the anti-imperialists also saw opposing colonial expansion as the just expression of their party's anti-slavery roots.[96]

There were also those who argued that other races were incapable of governing themselves, and that the United States should keep away from populations that could debase its own civilization.[97] Schurz worried about "Asiatics," while the Missouri congressman Champ Clark tried and failed to imagine "almond eyed, brown skinned United States senators." What's more, he argued, "No matter whether they are fit to govern themselves or not, they are not fit to govern us."[98] Then there were the elites who offered that subduing alien races was simply an impossible job that would ruin the country. The sociologist William Sumner Graham declared that the United States had never been able to "civilize lower races" and trying to do so would "lead [the country] to ruin."[99] Senator Donelson Caffery pointed out a puzzling paradox: "In order to Christianize these savage people we must put the yoke of despotism on their necks [but] Christianity cannot be advanced by force."[100]

Many businessmen financed the anti-imperialist movement and subscribed to its views. Andrew Carnegie even toyed with the idea of personally buying the Philippines and then granting it independence.[101] The rationale of such elites was economic. Military adventurism and the responsibility of imperialism did not come cheap. The costs of this, it was feared, would be borne by American farmers and workers. The expense of subduing and then maintaining the Philippines would take resources away from domestic industrial development.

Moreover, the United States would encounter problems arising from any trade relations established with colonized territories. Free trade would push down the value of America's agricultural products if goods such as sugar, tobacco, and flax from a colony were admitted duty free. On the other hand, imposing tariffs on goods from a colony would ruin its economy and violate the Constitution. If the United States opened the Philippines to free trade with other nations, American producers would have pay exorbitant shipping costs compared to European powers, given the distance of the United States from its colony. If it closed trade or taxed European goods sold to the Philippines, the United States could face economic punishment or even be pushed out of the region.[102] Finally, some anti-imperialists argued that the United States needed to become a great power and lead by example. Following the path of empire would result in the downfall of free institutions and perhaps even the country itself. Democrat Senator Benjamin Ryan Tillman announced, "we assert that no nation can long endure half republic and half empire."[103]

Despite the popularity of the anti-imperialist point of view, the foreign policy elites were ultimately dominated by the imperialists, who offered strongly opposing arguments. There were those such as Alfred Thayer Mahan, of course, who thought the United States needed a large navy and overseas bases to protect its commercial and strategic interests.[104] Then there were others who thought that the European foreign powers needed to be challenged, that expansion would develop American character and strengthen national pride. Still others were businessmen who pushed to build a commercial empire in Asia and Latin America.[105]

But, most crucially, highly influential luminaries had dreams of international greatness and of America taking its rightful place on the world stage, a place that would be guaranteed by being a colonial power. Senator Henry Cabot Lodge urged Americans to realize their place "as one of the great nations of the world."[106] In a passionate speech delivered on the Senate floor, he also declared, "I do not think the Filipinos are fit for self-government as we understand it, and I am certain that if we left them alone the result would be disastrous to them and discreditable to us . . . I hope we have too much self-respect to hand them over to European powers with the confession that they can restore peace and order more kindly and justly than we, and lead the inhabitants on to a larger liberty and a more complete self-government than we can bestow upon them."[107]

The dominant imperialist vision of American greatness equated "the cause of liberty with the active pursuit of national greatness in world affairs."[108] Theodore Roosevelt subscribed strongly to this view: "Nations that expand and nations that do not expand may both ultimately go down, but the one leaves heirs and a glorious memory, and the other leaves neither. The Roman expanded and he has left a memory which has profoundly influenced the history of mankind."[109] In his opinion, colonialism was not contradictory with American greatness. While he considered some races sufficiently civilized (Russians, Japanese), others, he thought, needed to be governed by more "advanced" people. Thus, he believed America (and other advanced powers) should take on the mantle of imperialism as long as doing so did not impair its interests. It was simply natural, in his opinion, that the civilizations that were best suited for expansion and self-government should have authority over the less civilized parts of the world.[110] Moreover, America was nothing like Spain and would never deny the Filipinos progress. Rather, it would help make them fit for self-rule.[111] He thus explained the post-1898 American colonialism: "It is our duty toward the people living in barbarism to see that they are freed from their chains, and we can free them only by destroying barbarism itself. . . ."[112] We hope to do what has never before been done for any people of the tropics—to make them fit for self-government after the fashion of the really free nations."[113] Others echoed his sense of colonial great power responsibility and authority, along with the drive to shape perceptions of America in the world. Senator Albert J. Beveridge (Indiana) declared:

> Such [colonial] administration of government is nature's method for the spread of civilization. Throughout all history administering peoples have appeared. These advanced peoples have extended their customs and their culture by the administration of government to less developed peoples. Thus . . . these backward peoples have evolved those qualities of mind and character and that mode of living called civilization . . . and now this same duty that has come to every people who have reached our present state of enlightenment and power must be performed by the American people.[114]

Roosevelt, along with Mahan and Lodge, also viewed colonial acquisitions as a path to domination of the Latin American and Asian markets.[115] While there is controversy over the exact motivations of President William McKinley that led him to intervene in the Spanish-Cuban conflict and acquire the Philippines,[116] there is evidence he was acutely sensitive to and influenced by the debate over the United States' changing status.[117] Even before he took office, the themes of his election campaign outlined the key US foreign policy goals of spurring commerce and "civilizing" other peoples around the world.[118]

The imperialist narratives ultimately prevailed. On February 7, 1899, the US Senate ratified the provisions of the Treaty of Paris by the exceedingly slim margin of two votes, and America was soon embroiled in a war to quash the Filipino insurrection. With the ratification of the treaty, American power now reached to Asia. The imperialists saw this period as the closing of the first chapter of American history and the start of a new era of great power. They posited that victories in international relations were often decided by violent means in addition to peaceful competition. This was a new concept, because before this period Americans had viewed war "as an evil to be avoided not cultivated."[119]

The narratives of this time spoke to the United States' status as a rising active power. They focused attention on goals that were attainable—acquiring overseas territories in the pursuit of power in the fashion of the great powers of the day. They also explained for a domestic audience the deviation from the hitherto held policy of non-intervention and the flexing of military muscle as necessary for not just national but international greatness. They focused attention on the United States' regional role (the dominance of markets in Latin America), and its relationship with the superpower of the day, Great Britain. Imperialists, in fact, often explicitly emphasized the latter by arguing that the use of military force and simultaneous cooperation with Great Britain would enable the assumption of power by the fittest race, the Anglo-Saxons. In Roosevelt's mind, even among the more advanced peoples, the English-speaking races were preeminent.[120] Thus, he believed, the Anglo-American alliance needed to be developed.[121] These narratives talked about how the United States could and should mold the international system because it was its responsibility as a civilized advanced nation to take on colonies. In short, the narratives in America at the time acknowledged the current norms of great power, debated its international responsibilities in that context, and outlined its relationship with the status quo power(s) and the current international order. Moreover, they explained for a domestic audience why it should take on (or refrain from taking on) such responsibilities.

Conclusion

By the late 19th century, as we have seen, the United States was firmly on the path to great power. It not only strengthened its economic and military power, but it began behaving like an active power. It globalized its authority, and shaped perceptions of it as a great power to be. And as it did so, it was accommodational of the great power norms of the day—it accepted and conformed to the notion that great power meant imperialism and the possession of overseas colonies.

As discussed in chapter 1, and in this chapter as well, there has long been much debate on whether the United States was always an empire, and had always been colonial.[122] It has been argued that its policies toward indigenous populations and its expansion in the West long smacked of both.[123] Historians including Williams Appleman Williams put forth a different view, that the economic prowess of the United States was synonymous with empire because of its colonial exploitation of foreign markets.[124] However, as the work of Elizabeth

Hoffman and others points out, despite its history of suppressing native peoples, the "one and only period" in which the United States acquired an "actual" formal colonial empire, as opposed to a "metaphorical" one, was when it took over the Philippines in 1898.[125] In this behavior it was active and accommodational, in that it behaved precisely as the world of the time would expect of a colonial great power.[126] Eventually, the United States transitioned from an active to an activist power and began revising the norms and setting the agenda of great power. This included a rejection of the norm of colonialism,[127] evidenced, for example, by its move to cancel "America's membership in the imperialist club by passing the Philippine Autonomy Act in 1916, followed by the Philippines Independence Act in 1934."[128] The United States no longer had to act in keeping with the later 19th-century norms of great power.

The active and accommodational rise of the United States was accompanied by prolific narratives about great power. The narratives debated whether the United States should indeed become a colonial great power, what it would mean for the United States to acquire colonies, or to intervene in the affairs of other nations. While there was dissent, there was also justification of why the United States should move away from its long-held identity of being a non-colonial power. These justifications and their rebuttals were not organic—rather, they had historical roots and were drawn from interpretations and reinterpretations of long-held foreign policy ideas in America.

In these narratives about whether and how to acquire colonial great power, America was not unique. Japan, a country vastly dissimilar to the United States in history, culture, government, and people, was also rising in the same time period. And, as we will see, it too had such narratives, in addition to its increasing capabilities. And like the United States, it too subscribed to the norms of the prevailing international order and to the idea of colonial greatness. But first we need to turn to another case of a country that rose materially—it became one of the wealthiest nations in Europe, it began reforming its military, and it already held overseas colonies. Yet this country, the Netherlands, not only shied away from active behavior, but displayed reticence that was surprising even when compared with smaller European nations.

The Reticence of the Netherlands

By the late 19th century, it was clear that the United States had arrived as a power to be reckoned with. It had defeated a major power, Spain, and, after much debate and soul searching, had acquired a colony, the Philippines. With increasing military capabilities, an expanding economy, and ideas about acquiring great power, it was now an active rising power, a country on the path to great power. America would, soon after World War I, upend the international status quo and become activist. But, in that same era of the United States' ascension as an active power, there was another country, a European nation, that had once been a great power. By the late 19th century, this country had three of the material attributes we often associate with rising powers of that era: it held colonies and was considered to be the second greatest colonial power after Great Britain; it was one of the richest nations in Europe, with a booming economy; and it began to take steps to modernize its military and navy and build up its defenses. This country was the Netherlands. During the years 1870–1910, the Dutch entered what many have called a "Second Golden Age" (its first Golden Age[1] was during the 16th and 17th centuries), yet it never again aspired to achieve great power.[2]

What is surprising about the Netherlands during this period is not that it was no longer able to play in the up-and-coming great power league of the time; it faced strong geopolitical constraints, given the strength of both Great Britain and Germany. It was that the Dutch, even with lower-risk opportunities to play a more assertive role, showed little interest in doing so. They were curiously reticent, almost "passive," even when compared to smaller and weaker European countries like Belgium. As one historian commented, "[Their] determination to play a passive role in world politics was so strong as to amount almost to an obsession."[3] And interestingly, the Dutch elites in the late 19th century were convinced that their nation as a small country should have correspondingly small ambitions. Not only that, despite already being a highly successful colonial power, they rejected any notion that their country was imperialist—the very foundation of great power at that time. Rather, Dutch narratives painted

Why Nations Rise. Manjari Chatterjee Miller, Oxford University Press (2021). © Oxford University Press.
DOI: 10.1093/oso/9780190639938.003.0003

the Netherlands as a benevolent, even ethical, power that was non-martial, non-aggressive, and unambitious.

The Netherlands in the 19th-Century World

By the early 19th century, the Netherlands had long ago lost its vaunted position as one of the European great powers. The century that had marked it as a European power with international greatness was from the mid-1500s to the mid-1600s, when the country had constructed new economic initiatives that made it competitive in the global economy. The Republic (comprising seven states: Friesland, Gelderland, Groningen, Holland, Overijssel, Utrecht, and Zeeland) was an "economic powerhouse," dominating maritime commerce and expanding overseas through the Dutch West India Company (WIC) and the Dutch East India Company (VOC).[4] With a modernized navy, domination of overseas trade, and a domestic flowering of culture, knowledge, and the arts, this period for the Netherlands is rightly considered a "golden age" and, even today, the Dutch draw much of their identity from this era of achievement.

The early 19th century, on the other hand, seemed to be an age when the Netherlands was declining. Particularly, it suffered a blow in 1830 when the southern provinces of the country, with primarily a Flemish and Walloon population, erupted in a rebellion against the north. The ensuing civil war led to the breakaway, creation, and establishment of the kingdom of Belgium under Leopold I, which was given finality when it was endorsed and recognized by the other European states at the London Conference later that year. It would take the Netherlands almost a full decade after the London Conference to finally accept its decision and recognize Belgian independence.

Thus, by the mid-nineteenth century, the Dutch had to take stock of the world around them. The revolt, the subsequent loss of southern territory, and the creation of an independent Belgium in 1830 was a bitter event, compelling them to reflect on past days of glory and rethink who they were as a nation. They now perceived Europe as a world of rivalry between three great powers—Britain, France, and Prussia. In this world, they had little means to defend themselves, and yet they needed good economic relationships with all of their European rivals. The overseas Dutch colonies were somewhat dependent on British protection, leaving them unable to afford an explicitly anti-British policy.[5] But neither could they alienate France or Prussia. Consequently, they adopted a policy of neutrality in 1840, a policy that would stay in place until World War II. The policy declared Dutch neutrality in peacetime on the rather confident assumption that the Netherlands was so strategically valuable that, should it ever be attacked, other European powers would inevitably come to its aid.

But by the late 19th century, the Netherlands had cemented its material power in three ways—it held on to extremely profitable colonial territories, particularly Indonesia and islands in the Caribbean, keeping it "among the first rank of colonial powers";[6] it rapidly industrialized to become one of the richest countries in Europe; and it undertook significant and expansive reorganization of the military, as well as investing in its navy.

The Material Rise of the Netherlands

In the 19th century, the Netherlands had a crucial attribute that only the great powers of the day possessed—it held colonies. Dutch colonial holdings went back to the 16th century and its Golden Age. With the founding of the Dutch East India Company in 1602 and the Dutch West India Company in 1621, the Netherlands, following the path of the other European countries of the time, expanded into Africa (South Africa, Gold Coast), Asia (in Indonesia, Taiwan, Sri Lanka, Malacca, Japan, and India), and the Americas (states on the North American East Coast, the West Indies, Suriname, Guyana, Tobago, and Brazil).[7] Thus, by the late 19th century, it had already been a colonial power for quite some time, though by 1870 the Netherlands had lost some of these colonies. Dutch territories in North America and Brazil were lost in the 17th century; South Africa, Guyana, and Ceylon were lost in the early 19th century; and in 1824, through the Anglo-Dutch treaty, the Dutch gave up its claims to any remaining territories in India and Malacca to the British in exchange for British territories in Sumatra. Nevertheless, despite a reduction in its colonial holdings, the Netherlands retained extremely profitable colonial territories—the East Indies, the West Indies, and its Gold Coast territories in Africa, and it maintained close ties with the Boers in South Africa.

Not only were these colonies profitable, but the Dutch had perfected the art of exploiting them. In 1830, the Dutch government had established a highly lucrative "cultivation system" (*cultuurstelsel*, also sometimes translated as the "culture system") in its territory of Indonesia. According to the rules of this system, a full 20 percent of arable land had to be cultivated with profitable crops, such as indigo, coffee, and sugar, requisitioned by the Dutch government. Thus, the native population was taxed in kind as the crops were turned over to the Dutch for export to Europe. The cultivation system was incredibly abusive and unjust to the native population. In return for their labor, the natives received a wage that was determined by the government, and was completely unrelated to the actual value of the crops they were forced to cultivate.[8] But the cultivation system contributed substantially to Dutch wealth. The profit from the crops, or *batig slot* as it was known, comprised in the 1850s, for example, almost half of all government revenues. This ruthlessly efficient and exploitative cultivation system was one of the reasons the Dutch were internationally admired by the great powers as a colonial model to emulate—they displayed a remarkable prowess for squeezing every last drop of profit out of their colonies at the expense of the native population. The French talked of the Netherlands as a "model for all colonies," with its "magnificent prosperity" and its "perfect order."[9] The Germans envied its "exploitation of its rich colonies" and aspired to the ideal of succeeding in Africa as the Dutch had done in Indonesia.[10] The British published a laudatory volume, *Java; or, How to Manage a Colony: Showing a practical solution of the questions now affecting British India*, which praised the cultivation system as having magically transformed Java into a model colony.[11] Thus, despite its position by the late 19th century as a "diminutive democracy" in Europe, the Netherlands was still a "colonial giant" outside of it, a "small mother country [but] a wealthy colonial empire."[12] It has even been called, during this time period, the "greatest colonial power after Britain."[13]

In addition to holding colonial wealth, the Dutch now also rapidly improved their economy, moving away from being a primarily agrarian economy to industrialization. The Netherlands had been industrializing gradually, more slowly than some of the European great powers.[14] But post-1870, there was a significant economic shift, as the country entered a period of "modern economic growth."[15] That is, it now enjoyed "virtually permanent high growth combined with structural economic changes such that agriculture became relatively less significant while manufacturing's share of national income increased."[16] The expansion of industrialization that led to a boom in the economy was a result of both the liberalization of international trade, leading to specialization in certain goods (which benefited parts of Dutch industry), and the rising competitiveness of Dutch industry as a whole.[17] Having lost its industrial connections to Belgium, the Netherlands adopted a policy of enforced industrialization, driven initially by steam power. This particularly revolutionized the shipping industry, which grew at a phenomenal rate, with its merchant marine becoming one of the largest in the world.[18] The country increased its investments in railways and canals, which stimulated the growth of construction companies.[19] After 1889, there was an increase in the establishment of large businesses,[20] while post-1894 Dutch banking also entered a period of "unprecedented growth."[21] Even the agricultural sector was able to emerge and recover in the 1890s from the brief period of severe depression created by industrialization. Rising urbanization and increases in the population created a new demand for agricultural products, leading in turn to innovation in agrarian cultivation methods.[22] Besides the domestic market, the economy diversified and reaped the benefits of international trade. Economic ties with Germany, for example, were particularly important. The German demand for both natural resources and Dutch agricultural products stimulated the Dutch economy.[23] As the German economy expanded, so did the Dutch. Between 1870 and 1910, Dutch foreign trade boomed with both exports and imports rising rapidly.[24] The Dutch would become and remain "one of the world's major investors in other countries, despite its small size . . . recurrently the third or fourth international investor after the [UK], at a level comparable to Germany and France."[25]

Unsurprisingly, Dutch per capita income rose during this time, from $2,750 in 1870 to $3,850 in 1914. By the early 20th century, both Dutch GDP per capita and labor productivity were not only roughly on par with Germany but nearing that of Great Britain.[26] Jan Luiten van Zanden and Arthur van Riel point out that it was actually quite remarkable that the Dutch economy expanded so swiftly after 1870, given the country's late industrialization, and that the base of the previous economic growth—the agricultural sector—had gone through a period of severe depression.[27]

With colonial and economic wealth, the Dutch could afford to turn their attention to the state of their military and navy. Up until the 1860s, the Dutch had considered France the most powerful continental power and their "hereditary enemy."[28] A committee to review Dutch defense strategy convened in 1860 had concluded that, in fact, France was really "the only important potential enemy."[29] But two important events would lead the Dutch to both reconsider their strategic position and realize their limits. First, in 1864, Prussia went to war with Denmark. Even though the United Kingdom had been a guarantor of Danish independence, it refused to intervene in the conflict and help Denmark. This led not just to Dutch uncertainty about the European balance in power and the value of relying on allies, but also to a decline of trust in the promises of the English.[30] The Dutch leadership now acknowledged that if there were a war, they would have to be prepared to fight it on their own. Second, and importantly, the rise of Prussia jolted them. Particularly, the Prussian victories against France in 1870 shocked the Dutch military establishment, which had always thought of the French army as superior to the German one. The unified German empire now posed a serious threat to the Dutch eastern border. As Willem Bevaart points out, "as the Dutch military let themselves be led by the French after 1815, [so] they let themselves be led by the Prussians after 1870."[31] Reassessing this geopolitical situation, the Dutch believed they had four options for increasing their security: rely on complete demilitarization (which some Dutch pacifists advocated); rely on the capricious support of the European great powers; shore up their defenses to make invasion very costly for an attacking power;[32] or strengthen the military and navy.[33] After much debate about the logistics, they chose both of the latter. Post-1870, they thus began the process of strengthening their defenses, evaluating their defense strategy and reorganizing the military. In other words, they moved away from preparing for yesterday's war.[34]

There was a growing realization that the Dutch army was in dire need of improvement. The *Militaire Spectator*, an influential journal that regarded itself as a marketplace for the expression of different military voices, argued that the Netherlands needed to learn from the German success of 1870, and to reorganize the army by turning to the methods, tactics, and training utilized by the Prussians.[35] Military officers advocated for dramatically expanding the army, increasing its prestige, and involving the entire population in the defense of the nation. Consequently, there was considerable military pressure on Dutch politicians to take action.[36] While politicians agreed that investments in the army had become necessary—materials, technology, organization, and preparation for mobilization all needed to be overhauled—they were divided about the priorities, the process by which an overhaul would take place, and whether the reorganization should indeed mimic that of the Prussians. Despite debates, between 1870 and 1907 there was a significant overhaul of Dutch defenses, and the reorganization was very similar to the military organization of neighboring great powers.[37] The overhaul proceeded along four lines—a reorganization of key structures in the army, the shoring up of fortresses, investing in rapid mobilization, and a buildup of the navy.

In terms of the army, prior to 1887, Dutch forces consisted of three loose divisions: one that was made up of volunteers from all over the country; a national militia relying on conscripts from all over the country (with every man over the age of 18 drawing lots); and a civil militia organized on a municipal or village level, which also drew on conscripts. The conscripts could rely on a replacement system to get out of service. That is, they could pay someone else to serve in their place, or they could pay someone who had been given an exemption and swap lottery numbers with them. Unsurprisingly, this system of organization was deeply problematic. To begin with, the conscripts were given minimal and irregular training[38] and were not required to stay in the barracks. At the same time, because there were simply not enough volunteers who could be trained regularly to meet the military standards of the day, the Dutch effectively lacked a suitable standing army. Moreover, the replacement system meant that national service could be easily avoided, especially by the wealthy. Around 20 percent of men escaped military service by paying between 600 and 800 Dutch guilders to be replaced.[39] Since the Dutch attributed Prussian victories to an army which was composed of "the economic and intellectual leaders" of Germany society,[40] the avoidance of service by the Dutch elite was believed to have led to the deterioration in the quality of the army.[41] Moreover, the professionalism of ordinary Prussian soldiers was seen as worthy of emulation.[42]

Thus, between 1887 and 1907, the Dutch army was remodeled along Prussian lines. The volunteer army and national militia were merged to create a standing army. *Conscriptie-achtige dienstplicht* (literally "conscript-ish conscription") based on the Prussian system was put in place—men were conscripted or volunteered into the army, trained for two to three years, and remained in army service for eight years. Moreover, beginning in 1901, the civil militia was replaced by the *Landweer* (modeled after the Prussian *Landwehr*), which was an army reserves corps, functioning as both a territorial defense force (which could be mobilized both before and after the army was called up) and as a border protection force.[43] After eight years of service, professional army soldiers and conscripts automatically became a member of the *Landweer* for another seven years. By 1903, some 67,000 men were serving, and by 1910, this had increased exponentially to 190,000 men (135,000 in the army, and 55,000 in the *Landweer*).[44] For comparison, in 1910, the United Kingdom, a great power, had 571,000 men, and the United States, a rising power, 127,000 men.[45] Moreover, the officer corps was also significantly enlarged by introducing conscription. Also, the reorganization finally led to the abolishing in 1898 of the Dutch "replacement system" that had been embedded in the structure of the army. This had been one of the biggest demands of the military who used, as mentioned earlier, both social and military arguments to support their position. Conscription led to not only a bigger army but also a stronger one, allegedly due to the "higher" intellect of the upper classes who could no longer avoid service.[46]

At the same time, the Dutch invested in military technology and weapons (introducing the breech-loaded gun, expanding field artillery to become one of the most modern in Europe, and investing in pioneering weaponry for the infantry); laid plans for more rapid mobilization (repositioning the army, investing in railways and the telegraph system, etc.);[47] and shored up their traditional fortress system, which was hitherto, given their lack of military strength, their primary defense against an invasion. Equally importantly, in 1907, the Dutch, uniquely in Europe, introduced a peacetime command of the standing army, showing the enlarged significance of its military force.[48] The Dutch also turned their attention to the navy, investing in the purchase of a range of different ships, including *panterschepen* (armored ships), after 1893. Between 1869 and 1910, the budget for the War Ministry almost doubled, growing from 14.7 million guilders to 28.7 million guilders; during this time it comprised from 15 percent to 20 percent of the total government budget. Meanwhile, the budget for the navy comprised 8 to 12 percent of the total budget (growing from 9.4 million guilders in 1869 to 20.1 million guilders in 1910).[49] Due to the increasing trade between the East Indies and the Netherlands, the Dutch shipping and shipbuilding industry was revived to the extent that the Netherlands came to possess the fourth largest maritime fleet in the world,[50] with huge growth toward the later 19th century.[51]

Thus, the Netherlands possessed lucrative colonies, a booming economy, and a reformed and strengthened military. Yet despite these material attributes, the Dutch were peculiarly passive on the world stage. Why?

The Reticence of the Netherlands

Curiously, the Netherlands showed little propensity to *behave* in a manner commensurate with its position as one of the richest countries in Europe with colonial holdings. Not only did it abstain from taking on global authority or seeking recognition of its growing wealth, but it was reticent to the point of "turning away from engaging in international power politics,"[52] a "colonial giant but a political dwarf."[53]

We can particularly observe this through its behavior with respect to colonialism and colonial territories. Owning large numbers of colonies was, as we have seen, the hallmark of great power in the late 19th century, and a source of pride for the countries that owned them. The Netherlands was acutely aware of this. Yet it displayed surprising caution and reticence with respect to colonies, passing up opportunities to engage in colonial expansionism, reducing its number of colonies, and changing its economic policies for the ones remaining. Since the 1840s, the Dutch government had formulated a policy of "abstention" from colonial expansion, theorizing that expensive expeditions would undercut their profits from colonial territories. But this policy continued into the late 19th century,[54] even after the country was well able to shoulder potential financial risk; and post-1870, the Dutch passed up opportunities to expand beyond their territorial holdings, and even bartered away colonial territories. In addition, within its colonies, the Dutch government re-evaluated its long-administered exploitative policies of economic extraction—policies that other European powers of the day not only envied but saw as a profitable model to be emulated—and attempted to instill what they perceived as non-imperialistic moral policies.

Dutch reticence was on particularly full display with respect to Africa. Like other European countries, the Netherlands drew from Africa economically; in addition to its possession of the Gold Coast, it also had extensive trade interests in other parts of West Africa, as well as in the Congo. We know from diplomatic reports that Dutch commercial interests in the Congo were possibly the largest of any European power.[55] But, unlike the other European powers, during the last part of the 19th century it voluntarily ceded its colonial holdings in Africa, and it also chose to stay aloof from the European scramble for territories in the continent.

To begin with, between 1870 and 1872, the Netherlands concluded three treaties by which it ceded its Gold Coast region to Britain, and gave the latter equal commercial rights in the territory of Siak in Indonesia in exchange for Britain recognizing Dutch sovereignty over Siak and other parts of the island of Sumatra. These treaties faced intense Dutch political opposition. The Dutch Privy Council pointed out during the negotiations, "It may be true that [the Dutch] can also trade without colonial possessions, but such an assumption would lead to giving up all our colonies. And what would the Netherlands be without colonies?"[56] One of the most hotly contested issues was that, at first, the Dutch government did not ask the British to recognize Dutch sovereignty over the Aceh Sultanate, a territory within Sumatra where the British had guaranteed independence (indeed the British would continue to refuse to recognize Aceh as part of the Dutch sphere of influence). Opponents of the treaties argued that the Dutch should not cede the Gold Coast unless the British recognized Dutch sovereignty over the entire Indonesian archipelago plus the island of Borneo. They also objected that giving Britain rights in Siak would harm Dutch economic interests. Ultimately, the treaty ceding the Gold Coast passed Parliament by 34–30 votes, but the Siak treaty was defeated by 36–28 votes. The Dutch government responded by drafting and this time successfully passing another new treaty that guaranteed Dutch sovereignty in the whole of Sumatra, including Aceh, while giving British and Dutch trade and shipping equal status.[57] In short, with these three treaties, the Dutch volunteered to give up colonies in exchange for very little. Later this would be mourned as "political short-sightedness ... and turning a blind eye on the promising future of that land which even non-colonising nations saw as the economic Jerusalem."[58]

The Netherlands also displayed remarkable reticence with respect to the acquisition of new colonies in Africa. In the 1880s, the colonial expansion in Africa, or "steeple chase" for colonies, was a race by each European country to gain territory, cement economic holdings, expand trade, and increase both its power and prestige. Not only did the Netherlands decline to enter this race to expand spheres of influence, but "as far as was possible kept aloof from the partitioning of Africa," seeming to pursue the "exact opposite of imperialism in its foreign policies."[59] As historian Maarten Kuitenbrouwer pointed out, "nobody seemed to regret that the Netherlands itself [had] definitively renounced the option of acquiring further colonies in Africa."[60]

The Dutch pursued diffident policies even in areas that were key to their control of the Asian colonies that they did retain. In the 1880s, Egypt and the use of the Suez Canal became an international issue. The Netherlands, which relied heavily on the canal to reach its colonies in Asia, was divided on whether it should actively participate in international negotiations about the control of the canal; the country compromised by sending a force to simply protect its Dutch diaspora and goods. In the Congo, where the Dutch had a large economic stake (in 1890, for example, about 60 percent of all exports from the Congo went to the Netherlands), the Netherlands concentrated its diplomacy on obtaining guarantees of free trade and free navigation of the Congo and Niger rivers. At the seminal Berlin Conference of 1884,[61] the Netherlands played a diffident role. The conference, which came to be seen as the meeting where the fate of Africa was decided by Europe, triggered a scramble for African colonial territories.

(Kwame Nkrumah, the former president of Ghana, would famously claim that "the original carve up of Africa [was] arranged at the Berlin conference."[62]) The great powers of France, Britain, and Germany, along with smaller powers and declining powers, including Belgium and Portugal, participated enthusiastically in the agenda for the conference, which included discussing freedom of trade in the region of the Congo river, freedom of navigation of both the Congo and Niger rivers, and the setting up of rules for further occupation of African territory by European powers. The Berlin conference would cement a colonial empire for Belgium through its control of the Congo, while the Portuguese, who had an established presence on the continent, suffered some losses but also made significant gains (Mozambique and Angola). For European nations, it was a conference "not of the past but of the future," a competition with "only winners."[63] But the Netherlands either caved to demands or stayed aloof. When the British demanded that the region of the Niger River fell under the British sphere of influence and should not be considered the same way as the Congo, the Dutch agreed. The Dutch also accepted Belgium's assurances of free trade and promises of exemption of Dutch citizens from import and transit duties. In return, they recognized Belgian Congo's sovereignty and definition of territory. "The small countries had enough opportunities [to play a role in the Conference], as was proved by Belgium and Portugal," but the Dutch did not want to "play a political role" and remained "the only uninvolved Western European power."[64]

Even within Asia, the Netherlands would refuse to make any push to acquire more colonies. In 1900, during the slicing up of China into Western spheres of influence, the Dutch government came under pressure from Dutch officials in China to open up colonial outposts. The Dutch had participated, albeit in a limited way, in the international quelling of the Boxer Rebellion, and they had extensive economic interests in China because of the use of Chinese contract labor in the East Indies. Yet when the opportunity presented itself to increase its colonial influence, the Dutch government decided to tamp down any territorial aspirations in China.[65]

In Southeast Asia, the Netherlands' behavior as a colonial power was also markedly unusual. Rather than use the East Indies as a base for colonial expansion into more of Southeast Asia, the Dutch followed a process of internal colonial consolidation and extension of power over the East Indies itself, a territory they controlled. And even this initiative for the consolidation and extension of power was not spurred by the Dutch government, but by the local colonial government. In 1873, for example, the Dutch went to war in Aceh in Indonesia. Prior to the Anglo-Dutch treaties of 1870–1872, as we saw earlier, the British had guaranteed the independence of the Sultanate of Aceh in Sumatra. But the signing of these treaties had given the Dutch control throughout Sumatra in exchange for their territories in Africa. Shortly afterward, the Dutch declared war on the Sultanate, citing its sponsorship of piracy and its diplomatic relations with the United States. The war was long, lasting from 1873 to 1903, and resulted in terrible casualties.

At first glance, it could seem as if here, in Indonesia, the Dutch behaved *actively*, engaging in colonial territorial expansion. But the Aceh war, in fact, represented something of a puzzle, in that the usual expansive motives of colonial powers for wars were absent. As Henk Wesseling has pointed out, the war, initiated by the colonial government, was deeply unpopular not simply with the tax-paying public, but also even with the Dutch government. Moreover, it was difficult to discern any economic motives for the Netherlands to invade Aceh—the war wasn't driven by a need for markets or raw materials, or even capital investments. Some historians have pointed to the existence of petroleum resources as a possible motive, but those resources were not discovered until about 1895—long after the war was underway.[66] Rather, many argued that the Aceh war represented a "frontier imperialism"[67] at best—the Dutch were simply consolidating their existing authority in the region, and maneuvering against any potential British influence. Some others, most notably Dutch historian Maarten Kuitenbrouwer, have disagreed, pointing out that post-1870, Dutch policies in its colonies and the Aceh war were remarkably similar to the behavior of other European imperialists.[68]

Despite disagreements about whether the Netherlands was imperialistic in the style of the other European nations, many Dutch academics are cautiously in agreement when discussing whether the Dutch engaged in *colonial expansionism*, particularly since Indonesia was indisputably already a part of the Dutch colonial empire.[69] As the economist J. Thomas Lindblad acknowledged, if colonial expansion constitutes "formal annexation of new territories," then "it follows logically, there was no Dutch imperialism in South East Asia" in the late 19th century. Rather, he suggests that "Dutch hegemony" over Indonesia changed in the century between 1816 and 1914, in that the war established a Dutch, indisputably colonial, administration. This concept of expansion but only *within its own colony* is the core of why the Dutch have been said to be unique among imperialist countries of that time.[70] It was not that the Dutch were *not* imperialist, or that they had *no* commonalities with other European colonists. But Dutch expansion was different from the way other colonial European countries expanded—the Netherlands extended its power and established political domination, but within "already nominally fixed and recognized boundaries," and in response to local incidents, rather than as a grand deliberate initiative for expansion from the Dutch government at The Hague.[71] Moreover, the Dutch would eventually link even this internal projection of power to the implementation of what it termed an "ethical policy," or a policy ostensibly aimed at promoting the welfare and civilization of the native population,[72] distinguishing them further from the other European colonists. Whereas other European countries, such as the French, used policies aimed at civilizing the heathen natives (*mission civilisatrice*, as it was called by France) to expand and justify conquest (such arguments, as we have seen, were also advanced by some American elites), the Dutch implemented the so-called ethical policy in territories that were *already* under their colonial occupation, thereby further justifying Dutch authority.

Moreover, the Dutch government took steps to dismantle existing and successful economic structures in Indonesia in the late 19th century, including the highly profitable cultivation system. By 1878, "the traditional surplus on the budget of the Netherlands Indies [had] turned into a deficit."[73] As the government retreated, profiteering from the colonies was instead left to private enterprises.

Thus, in the late 19th century the Dutch entered what could be plausibly dubbed an age of paradox—a rich country with profitable colonies, but a peculiarly reticent imperialist. It possessed, as we have seen, many crucial material resources. In that sense, the Dutch were indisputably European imperialists—they followed colonial patterns of economic exploitation; they set up the economic foundations of a colonial state;[74] and they decimated the Javanese peasantry through famine, epidemics, and death caused by these Dutch colonial policies.[75] That wealth was used to power its military modernization and rejuvenate its society. Even in the arts, literature, and science, the country during this time birthed initiatives that revived its lost glorious achievements.[76] Some historians call the period from 1870 to just before the outbreak of World War I an "age of achievement," a second Golden Age for the Dutch.[77]

Despite being a wealthy power, during a time when imperialism and imperialist expansion were *the* foreign policy issues of the day, the Dutch were very strange and reticent imperialists. They engaged in actions contrary to the norms of the established international order of the day. Not only did they refuse to participate in the scramble for Africa, they voluntarily ceded their African colonial holdings. They did not engage in expansion or consolidation beyond the territories that already were under their control. They engaged in extension of power only within their colonies, but not at any behest of the Dutch government. And they ended a profitable colonial system of enrichment that had earned them the envy of other European colonial powers, and underlined this colonial policy in controlled territories with an ostensibly strong commitment to ethics.

Why was this the case? Why did the Netherlands show little interest in seizing opportunities for further colonization, colonial enrichment, and fulfilling a promise of again becoming one of the European great powers? Part of the explanation certainly lies in the Netherlands' insecurity about its size, its strategic position with respect to the rise of Prussia, and the jockeying between the English, Germans, and the French for power. But it cannot be the whole explanation—it does not explain, for example, why during the Berlin Conference, the Netherlands, as the second largest colonial power in the world with significant economic interests in the Congo, would not play a strong political role and would choose to remain uninvolved in Africa. As Wesseling wrote, "Its political will to operate as an imperialist power [in Africa] was nonexistent."[78] It also does not explain its reticence in other parts of the world.

In 1906, historian J. Ellis Barker scornfully wrote of the late 19th-century Dutch that they lacked the "will" for national success and greatness:

> [N]ot inanimate resources but men, make a nation . . . the greatness and prosperity of a nation depend not upon the size of its territory and its natural resources, and the quantity of commodities exchanged but upon its ability and upon its will, and principally upon the latter; for will can create ability but ability cannot create will . . . the history of the Netherlands is a history of missed opportunities and of opportunities deliberately thrown away.[79]

This unduly harsh condemnation is not my argument. No country can will itself to great power, and neither could the Netherlands, even in the late 19th century, constrained as it was by three European great powers on its doorstep jockeying for influence.

However, if we look to Dutch narratives of this period to see what the elites *did* want, we find an interesting paradox—the Dutch were successful imperialists who now rejected this very identity. Not only did they lack any narratives about playing a more active role in international politics, let alone about regaining great power, but the "traditional self-image of the Dutch [made] it very difficult for them to consider themselves as an imperialist nation."[80] This, in turn, helped make them a very cautious, passive, and *reticent* player in the international politics of the time, even when their material strength increased.

Dutch Narratives in the Late 19th Century

What was indeed striking about Dutch narratives during this time was how little they reflected on what the Netherlands *could* achieve given its material capabilities. Active powers that have idea advocacy reconcile their material capability *with* the constraints of the international order—they focus attention on those goals that are perceived to be materially attainable given the constraints of the current order. They also acknowledge the current norms of great power and aspire to them, and they explain their purpose and goals for both a domestic and international audience.

The narratives in the Netherlands, on the other hand, not only did no such thing, but they seemed both indifferent to their capabilities and rejecting of the label of great power that they *could* indeed plausibly lay claim to—colonial greatness. Instead, Dutch narratives were broadly characterized by three elements. First, the Dutch had what has been termed a "small state mentality"—the idea that it was both physically and metaphorically "a small country with a big past"[81] that had to survive the machinations of bigger powers. Second, the Netherlands drew a strong contrast between itself as a benevolent and moral country, and the power-hungry and grasping European nations around it. Third, the Dutch firmly believed themselves to be non-imperialistic—this, despite both owning and successfully exploiting colonies. Consequently, the very notion of the Netherlands as a country that could be assertive, let alone again become or ever act like a great power, was absent.

By the 19th century, the Dutch had an acute sense that their era of great achievement was past. The civil war and creation of Belgium in 1830 seemed to deal a final blow to the glories of the Golden Age. Before the partition, the Dutch had imagined themselves as a kind of Prussia, a solid, northern, important country.[82] But the loss of Belgium shifted their thinking. As previously mentioned, the Dutch developed a "small state mentality." What did this mean? Certainly the Netherlands itself was (and is) a small country, physically speaking. Its land today comprises only about 13,000 square miles.[83] But, curiously, even after 1830 when it lost the territory of Belgium, its physical size was, in fact, not much different from its size at the height of its first Golden Age. Yet the Netherlands now viewed itself differently: it accepted itself as a small state, both physically and metaphorically, among the European great powers. As one Dutch academic points out, the Netherlands was just too small to count for much in either European or world history to the extent that "even modern historians tend to think disparagingly of their own national history."[84] The Netherlands was said to have the "touchiness of a small nation with a great past."[85] Like every other small European country, it had to maneuver to survive great power machinations—in a sense, the quest to survive trumped any ambitious desires or even thoughts of again seeking great power. As Abraham Kuyper, the Dutch prime minister elected to power in 1901, before the Aceh war had ended, once declared, "To own colonies is an honor; increases our prestige; brings us into a different position in Europe than we would have had without them; lets the glory of a famous past shine over our the weakness of our current nation; and for that reason it should be regarded as a privilege for which not a few envy us, and whose defence must therefore be valuable to us."[86] The Dutch "national feeling," or *vaderland gevoel*, which developed in the 19th century was a "heightened sense of history," involving a nostalgia for the Golden Age as well as a sense of lost confidence. Both self-fulfilling and justified, *vaderland gevoel* was distinct from nationalism as we conceive of it, for it lacked any activism or even ideological content.[87] But it impacted Dutch beliefs about their place in the world.

When discussing the Netherlands' treaties with the British, for example, Dutch politicians struggled with their own self-image as a great colonial power but a small state. Many from the Dutch Conservative Party opposed relinquishing the Gold Coast, and some Liberals joined them. The latter pointed out the historical and economic significance of the Gold Coast, while the conservative Dutch newspaper *Dagblad* spoke for many Conservative politicians when it blasted the ceding of the Gold Coast as "a suicidal and short-sighted policy."[88] Debating in Parliament, Conservatives lamented the mistake the Dutch were making in giving up Africa, "the land of the future."[89] On the other hand, some Conservatives joined Liberals in applauding the move. The Liberal newspaper *Algemeen Handelsblad* echoed the Liberal position that not only were commerce and free trade more important than colonies, but that owning colonies "imposed more obligations than before," with the colonial power having to bear the responsibility of "civilizing" the natives.[90] Conservative politician Eduard Herman s'Jacob agreed, asking sardonically, "Where are they—those Dutch Livingstones—who will risk their lives and property in the course of Africa's development and civilization?"[91] There was, thus, not necessarily a sharp ideological divide between Liberals and Conservatives on the treaties and the Netherlands' path forward so much as there was a debate. Dutch elites from both sides weighed the clear cost to the Dutch of ceding Africa to the British in the absence of both threat and material gains with the feeling that the Netherlands, as a small country, should make do with Indonesia, and keep the British out of that territory.

Again during the Berlin Conference, and later when the great powers held the Suez Convention in Constantinople in 1888 to regulate the use of the Suez Canal, Dutch angst was on display. At Berlin, a member of the Dutch Parliament lamented that the country, the second largest colonial power in Asia and the third largest to use the canal, was making itself "smaller and less important" than it actually was. Another member of Parliament questioned why the Netherlands, a country with "a major [colonial] role to play" did not ally with Spain and Portugal to protect its colonial and maritime interests.[92] Eschewing the bold steps of a fellow small country, Belgium, which staked its own lucrative claim in the Congo, the Dutch would confine themselves instead to praising its actions: the annual report of the Rotterdam Chamber of Commerce lauded Belgium's King Leopold as "that excellent monarch," and praised his vision of a free state with free trade.[93]

In Constantinople, the Dutch government dithered so much on signing and ratification that Dutch lawyer Tobias Michael Asser (later awarded the Nobel Peace Prize for his work in international law) had to take the Dutch ministerial delegate to task—reminding him that the Netherlands was one of the "most important" users of the canal and "should not allow itself to be pushed into the background because of prudence taken to extremes."[94]

The Dutch thought of their country in moralistic terms. After significant struggle, a new liberal constitution had been drafted in 1848. This constitution curtailed the monarchy, separated church and state, and established many freedoms, including freedom of the press, direct elections, and ministerial accountability. These changes had been championed by the Liberal leader Johan Rudolf Thorbecke, and under his aegis the language of principles began creeping into Dutch foreign policy. With the glorious past behind them and having no further pretensions to great power, the Dutch not only thought of themselves as a moral country, but also correspondingly as virtuously lacking international ambition. They were different from those nakedly ambitious Europeans surrounding their small country. Thorbecke declared, "the Dutch policy, being itself free from lust for power, is the most impartial judge of other nations' lust for power."[95] As one historian wryly pointed out, the Dutch government tended to judge "itself by its motives, and others by their actions."[96]

Now, far from being militaristic, the Dutch national character was said to have evolved, as Henk te Velde has argued, to be stereotypically *burgerlijke*—that is, bourgeois, middle class, and devoted to civic virtues.[97] The term *burgerlijke* stemmed from Dutch cultural historian Johan Huizinga, who summed up the beliefs of the time in his work *Spirit of the Netherlands*. While Huizinga wrote his treatise in 1934, the origins of his argument can be traced to the 19th century. Many intellectuals thought the Dutch middle class was the "core" of the nation, providing, as the scholar Robert Fruin pointed out, "reliable but conventional workers" who would "determine the course of the nation."[98] This bourgeois Dutch national character was the embodiment of civic freedom and virtues; the Dutch respected the rights and opinions of others; they were "neat and proper," "unheroic" and "lack[ed] military spirit."[99] Even children's books emphasized that it was better to be the most moral nation in the world than the most powerful nation in the world.[100]

This idea of the civic-minded, moral, and good country that they thought themselves to be extended to how they believed they were administering, or should administer, their colonies. By the mid- to late 19th century, the Dutch had developed a moral, and frankly paternalistic, sense of responsibility toward their colonies, the culmination of which would be the abolition of the cultivation system, and the establishment of what was dubbed the "Ethical Policy." A movement to understand the plight of the natives in the Dutch East Indies began during this period, spurred in large part by Dutchmen who had spent time in the colonies. Among the most famous of them, a Dutch civil servant in the East Indies colonial government, E. Douwes Dekker, returned to Europe and in 1860 published a novel under the *nom de plume* Multatuli. The novel, *Max*

Havelaar or the Coffee Auctions of the Dutch Trading Company, was a damning indictment of the Dutch government and the exploitative cultivation system. Centered on a greedy bourgeois Dutch coffee trader, Batavus Droogstroppel, and the arrival of a new assistant-resident[101] with a strong sense of fairness and justice, Max Havelaar, it exposed the sorry plight of Javanese peasants, forced to cultivate coffee and squeezed for profit by the local princes at the behest of the colonial administration. Dekker ended *Havelaar* with a plea to King William III to restore justice in the Dutch East Indies. The impact of *Max Havelaar* among the Dutch elite cannot be overstated: "There was not a single educated family in the Netherlands in which it was not read."[102] The novel deeply shocked the Dutch elite, violating as it did their image of the country as benevolent and civic and non-imperialistic. Abraham Kuyper spoke for many Dutch elites when he found it "an utter absurdity" to say that the Dutch in Indonesia were imperialists.[103] *Havelaar* was also published at a time when sentimentalism as a literary technique had gained traction; it offered a glimpse into the lives of ordinary Javanese, gave the readers a window into suffering and how it could be stopped, and consequently made "intervention a moral imperative."[104]

Havelaar would notably influence one of the first architects of the ethical policy, Conrad Theodor van Deventer, a civil servant and lawyer in the Dutch East Indies. In 1899, van Deventer penned an article for the liberal Dutch journal *De Gids*, titled "A Debt of Honor" (*Een Eereschuld*). In it he argued that he believed the Dutch had failed to do their duty in their colonies, and that while the Dutch government had the right to use revenues from the colonies to pay their own debts, they also had to look after the welfare of the Javanese, and stop colonial transfers of money when any budgetary problems had been resolved. Fundamentally, the Dutch owed the Javanese "a debt of honor" which was equal to the colonial transfers of money to the Dutch budget after 1867.[105] (The year 1867 was when the Compatibility Law—*Comptabiliteitswet*—went into force, mandating a separate colonial budget that had to be approved by the Dutch parliament.) van Deventer's article landed in the Dutch parliament with a bang, leading to impassioned discussions on future Dutch policy. P. Brooshooft, a Dutch journalist at the time for several newspapers in the East Indies, averred that van Deventer's article was the single most influential piece of writing on colonial policy since *Havelaar*.[106] Brooshooft went on to argue that the Dutch had a special duty to care for the Javanese as a "good father" and to improve their well-being. In return, they could demand two things from the native population: obedience to Dutch authority and the paying of taxes.[107] Administration such as the cultivation system was not wrong per se, he continued, but stood in need of improvement to minimize exploitation by private interests.[108]

Prime Minister Kuyper agreed with such moral sentiments, arguing that the system of exploitation was morally wrong, and that any reform of the Dutch colonial system needed to raise the morals of the native population, make the system profitable for the Dutch and the natives, and eventually give the colony more autonomy. The Dutch needed to ask themselves not " 'what does Java yield to us?' but only 'what does God want us to be to Java?' "[109] In 1901, the new queen, Wilhelmina, gave a speech to the nation making an official statement about the ethical policy. In it she declared:

> As a Christian Power the Netherlands are obliged to improve the legal status of the native Christians on the Indian Archipelago, to provide the Christian mission support on a more fixed basis, and to base the whole policy of the government on the awareness that the Netherlands have to fulfill a moral obligation towards the peoples of these regions. In this respect, our particular attention is drawn to the lesser prosperity of the native population on Java. I want to set up an investigation into the causes of this. The regulations to protect the coolies who are under contract, will be strictly enforced. We strive for administrative decentralisation.[110]

The thrust of these beliefs, including *Havelaar* and similar other works, was not to deny that the Netherlands should own colonies or even to directly attack the cultivation system, but to advocate for a more fatherly, benevolent, and gentler approach. As Cees Fasseur points out, the cultivation system went into decline "not primarily for socio-economic reasons . . . but because it collided with the liberal ideology which prevailed more and more in Dutch politics after 1850."[111] This climate led to a spate of reproaches, and to a search for a more ethical policy that would allow the Netherlands to continue to profit while civilizing the natives with a rod of bamboo perhaps, rather than iron. The natives were considered helpless and in need of Dutch protection, which the Netherlands had a moral obligation to provide; this was in keeping with its narratives about its own image as a morally upright and civilized Christian nation.[112] And reflecting the beliefs of this period, histories of Dutch colonialism written in the early 20th century by Dutch historians largely avoided the terms "imperialism" and "empire"[113] and replaced them with more neutral phrases such as "rounding of the state," "the unification of Indonesia," and "the establishment of Dutch authority."[114]

Conclusion

As we've seen, the Netherlands viewed itself as a benevolent, ethical power,[115] and as an exemplar country (*gidsland*, or literally "good state," implying a "guiding state")[116] that was non-martial, non-aggressive, and unambitious. It could not, therefore, accept the idea of itself as a colonizer or imperialist in the mold of the colonizing great powers of the day. Even though, in many respects, the Dutch modus operandi in its colonies was similar to that of the other colonial powers of the time (post-1870), it was a "reluctant imperialist."[117] This "reluctance" was different from the reluctance of some American elites to embrace colonialism and colonies. The debate in the United States was whether to become a colonial power at all. In contrast, the Dutch both accepted and profited from their colonies. Their "reluctance" stemmed instead from their belief that Dutch colonialism was only very superficially similar to the colonialism of other powers.

Simultaneously, Dutch behavior on the world stage differed from the other European colonizing nations, despite its status as one of the richest countries in Europe and the second largest colonial power in the world. The Netherlands preferred passive over active diplomacy. One set of historians called Dutch policy during this time one of "passive neutrality." Indeed, they continued, "[t]he Dutch developed the small power policy to a point little short of perfection. [Their] determination to play a passive role in world politics was so strong as to amount almost to an obsession."[118] Thus, an issue such as Dutch diplomacy around the Congo question was discussed only very superficially in Parliament—it simply was not a huge topic of interest in the 1880s despite the Netherlands' status. As Wesseling stated, "No one really cared very much about Africa." The Berlin Conference mattered only inasmuch as it was a part of international relations and forwarding the interests of "civilized nations."[119] The Dutch expanded power within their areas of territorial control in Southeast Asia, but these decisions were made in response to local imperatives by the Dutch colonial government, rather than driven by a policy initiative from The Hague. And they both hesitated to expand beyond the Dutch East Indies and stayed aloof from Africa and China, other lucrative areas of colonial opportunity.

Within the East Indies, the Dutch gradually dismantled the highly profitable cultivation system, which had a huge impact on revenues—by about 1878, the traditional surplus in this area of the Dutch budget had turned into a deficit partly as a result of the shift.[120] They were still determined to hold on to and profit from the Dutch East Indies—extending authority within the colony and establishing a colonial state but at a micro-level, without intent of expansion beyond the colony.[121] But they were determined to do so in a manner that fit their perception of themselves as a different kind of colonizer. The ethical policy was declared official doctrine, "making explicit that the Dutch had the aspiration to 'elevate' the colonized subjects economically and culturally."[122] As historians have pointed out, this did not actually mean that the Dutch were not exploitative imperialists,[123] even if their practices differed from the other European powers, but rather that the Dutch narratives of the time painted the Netherlands as different. The Dutch saw themselves not as modern imperialists but as the

guardians of native tradition and welfare, offering enlightened and efficient administration.[124] The very idea that the Netherlands could ever again even move
toward great power was absent—the Dutch put their glory days firmly in the
past, and moved on by embracing the notion of themselves as virtuous and
moral, a small shining example to the rest of the world. Good powers could not,
by definition, be imperialists. By the norms of the international order of the day,
if they were not imperialists they could not be great powers. And it was, after all,
better to be a good power than a great power.

The late 19th-century Netherlands is a fascinating and important lens
through which to understand reticence. It shows us not only the problems of
simply using material power as a yardstick to understand rising powers, but
also how some countries are puzzlingly reticent, even when taking into account
other factors such as geopolitical constraints. The Netherlands was reticent not
compared to the great powers of the day. It was reticent given its opportunities
and the behaviors of other European nations. The Netherlands case also shows
us that narratives of great "power-dom," if you will, do not necessarily stem from
material attributes. The Netherlands was a great colonial power, but not only did
it refuse to describe itself as such, it eschewed colonial ambition.

Thus, the United States and the Netherlands behaved very differently in the
age of colonial great power. They both acknowledged the norm of the day, that
great power meant owning and exploiting colonies. But they responded to that
norm differently. The United States would ultimately conform to that norm, and
it continued to rise as a great power-to-be. The Netherlands accepted only a portion of the norm—great powers did hold colonies and were imperialistic. But in
terms of how the Netherlands saw itself, the country was not imperialistic, despite its colony, and could not ever be like the implicitly immoral great powers.
But as we will see in the next chapter, the idea of equating colonies with great
power was not confined to Anglo-Saxon elites. Meiji Japan also wholeheartedly
embraced the late 19th-century European-imposed international order. It was
an active rising power. But after World War II, when Japan rose again in terms of
material strength, its embrace of the international order was reticent. And, by the
1990s, the notion of Japan as a rising power had disappeared, to be replaced with
warnings about the rise of China and India. The vignette of Japan in two time
periods serves as a bridge between the late 19th and late 20th centuries, from a
Western century of great power to the beginning of what has been dubbed "the
Asian century."[125]

Meiji Japan and Cold War Japan

A Vignette of Rise and Reticence

Japan presents a fascinating case of a country that rose in at least two different time periods over the course of a century—1870–1914 and 1960–1989—but emerged as a great power in only the former. It also behaved very differently in these two time periods. During the Meiji era of the late 19th century, Japan was an active rising power. By World War I, Japan's status as a major power was established—it defeated a Western country (Russia) in a war in 1905, it joined the World War on the winning side of the Allies, and after the war was invited to join the newly created League of Nations in 1920, and the Washington Conference to create the rules of order in the Pacific in 1921–1922. In the interwar period, Japan was frustrated with the West, particularly the United States, and turned to activism and challenged the international order—it exited the League of Nations and the Washington system, and grew closer to Germany and Italy to form an alliance during World War II.[1] Though World War II ended in Japan's defeat, after the war Japan would rise again, and its rise would be recognized and feared by the international community. But Cold War Japan would remain reticent and would not fulfill international expectations. Similar to the cases of active and reticent powers discussed thus far, Japan developed narratives about becoming a great power during the Meiji period, but did not in the era after World War II. This chapter is a vignette of Japan, its similar material rise, its dissimilar behavior, and the presence and absence of narratives in these two time periods. The contrast between Meiji Japan and Cold War Japan is an important story for us to touch on for several reasons. Japan shows us that narratives about becoming a great power in the style of the great power of the day were not simply a Western phenomenon in the late 19th century. Moreover, it re-emphasizes that rising powers do not rise by becoming revisionist. They rise by accepting the international order. Meiji Japan rose to become a great power not because it revised the international order, but because it adhered closely to

Why Nations Rise. Manjari Chatterjee Miller, Oxford University Press (2021). © Oxford University Press.
DOI: 10.1093/oso/9780190639938.003.0004

it, embracing Western norms of great power before it became revisionist. At the same time, it is not a given that a once great power will always rise again and produce narratives about great power, even if it has the material power to do so. Post–World War II Japan was said to be *the* next great power to fear. Yet by the late 1980s Japan's influence had petered out, and international society turned its eyes instead, as Chapter 5 details, toward China as the next possible threat to world peace. Meiji Japan and post–World War II Japan were different not just because they had different regimes and leaders, but also because the former had narratives about greatness while the latter did not.

The Rise of Meiji Japan: 1870–1914

From the Tokugawa Regime to the Meiji Restoration

For centuries prior to 1854, Japan was closed to the rest of the world, and was ruled by the Tokugawa dynasty through a *shogunate*—a hereditary military dictatorship in which a *shogun* (general) ruled in the name of the Japanese emperor with the help of officials collectively referred to as *bakufu* (tent government). Japanese elites had very strongly ethnocentric perceptions of the world outside of their borders. They regarded the "Southern barbarians" (Europeans but also Indians and Southeast Asians) as uncivilized peoples whose culture and morals were beyond the pale.[2] But in 1854, a seminal crisis occurred: the American Commander Matthew Perry led a naval expedition to Japan and used military and diplomatic pressure to forcibly open the country to the West, ending Japan's 200-plus years of isolation. This crisis foreshadowed a series of events, the most important of which was the Meiji Restoration of 1868, which would eventually lead to the complete transformation of Japanese society, nation, and state.

Once Japan was opened to the world, it was coerced into signing a series of treaties with the United States, the British, the Russians, the French, and the Dutch. These treaties forced it to cede trading rights, open new treaty ports, extend special legal protections which would allow foreigners to travel through Japan, and establish both trade and diplomatic relations with foreign countries, which it had steadfastly refused to do for centuries. With the end of the policy of isolation, Japanese elites now realized that expelling the Westerners from their country was a futile quest. As they saw it, the only alternative remaining to them was to make Japan "as strong as the foreigners through a policy of 'national wealth and strength.'"[3] But this would require unification of the country and the sweeping away of the Tokugawa dynasty which had formed the ruling *shogunate* since the 16th century.

Thus, in January 1868, a military coup led by rebel samurai toppled the shogunate. The rebels established the reign of the young Emperor Meiji, the son and heir of the Emperor Komei who had been a mere figurehead through whom the *shogun* and samurai elite had wielded power, as the rightful ruler of Japan. They claimed to sweep away the traditional administration and restore imperial rule by setting up a new imperial government.[4]

The Meiji Restoration revolutionized Japan. While the actual events of 1868 in fact simply heralded a shift of power between established elites—the rebellion originally came from lower-ranking samurai, but soon power in the Meiji court was reconsolidated in the hands of the old samurai elite who had neither popular support nor representation[5]—the process that was the Meiji Restoration eventually demolished the class of samurai warriors altogether,[6] converting the Tokugawa feudal society into a modern centralized state led by a modernized monarchy.[7] Under the Tokugawa dynasty, Japan had been unified only in a cultural and historical sense rather than a political one. Not only was there no single government that maintained order throughout the country, there was also no single political center to which people pledged total loyalty. Thus, the priority of the Meiji regime was the consolidation of control over the whole of Japan, and the creation of the idea of Japan as a single nation under a powerful emperor. This was a first step toward overcoming the "national humiliation" that Japan had suffered at the hands of Westerners.[8] The Meiji emperor was reinvented to be the focus of all political loyalty. While many modern countries of that time were monarchies, the Meiji imperial system was different. Japanese elites deliberately created a centralized imperial system whereby the military and bureaucrats were authorized by the sanctity accorded to Emperor Meiji's personage—the emperor was made a symbol of both national unification and legitimacy. This enabled the elite to give the rapid modernization and reforms that would occur under his aegis an imperial legitimacy, and thus gain acceptance for them in Japanese society.[9]

The task of building Japan into a great power began in earnest with radical reforms implemented in the late 19th century. This meant a complete military and economic transformation of Japan, and also, importantly, the acquisition of that hallmark of great power in the 19th century, overseas colonies.

The Rise of Japan's Material Power

The Meiji Restoration and Japan's rapid reform of its military and economy during this period were nothing short of astonishing. The British historian John Keegan declared the Meiji reforms to be "one of the most radical changes of national policy recorded in history."[10] During the Tokugawa era, Japan had a quasi-feudal society, and its economic development during that period was considered to be similar to Western Europe during the Middle Ages. But after the Meiji Restoration, along with sweeping internal reforms to restructure land, property, and trading rights and demolish the feudal system, Japan now opened itself up to the Industrial Revolution, and the corresponding growth of modern capitalism.[11] There was now a "feverish process of modernization."[12] The Meiji government reorganized the banking system, stabilized and refunded the national debt, and improved Japan's international credit standing, while also modernizing the army and navy, improving transportation and communications, and establishing new industries.[13]

Between 1868 and 1878, Japan's foreign trade more than doubled.[14] In 1866 Japan had built its first steamship and initiated steamer service between Yokohama and Nagasaki. It had also opened its first silk factory, cotton spinning mills, and factories that would produce cement, sugar, beer, glass, chemicals and many other goods that appealed to the West. Between 1876 and 1896, mineral production increased sevenfold. Between 1870 and 1872, Japan constructed its first railroad from Tokyo to Yokohama with a loan from the British. By 1893 Japan had built or acquired 2,000 miles of operating railway lines, 100,000 tons of steam vessels, 4,000 miles of telegraph lines and "shipyards, arsenals, foundries, machine shops, and technical schools," all established or modernized with the help of foreign aid and equipment and the advice of foreign experts. The country became a leading exporter of raw silk (which accounted for up to 42 percent of Japan's total exports abroad) as well as tea, rice, copper, coal, and handicrafts.[15]

As a result, the 1890s were revolutionary for the Japanese economy. Building on the foundations of the earlier Meiji years, Japan now entered an era of industrial output. By 1914 total production and real income in Japan had increased between 80 percent and 100 percent.[16] Its imports and exports had doubled in the 1890s and doubled again in the 1900s. This provided valuable foreign exchange with which Japan could buy foreign machinery, equipment, and raw materials to meet both industrial and military requirements. One measure of industrial activity, coal consumption, increased to 15 million tons in 1915 (up from 3.6 million tons in 1896[17]). Japan was not in the front rank of industrial powers, but its capabilities were changing rapidly. Clearly, Japan was undergoing an Industrial Revolution with corresponding increases to its GDP and power.[18]

Simultaneously, hand in hand with its large-scale industrialization, Japan undertook a massive revamping of its military. There were two stages of military reform in the post-Tokugawa period. At first, these reforms were focused on the idea of national conscription and the modernization—that is, the Westernization—of the organization, training, and equipment of its armed forces. Prior to the events of 1868, and struck by the obvious superiority of Western technology and Western military forces, Japan had already adopted "defensive Westernization"[19]—many powerful elites looked to both Western technology and recruitment practices, relying particularly heavily on the advice of the French. This would later come in handy to defeat the *shogun* who had been forced to open Japan to the West. But Japan now realized it needed to acquire modern lethal weapons and transform the samurai, an "army of occupation" that had enjoyed a long period of peace, into rifle companies.[20] Thus, with the Meiji Restoration, Japan undertook major military reform. In 1871, not coincidentally, the year when fiefs were abolished and the power to tax became the sole province of the central government, an Imperial Guard of 10,000 was established that was to be controlled directly by the central government. In 1873 the Guard was dissolved, and instead universal conscription for all Japanese men of the age of twenty and in good physical health was adopted. The army was now modeled on both the French and the Prussian armies—in the organization and training of the army, Japan followed the French, while conscription was based on the Prussian notion of universal military service.[21] In 1882 an Army Staff College was established, and by 1886, the Japanese army was a "flexible, mobile, offensive force" with seven divisions that could also operate as independent units. It was an army that could "mobilize, prepare for and execute large-scale war."[22] Japan also undertook a major reform of its navy. In 1869 a naval training school had been set up to train Japanese officers with the help of British officers. Unsurprisingly, given Britain's global naval superiority, the navy was modeled along British lines. By 1875 Japan had launched its first warship, and by the 1890s a modern fleet began to emerge—by 1894 Japan had 28 ships totaling 57,000 tons, and 24 torpedo boats; by 1903 it had 76 warships of 250,000 tons and 76 torpedo boats.[23] These innovations were not radical simply because they were new to Japan; rather, they were also radical because this was the first time such reforms had been enacted on a national scale.[24]

It is important to note that economic development and military reform went hand in hand. That is, Japan's economic development and industrialization fueled the military reforms, but the military reforms in turn also fueled development. The Meiji government tried to standardize and modernize the manufacture of munitions because acquiring and directly managing its arsenal allowed it to develop economically but also strategically. By 1877 almost two-thirds of the government's total investments were targeted toward the military.[25] Modern transportation, communication, and the acquisition of heavy industrial technologies were all seen as intertwined in the goal of building great power. By the eve of World War I the Japanese had achieved self-sufficiency in the production of military and naval weapons,[26] and its economy was well integrated with the rest of the world.

Japan, however, was not simply a rising power because it had rapidly increased its economic and military capabilities. Meiji Japan also began behaving like a great power-to-be, globalizing its authority and seeking to shape internal and external perceptions of the nation. And importantly, it sought that great power symbol of the day: the acquisition of colonies.

Meiji Japan: The Active Path to Great Power

Japan's path to becoming a colonial power began with its increasing encroachment on Korea beginning in 1869, would lead to an eventual war with China in 1894, and would culminate in 1904 with a surprise attack on and defeat of Russia's fleet stationed in Port Arthur. The acquisition of colonial territories through these conflicts would mean that Japan would eventually be recognized by the West and admitted into the ranks of the colonial powers.

Japan's colonial designs on Korea can be traced back to 1869, just after the Meiji Restoration. Korean officials challenged Japanese authority and the foundation of the Meiji Restoration by questioning the very idea of Meiji as an emperor rather than a king. The East Asian regional system had hitherto been organized around the idea of China and its imperial authority at the center of a tributary system, with neighboring countries occupying a lower tier in the hierarchy.[27] Thus, for the Koreans, Meiji was a mere king, for only the Chinese could possibly have an emperor whom neighboring vassal countries recognized. For the Koreans, changing this perception of Meiji would cast the Korean monarch as a vassal of the Japanese emperor.[28] The Korean refusal to recognize an Emperor Meiji was an inauspicious greeting of the Meiji Restoration and set the stage for the gradual deterioration of the bilateral relationship. By 1873, the relationship entered crisis mode: the Japanese resented Korea's treatment of its envoys and merchants, along with Korea's steadfast denial of the change from *shogunate* to imperial rule, with the Korean government refusing even to accept the official greetings of the Japanese emperor.[29]

By 1876 the Japanese had used military and naval force to compel Korea to sign the punitive Treaty of Kanghwa. Under the treaty, Korea was now an independent and sovereign state; Japan declared that Korea was no longer a vassal state of China, and as such could no longer look to it for foreign policy decisions or support. Thus, Japan forced Korea to open three ports for trade, and to accept Japanese officials in these ports along with the right of Japanese ships to come to Korean shores for "wood, water, and shelter."[30] Later treaties forced Korea to accept a diplomatic exchange, and gave Japan the right to survey Korean waters and the right to extraterritoriality. Another supplementary treaty went even further: Japanese could now buy Korean goods with Japanese currency at face value; there would be no Korean tariffs on Japanese imports and exports; and in turn there would be no duties levied by Japan on goods going to or coming from Korea.[31] Japan's early machinations in Korea did not yet involve territorial control of the country—Japan would not formally annex Korea until 1910—but they represented Japan's gradual steps toward becoming an imperialist country in two important ways. They set the stage for the war with China and the war with Russia, both of which would yield colonies for Japan.

In 1890, Prime Minister Yamagata gave a speech to the legislature arguing that it was crucial for an independent Japan to maintain "a line of sovereignty and a line of advantage."[32] By this he meant that Japan needed both a secure homeland and a buffer zone—Korea—to protect it. Moreover, this buffer zone needed to be protected from both the Chinese and the Russians.[33] Thus, in 1894, when the Korean government asked China to send troops to help it quell a domestic rebellion, Japan accused Beijing of intervening in an independent Korea, and in turn, dispatched its own troops to the country. On August 1, Japan formally declared war on China to great public approval in Japan. By 1895 Japan had won the war and had imposed on China the punitive Treaty of Shimonoseki. The war and the defeat of China were an utter shock to the regional balance of power. The Treaty of Shimonoseki, which gave Japan vast rights, heralded its changing regional status—no longer was it the little brother to China. Instead, China was forced to allow Japan special commercial rights, pay it an indemnity of nearly ¥350 million, and recognize Korea's independence. Moreover, the treaty yielded a rich prize and symbol of great power—colonies. Japan obtained the Pescadore islands, Taiwan, and the Liaodong Peninsula, which was the southern part of Manchuria.[34] Japan had begun a colonial empire.

However, while Japan was allowed to retain Taiwan as a colony, the Western powers—Russia, Germany, and France, in what was to be dubbed the "Triple Intervention"—forced Japan to return the Liaodong Peninsula to China in exchange for an increase in indemnity. Lacking the military strength at the time to challenge them, Japan reluctantly agreed. But the issue was far from settled. The following years saw the development of a rivalry between Russia and Japan in Korea, with the Russians adopting the role of the protector of the Korean king. Moreover, by 1898 Russia also secured its own control over the Liaodong Peninsula by moving Russian troops into Manchuria after the Boxer Rebellion in China—a rebellion that Japan had helped end by contributing troops to the international force—and then failed to follow a promised timetable for withdrawing the troops. By 1904 Japan was incensed by both Russian control over Korea and Russian control of Liaodong, which the Japanese had been forced to give up just a decade before.

Thus, on February 8, 1904, Japan embarked on its second imperialist war by launching a surprise attack on Russia's fleet stationed in Port Arthur, at the very southern tip of the Liaodong Peninsula. In hindsight, the hostilities between Russia and Japan that would culminate in the 1904 war had been building for decades. While the immediate purpose of the war was to protect Japanese interests from Russian encroachment in Manchuria, the underlying and more important reason was Japan's fixation on maintaining its rights in Korea. Military action against Russia was in a sense inevitable when that country would not acknowledge the special rights that Japan had in Korea. And controlling Korea, the

Japanese had long believed, was crucial to Japan becoming a great power. While Taiwan was Japan's first colonial territory, the first step on the road to empire, "the heart" of Japan's strategic colonial concerns was in Korea.[35]

Japan decisively won the war against Russia, obtaining Russia's rights in southern Manchuria/Liaodong Peninsula, its recognition of Japan's interests in Korea, and sovereignty, in perpetuity, over the southern half of Sakhalin Island. It is difficult to overstate the international importance of Japan's victory. Defeating China had changed the distribution of regional power and hierarchy in East Asia, but defeating Russia put Japan firmly within sight of great power. This was the late 19th–early 20th century world where owning colonies had often been justified by the great powers that held them as "the white man's burden." A "non-white" nation defeating a "white" nation was "stunning" to the West.[36] This defeat of a Western great power by a small Asian country was the final step in sealing Japan's reputation as a colonial power. It not only heralded the arrival of Japan as a great power-to-be, but also overturned the racial notions of the time that great powers could emerge only from the West.

Thus, Meiji Japan's economic and military modernization in the late 19th century was accompanied by Japan's acquisition of colonies. This was active—not revisionist—behavior. Japan was attempting to globalize its authority and shape both domestic and international perceptions of its rise, but in a manner that not only was accommodational of prevailing great power norms and the international order, but also was *seen* as accommodational by the great powers.

Active and Accommodational of Great Power Norms

As Japan became active, launched its imperialist wars, and began acquiring the symbol of great power, colonies, it was exceedingly careful to do so, both domestically and internationally, according to established Western symbolic and legal norms, practices, and administrative styles.

From the very beginning of the Meiji Restoration, Japan was keenly aware of Western great power, and sought to adopt its mores within the country, both symbolically and militarily. Once the Emperor Meiji was established as a symbol of unification, the Japanese government installed visibly Western symbols of the nation-state, including a flag, a national anthem, and national holidays such as the emperor's birthday.[37] Moreover, they reformed their military in the style of Western militaries of the day. Acquiring Western weapons, technology, and training became crucial to their military advancement.

In the years after its forced opening to the West, when anti-foreign sentiment ran high, Japan banned any assaults on foreigners, and launched a propaganda campaign to educate the people on abandoning what were seen as the old, bad habits of being anti-foreigner. This in turn allowed foreigners to travel freely through Japan, not needing any of the special systems of legal protections that were included by the West in treaties imposed upon Japan. This would later allow Japan to push the Western great powers for treaty revisions leaving out these special protections.[38]

Internationally, Japan was meticulous about conducting itself—and being seen to conduct itself—by the prevailing laws of the international order, including the way it conducted war. For example, Japan adopted the first Geneva Convention, in 1864, as well as the Brussels declaration of 1874 and the Hague convention of 1899, governing the humanitarian treatment of prisoners and rule of conduct during conventional warfare. It also established a Japanese Red Cross, allowing impartial treatment of war wounded. Subsequently, in its 1904 war with Russia, Japan made an immense and intensely public effort to display legal military behavior and "civilized" standards. When the war started, the Japanese government issued regulations on how to treat enemy prisoners of war (POWs) humanely. Wounded Russian soldiers received prompt and efficient medical treatment, and captured POWs were "thoroughly looked after."[39] Moreover, Japan ensured that there were observers from the West who could testify to Japan's embrace of the laws set by great powers.[40] The treaties that Japan imposed upon Korea and China were the same kind of treaties that were the hallmark of the West, both in terms of legal structures and in terms of the humiliation of the countries in question. Japan proclaimed that the treaties were in accordance with "the law of nations," even as they privileged Japan at the expense of Korea and China. The Treaty of Kanghwa's imposition of the right of Japanese ships to come to shore in Korea for wood, water, and shelter emulated Commodore Perry's "wood and water treaty" when Japan opened its ports. Later impositions of Japan's right to survey Korean coastal waters and Japan's right to extraterritoriality emulated the 1858 Harris treaty that the United States had imposed upon Japan.[41]

Japan fit the definition of being accommodational not simply because it, too, along with the Western powers, aspired to hold and exploit overseas possessions of its own. Once Japan acquired colonies, it administered them domestically and justified them internationally according to the legal and political norms set by the other imperialist powers. Japan launched reforms in both Taiwan and Korea that were along the lines of colonial administrations set up by Western powers. The historian Mark Peattie points out that the Japanese transformed Taiwan from an "embarrassment to a colonial showcase" by adopting European colonial policies to administrate and develop the island and extract resources.[42] Similarly, in Korea, Japan set up an extractive colony; that is, the Korean economy was developed for Japan's advantage.[43] Japan sought to build and control railroad lines, telegraph lines, mines, and even the postal service in Korea. On top of that, as Japan extended its influence in Korea, it sought to depict itself as bringing Western legal order to a country that lacked civilized laws. Consequently, Japan completely reordered Korea's legal codes and judicial system,[44] incorporating European notions of criminal law, and operating courts according to the European three-tiered trial system.[45] Even prisons were structured according to established Western laws.[46] Japan's colonies therefore also had a clear distinction, just like European colonies, between the colonizer and the colonized. Moreover, Japan, as we will see when we examine Japanese idea advocacy, went to great lengths to establish that it was bringing "civilization" to inferior peoples, just as the European powers had claimed to have done.

It is important to note here that although Japan's behavior was accommodational of prevailing great power norms, this should not be taken to mean that Japan's imperialism was exactly the same as Western imperialism. Unlike most of the geographically distant colonized territories held by Western countries, Japan's imperialism centered on territories contiguous to it. Moreover, in line with its rapid domestic transformation, Japan's imperial expansion was also quicker than that of Western countries. Yet colonization it was, not mere conquest. Just like the Western colonizing nations, Japan created and expanded its sphere of influence, instituted patterns of economic and political exploitation, and created racial, political, and economic hierarchies of difference between itself and its colonized populations.

It is equally important to point out that Japan's active behavior was not a predetermined outcome of its growing material might. Japan's imperialist wars and colonizing undoubtedly strengthened its security and its economic strength. However, the wars it undertook were also risky wars. Japan attempted to extend its influence beyond its borders to acquire colonies at a time when no Western great power recognized its rights in the region. Even Asian countries questioned Japan's assumption of authority, as the authority in the region stemmed from the personage of the Chinese emperor. The war with Russia was a particular risk—Japan was substantially weaker than Russia militarily when it initiated war. Russia was capable of mobilizing an army of 4.5 million men, while the Japanese army numbered about 850,000. Even in naval strength, Russia far outstripped Japan—it had the fourth largest navy in the world in tonnage (510,000 tonnage to Japan's 260,000).[47]

Moreover, as historian Peter Duus shows, the industrialization of Japan "did not impel the Japanese leaders to adopt imperialist policy . . . but merely empowered them to do so." In other words, while industrialization was necessary for Japan to acquire colonies, it did not make that acquisition inevitable.[48] Noted historian Akira Iriye agrees, calling the Russo-Japanese war a "quintessentially imperialistic war," fought as it was between two countries over issues outside of each country's boundaries at the expense of other ethnicities who had no say in the matter at all. The war was not a product of economic interests—Japanese trade with Korea was not so extensive that it needed to defend it at that point. Even Japan's interests in Manchuria did not occupy a substantial portion of its total trade.[49] It was also not obvious that in order to modernize, Japan would have had to acquire Western ways and conform to Western norms and order. We can see the contrasting example of another Asian country, China, which also modernized, but slowly, reluctantly, and resentfully. When China also adopted Western weapons, for example, they rejected the Western civilization from which such military technology emanated. Japan, on the other hand, as we will see, "acted as if the superiority of Western arms were an integral part of Western military institutions and Western civilization, as if to adopt Western weapons [also] demanded Westernization."[50]

To understand Japan's behavior, we need to understand that Japan was behaving like a great power-to-be. In addition to modernizing and strengthening its military and undertaking rapid economic and industrial development, Japan was also globalizing its authority. With the acquisition of colonies, Japan had unquestionably joined the ranks of the imperialist powers and began behaving like them overseas.[51] Both domestically and internationally, it was seeking to change the narrative of how Japan was perceived—as a small inferior Asian country—and to gain recognition as a great power in the making. Owning colonies was a crucial part of this process. Japan's accommodational behavior was accompanied by beliefs about how to be a great power in the late 19th-century world. Historians such as Iriye have argued that a war such as the one with Russia in 1904–1905 could in fact be seen as a product of the belief among Japanese elites that this was the only way the country could both show that it was modernizing and becoming a modern great power.[52] Thus, if we turn now to observe some of these powerful beliefs that were prevalent among the elite during the Meiji Japan period, we find that Japan, like the United States in the late 19th century, also had idea advocacy. Along with the acquisition of material power, Japanese elites were putting forth new narratives about Japan's appropriate behavior as a great power-to-be, and this included owning colonies.

Meiji Japan and the Narratives of Attaining Great Power

What were some of the narratives that were driving the discourse in Japan during this time? The Japanese elite who took control during the Meiji Restoration were driven by two broad beliefs—that in order to become a great power Japan needed to Westernize, and that Japan needed to gain the recognition of the other great powers of the day. These two beliefs were interrelated. The other great powers of the day were all Western powers. Ergo, Japan needed to become a great power in the mold of the West. And the beliefs shaped subsequent narratives about how to gain great power—narratives pertaining to Japan's military, to economic development, and crucially, to colonialism. Japanese elites believed, as we will see, that Japan needed to acquire colonies, needed to impose the kinds of humiliating treaties that the West had imposed on Japan, needed to justify its governance of the colonies to the West, and needed to display racial superiority over the colonized. In other words, Japan was extremely accommodational of the prevailing international order and the norms of great power. As Foreign Minister Inoue Kaoru believed, "The nation and the people must be made to look like the European nations and European peoples."[53]

After the Meiji Restoration, when Japanese elites undertook rapid military and economic modernization, they turned, as we have seen, to the West for guidance. Not only were they determined to acquire Western weapons and know-how, but they, in turn, accepted that using Western technology would result not just in a complete revamping of Japan's military, but also in large-scale industrialization.[54] This was the beginning of a larger process of Westernization, as Japan eventually adopted even "Western science, Western morals . . . [and] Western dress."[55]

After the opening up of Japan, influential intellectuals like Sakuma Shozan and Yoshida Shoin argued that learning from the foreigners was rational. Sakuma Shozan put forth that Japan needed to study the Western military arts to become a great power. Yoshida Shoin called for sending talented Japanese abroad to study in the West, with "learning encompassing all knowledge," in the hopes that they would come back and disseminate what they had learned.[56] Later Meiji leaders would adopt these calls because they believed that conformance to Western standards and practices would gain Japan acceptance into international society.[57]

In 1870, for example, two prominent military officers, Yamagata Aritomo (later prime minister of Japan) and Saigo Tsugumichi came back to Japan after a tour of Europe, where they had been sent to study the military establishments of leading powers. They would both (particularly Yamagata, who was a leading voice in the Japanese military until his death in 1922) be instrumental in building the modern Japanese army. Saigo Tsugumichi often expressed his admiration of the French army and Napoleon. And Yamagata Aritomo believed that while the French army was worthy of praise, it was overconfident, and it was rather the quiet strength of the Prussians that needed to be emulated.[58] Eventually such beliefs were what pushed Japan to emulate the British to organize their navy, the French to train their army, and the Prussians to organize and operationalize their land forces. Japanese naval training schools would be staffed with British officers, and they would recruit French and Prussian officers to train their armies and staff their military academies.

The ultimate goals of Japanese leaders became to "catch up and surpass the West," and to combine "Western technology with Japanese spirit."[59] Thus, the Japanese slogan of "enrich the country, strengthen the military" (*fukoku kyohei*) became popular not only to emphasize military and economic development, but also to change the fabric of Japan. Elites such as Japanese entrepreneur Godai Saisuke of the powerful Satsuma clan wrote that Western countries were dominating the world because they were rich nations with strong armies.[60] This pronouncement became the official and public endorsement of Western military and economic development. Another Japanese motto infusing the process of Meiji modernization was "being civilized"—it meant accepting Western civilization as both positive and the fashion of the day. Over time, the Japanese began to accept even the parts of Western civilization that were not related to either the military or the economy. The ideas of freedom, Christianity, and civil rights began to be introduced to Japan by elites like pastor Ozaki Hiromichi, and scholars and politicians Tsuda Masamichi and Kato Hiroyuki.[61] Kato Hiroyuki believed, for example, that an absence of civil rights indicated a lack of civilization, while Tsuda Masamichi suggested that the government expose the Japanese to Christianity because it was the predominant religion of a "civilized" people.[62]

The Japanese began to, in a sense, now consider themselves Western, and therefore different from the other Asian countries. Not only that, some Japanese emphasized that Japan should not identify itself as an Asian country at all. Like European elites, Japanese elites too now looked down upon other Asian countries as inferior to them. One of the most important intellectuals of the time, Fukuzawa Yukichi, famously counseled his countrymen to "quit Asia and join the West," for, he said, other Asians were too backward to reform themselves, and if Japan identified with them they would only be tarred with the same "brush of Asian backwardness."[63] Another intellectual, Hinohara Shozo, wrote an article for Fukazawa Yukichi's newspaper in 1894 titled "Japan must not be an oriental country." In it he exhorted Japan to become civilized and strong like Europe by adopting Western ways.[64] Greatness meant leaving Asia behind in order to, as statesman Ito Hirobumi declared in 1899, become the "most civilized country in the far east."[65]

In such narratives, Japanese citizens were encouraged to triumph over lesser Asian nations just as Western great powers had done. Fukazawa Yukichi penned an article titled "Oppression Can Be Pleasant" in which he argued that he did not feel sorry for the Chinese in Hong Kong for their suffering under British colonial rule, and that if Japan were to acquire a navy similar to the British they would be able to control the Chinese even more effectively than the British had.[66] Japan's victory in the Sino-Japanese war was celebrated as the victory of Japanese modernity over Chinese backwardness. No wonder, then, that Japan in its triumph imposed on China the same kind of humiliating treaties—being required to withdraw from Korea, pay large sums of money, relinquish Taiwan, and cede to Japan the Liaodong Peninsula in southern Manchuria—that were the hallmark of European great powers.[67]

But the narratives in Japan about Westernization were not completely homogenous, nor did all Japanese accept the complete Westernization of Japanese society. The Society for Political Education, formed by a group of young Japanese men, feared that the path toward Western civilization could result in Japan "forfeit[ing] its national character and destroy[ing] [the traditional] elements of Japanese society."[68] A predominant belief which married traditional identities with a changing Japan was that the traditional Japanese "spirit" could be combined with Western technology (Japanese began to use the expression *wakon yosai*, "the Japanese spirit, the Western skill") to produce superior results. That is, the Japanese remained superior to the West in morality, and thus could remain Japanese at heart even while Westernizing[69] and becoming a Western-style imperialist power.

But whether trying to strike a balance between Westernizing and retaining a Japanese tradition, or advocating complete Westernization, with regard to the norms of the international order that had been built by the European great powers, Japanese narratives were strikingly accommodational. For Japanese elites, the path forward meant accepting the rules of the current international order and placing great emphasis on "the laws of the world." Japan diligently reworked Western civil codes into Japanese, transforming international terms into Japanese practice.[70] And advocating Japan's adherence to these laws—laws created by the West and used to maintain the current international order—became integral to Japan's rise. The Japanese believed that accepting these laws of the Western great powers would help it "assert its prestige in the world."[71] One specific way to assert its prestige was to own and administer colonies in ways that were politically and culturally in sync with Western norms, which would also "legitimate [Japan's] imperialist expansion."[72] Japan would acquire and exploit its colonies legally—in the same manner as other imperialist powers—because that was the path to becoming (and being accepted as) a great power. As Iriye points out, "No amount of apologetic writing alters the fact that between 1880 and 1895 Japan established colonial enclaves and spheres of dominance over Korea, Taiwan, and parts of China. . . . [Colonial domination] was not an end in itself, a premeditated goal for its own sake, but an aspect of Japan's development in a world environment defined by the major powers."[73] If the West could perfect the art of establishing colonial protectorates and successfully use them for their enrichment, it was perfectly reasonable for the Japanese to follow suit, just as they had done in their military and economic development, and to establish their own "civilized" credentials. Colonial expansion would help Japan overcome its inferior status, and restore "imperial prestige." Japanese elites, thus, saw Japan's role with regard to colonies as both "tutor and military hegemon."[74]

An important initial step on this path was making, as colonizers did, a strong distinction between themselves as a great country and those whom they would colonize. Thus, embracing Social Darwinism became very popular in Japan in the years after it acquired colonies. Japanese elites were obsessed with ranking their country in the hierarchy of nations, and they strongly differentiated themselves from the native populations of Taiwan and Korea.[75] Unlike the United States, there were no bitter divisions in Japan's narratives about whether or not to become a colonizing country. There were dissenters who criticized Japan's imperialistic adventures, but they were the minority. Rather, the give and take of ideas were about why Japan should colonize, and how aggressively, and how it should administer its colonies and treat the people under its rule.

Politicians like Takekoshi Yosaburo asserted that, like the Western powers who had long shouldered the responsibility of colonizing and civilizing the world, Japan too was now rising as a nation to do its part and participate "in this great and glorious work."[76] Journalist Shiga Shigetaka declared that Japan should mark the accession and death anniversaries of the first emperor annually by annexing unclaimed territory, an act that would "excite an expeditionary spirit and the demoralized Japanese race."[77] Ukita Kazutami, another prominent intellectual, wrote in 1902 that imperialism was not only the fashion of the day but also an excellent way to build national strength.[78] There were colonization societies organized by leading politicians of the time which urged colonization through peaceful methods by encouraging Japanese emigration to the colonies.[79] Spreading their civilization through colonization was a way of cementing their position as a modern power—in their own eyes and in the eyes of the West.

The Japanese historian and intellectual Tokutomi Soho declared before the Sino-Japanese war, "Our future history will be the history of the establishment by the Japanese of new Japans everywhere in the world."[80] The Sino-Japanese war was redefined by politicians such as Ito Hirobumi (the first Japanese resident-general of Korea, and later prime minister of Japan) as the Korean War of Independence, in which Japan had acted as a "friend" to Korea.[81] Sidestepping the issue of whether the Koreans deserved a say in their own affairs, Japan's imperialist adventures and wars with China and Russia were presented as entirely necessary for Korea's well-being, which was in keeping with the prevalent great power norm of enlightened exploitation. As Ito stated, "Watching Russia try to annex [the Liaodong peninsula] who became alarmed for the sake of [Korea]? For the fate of the Orient? It was Japan. Japan took up arms and sacrificed life and property."[82]

When Japan was forced to relinquish the Liaodong Peninsula after the war, it displayed even more intense efforts to show it was a civilized Western great power that could uphold all of the trappings that came with that role. Japanese colonial bureaucrats like Kodama Gentaro and Goto Shimpei launched reforms in Taiwan that emphasized "colonial order and efficiency" in the service of the universal task of civilization, turning it into a "colonial showcase."[83] Using "biological principles" of social Darwinism, Goto Shimpei spoke of a "hundred year plan" to evolve Taiwanese society, whereby the natives would be gradually "evolved" toward becoming more civilized.[84] Similar sentiments accompanied the governing and reform of Korea. When the Japanese "opened" Korea in 1876, they did so in ways that echoed Perry's expedition to Japan while touting the benefits of the "civilization" they were bringing to the Koreans.[85] "The Koreans can be slowly and gradually led in the direction of progress," said Japanese historian and legislature member Takekoshi Yosaburo.[86] There were also those who saw Japan's colonial responsibilities as including humane policies to bolster its reputation as a responsible colonial power.[87] Intellectuals such as Nitobe Inazo (who was the first occupant of the position of chair of colonial studies established at Tokyo University in 1908) framed Japanese expansion within the context of global colonialism and pondered the merits of specific European colonial systems in terms of how Japan might apply them.[88] Thus the Japanese elite debated not *whether* Korea (or other Japanese colonies) should be reformed, but *how* it should be.[89]

Such narratives in Meiji Japan correspond with how we have seen idea advocacy play out in other settings—they focused on materially attainable goals given the constraints of the international order; they acknowledged the prevalent norms of great power, and how Japan needed to acquire global authority; and they explained Japan's increasing involvement in the world for both a domestic and international audience. Japan rose by acting like a great power-to-be and accommodating, not revising, the norms of the international order of the time. This would change in the interwar period with Japan's turn to activism. But after World War II, Japan's next rise played out very differently.

Post–World War II: The Rise of Cold War Japan

After the devastation of World War II, one would scarcely have expected that Japan, a defeated nation, would rise again like the proverbial phoenix. But rise it did. Japan recovered from the devastation of war to become the world's second-ranked economic power. In 1979, Japan was ranked the "number one" country in the world.[90] The historian Paul Kennedy argued that Japan would be the next new world power,[91] while *Newsweek* magazine went even further, suggesting that Japan was going to become the next superpower, "supplanting America as the colossus of the Pacific."[92] Japan's rise was seen as an astounding development during the Cold War era. In a very short period of time, not only had a vanquished nation transformed itself into a country seemingly on the path to great power, but international perceptions of it transformed from enemy to ally to increasing threat.

Japan's near-miraculous rise needs to be understood in the context of American dominance of the Cold War world. After its defeat in World War II, from 1945 until 1952, Japan was controlled by the "Allied Occupation." But the name was misleading because in effect the occupation was entirely controlled by the United States, and the influence of the other victorious powers was negligible.[93] The United States was determined to enact policies that would bring postwar Japan within its sphere of influence, modeling changes in Japan after American institutions.

Thus, under the command of General Douglas MacArthur, who was given the title of "Supreme Commander" encapsulating the massive amount of authority he held, Japanese political, economic, and societal structures were completely "revolutionized" to both modernize Japan and ensure that it would never again commit aggression.[94] That the United States introduced (or imposed, as some would term it)[95] a new democratic system and a new constitution to Japan, and in doing so embarked upon an unprecedented experiment in "induced democratization," is well known.[96] The new constitution, supported by Japanese liberals, included many new democratic provisions, such as implementing extensive women's and labor union rights. But, in addition, it included provisions designed not only to democratize the economy but also to weaken the old conservative elite—for example, by redistributing land and breaking up the trusts (large industrial and banking single-family-dominated combinations known as *zaibatsu*) that had driven the country's pre-war economic growth—even as the United States declared it would not bear any responsibility to either rehabilitate or strengthen the Japanese economy.[97] But Japan's extensive traditional civil bureaucracy that ran the daily administration of the country was left in place, as was the emperor, whose role was rewritten as a constitutional monarch, absolved of any responsibility for the war. The continuity of this civil bureaucracy meant that in the postwar era it was Japan's conservative elite that would eventually re-emerge to refashion Japan's politics, economics, and society. And it was under this elite that Japan would undertake extensive reforms, putting in place institutions that would result in high rates of economic growth. This elite would also seize opportunities provided by the later economic patronage of the United States, when Japan became a key component of its security policy in the Asia-Pacific region. The resulting high level of growth would astonish the world, and specifically the United States, which had not expected Japan to catapult again into the first rank of developed countries.

The Material Rise of Japan

After the war, the reforms of the occupation era created an environment ripe for economic change—the breaking up of the *zaibatsu* freed the Japanese economy from family domination, the number of enterprises increased, and a strong labor movement developed. But actual economic change was a result of what the political scientist Chalmers Johnson has called a "plan-rational" rather than "market-rational" system. Johnson explains that unlike, for example, economic growth in the United States, the role of Japan's bureaucracy as the driver of planned development and industrialization was crucial.[98] The Japanese bureaucracy strongly promoted particular ideas (in other words, plans or goals) for economic growth, and there was an expectation created that Japanese businesses would respond to these ideas. In return, the government would reward these businesses by facilitating access to capital, and approving their plans to procure foreign technology or establish joint ventures.[99] Accordingly, Japanese planners put forward a national plan of "priority production" that pushed for growth in four industries—iron and steel, coal mining, electricity, and shipbuilding—by making them the recipient of 50 to 60 percent of all government subsidies and grants, and by making capital available to small businesses and investors.[100]

To formulate and drive the details of this economic planning, Japan created several crucial bureaucratic organizations. One of the most important and powerful was the Ministry of International Trade and Industry (MITI). In keeping with the plan-rational system, MITI was "an economic bureaucracy but not a bureaucracy of economists . . . [instead it was dominated by] nationalistic political officials," and dubbed the "greatest concentration of brain power in Japan."[101] MITI's goal was to make Japan more competitive in the export market, promote modern technology, and allow for mergers and collaborations among the largest firms. Moreover, it had the power to allocate all foreign exchange, which meant that MITI could now influence the growth rate of the different industries as well as their capability to acquire new technology. MITI was also allowed to limit, restrict, and control investment from abroad, as well as the rights to own and participate in business in Japan.

In addition to MITI, the government also established the Japan Development Bank, which eventually was able, because of its access to the savings from the nation's postal system, to compile savings that were four times the size of the world's largest commercial bank. Consequently, the Japan Development Bank became the most important financial tool for the economic development of the country, working with MITI to finance industries for long-term growth. Another powerful Japanese ministry, the Ministry of Finance, enacted policies that would provide low-cost capital to leading industries, prod development particularly of industries that were seen as critical, impose high protectionist tariffs, reform the tax system in favor of growth, minimize the risks of adopting new technology, expand productive capacity by making the state the guarantor, relax restrictions on collusive behavior such as cartels, and limit foreign imports.[102]

In short, together the Japanese bureaucracy and bank implemented a detailed and far-reaching strategy that completely revamped the postwar national economy. Facilitating huge amounts of domestic investment, procuring modern technology, and enacting protectionist policies led to high export-driven growth.

In addition to these farsighted government-driven economic policies, many have argued that Japan's economic development was supported and encouraged by the United States. The United States both directly and indirectly created an international environment in which Japan's economic policies could flourish. The United States not only pushed for postwar treaties that secured for Japan most favored nation (MFN) trade status, allowed for unrestricted development of its industries, and made any war reparations voluntary,[103] but also provided economic patronage by, for example, arranging a series of low-interest loans which gave Japan the much-needed capital required for domestic investment.[104] This was not altruistic—Japan's postwar recovery was a crucial component of America's security policy.[105] What the United States did not expect was that Japan's economy would not just recover but would grow in leaps and bounds to catch up with the first rank of developed countries of the day.

Thus, only a decade after the war had ended, the Japanese economy returned to pre-war levels. And after this initial recovery, amazingly, Japan's growth accelerated—the average growth rate between 1945 and 1958 was 7.1 percent, and between 1959 and 1970, it was 9.1 percent. In terms of the real GDP growth rate between 1959 and 1970, it was above 10 percent in eight out of the ten years.[106] Economic growth was also accompanied by extraordinary rates of increase in asset and land prices.[107] *The Economist* magazine dubbed these astonishing achievements "the Japanese economic miracle."[108] By 1970, Japan not only had the third largest economy but was considered one of the most developed countries in the world. And it had achieved this by propelling itself from below average levels of development to the first ranks of the world economy in just a couple of decades.[109]

Japan's economic miracle transformed it, in the minds of international society, into a challenger state. By 1990, it was the "greatest creditor nation" in the history of the world, as well as the number one donor of foreign aid.[110] Aid policy had begun as reparation arrangements after World War II, whereby Japan negotiated "economic cooperation" arrangements.[111] But then, after the OPEC oil shock of 1973–1974, Japan expanded its aid policy as a tool that sought alternative sources of oil and energy in the Third World—following the oil crisis, Japan's aid dollars, which had been mostly flowing to Asia, now were directed toward Africa, Latin America, and the Middle East, places that could provide Japan with diversified sources of energy.[112] There was a proliferation of books in the West that cast Japan as a danger to the world. *The Enigma of Japanese Power* by Karel van Wolferen, for example, argued that amoral Japanese elites wielded massive power and remained virtually unaccountable, posing a danger to the world; *Agents of Influence* by Pat Choate warned, in a "bombshell of a book" as a *U.S. News & World Report* article blared, that Japan was out to dominate the United States through nefarious interference in American politics. Perhaps the most well-known was the novel *Rising Sun* by Michael Crichton; in this best-selling thriller, Crichton depicted Japan as out to systematically destroy American businesses. Newspapers too wondered whether Japan was the new threat; "The Danger from Japan" was one headline from the *New York Times* in 1985,[113] while another wondered in 1992 whether Japan was "out to get us."[114] A *Newsweek* article in 1989 conducted a poll showing that a majority of Americans believed that Japan was as much of a threat as the Soviet Union.[115] Yet, curiously, as many Japan experts noted in the context of their own research, during this time Japan remained a reticent power in many respects—militarily, politically, and arguably, even economically.

Japan's Puzzling Reticence on the World Stage

Japan's reticence was not just on display in the postwar era when it was a defeated power, but also when it was hailed and feared as a rising power. Perhaps the most glaring aspect of Japan's reticence was its pacifist policies and its consistent refusal to project military strength.

Originally, in the immediate aftermath of World War II, Japan's lack of rearmament was understandable in that this stance was imposed upon it during postwar negotiations. After the war, the United States was determined to avoid a militarily resurgent Japan. As a result, US-negotiated treaties included a clause by which Japan pledged to always avoid any kind of rearming that could be construed as threatening.[116] The rearmament clause was reinforced during the writing of Japan's constitution, which took place during the American occupation. The constitution included an article, Article 9, that stated that Japan would "forever renounce war as a sovereign right," and that it would never maintain "land, sea, and air forces" or other instruments of war. Instead, Japan's security would depend on the "peace-loving peoples of the world."[117] The Japanese government would eventually insert amendments to Article 9 that allowed for the establishment of a Self-Defense Force.

But there were two changes that occurred that could have spurred a more active role—Japan's growing wealth, and America's interest in having Japan become a participatory ally in East Asia.

From the dismal years just after World War II, it rapidly became the case that Japan could well afford to translate its economic wealth into military power. Yet Japan steadfastly refused to rearm and develop its military. As we've seen, by 1955, its economy was back to pre-war levels,[118] and by the 1970s and 1980s it was one of the richest countries the world. In absolute terms, Japan's defense budget was quite substantial—its aggregate spending made it one of the top two or three countries in defense spending.[119] Its budget was one of the smallest among industrialized countries—its defense budget was only 1 percent of its GDP as compared to other great powers who typically spend 1.5 to 3 percent of their GDP on defense. Moreover, it was an anomaly, because it spent substantially less on defense than we would expect of a country of its size and wealth.[120] Not only that, Japan's defense spending was paltry compared even to its neighbors with whom it had uneasy relationships—by the mid-1980s China's defense spending was at least 80 percent of Japan's defense spending.[121] Japan's distribution of financial resources in its military was also significantly uneven. While it had top-notch mine-sweeping and anti-submarine capabilities, for example, it completely lacked capability in key areas like nuclear weapons and nuclear-powered submarines, and it lagged far behind much smaller economies in necessary equipment for its ground army and air force.[122]

Even though Japan's neighborhood was not particularly friendly to it, Japan was incapable of launching offensive operations; it could not, for example, have carried out preemptive or retaliatory strikes against North Korean missile bases. In addition, its defensive operations also left much to be desired; it had limited ability to defend its vital sea lanes of communication and its shipping lanes, nor did it develop an adequate air defense system.[123] In short, during those years, Japan decided that its national interests could best be pursued by building industrial strength and transforming Japan into a powerful trading state. And its national security policy remained severely restricted. It refused to acquire "offensive" weapons such as long-range strategic bombers; it avoided acquiring power projection capabilities; and it adopted three non-nuclear principles (it would not own, manufacture, or allow the direction of nuclear weapons in its territory).[124]

On top of inadequate defense spending, Japanese leaders also consistently chose not to step up to the security role that the United States had envisioned for them. By the 1950s, the United States had modified its own position on the issue of Japan's security approach, admitting, as Vice President Richard Nixon did in 1953, that the disarming of Japan and the imposition of Article 9 were "mistakes";[125] the outbreak of the Korean War made the United States determined to forge a favorable security structure in the Pacific, and consequently Japan was now seen as important for American interests. The United States wanted Japan to help maintain the balance of power in Asia, and to play a role in containing communism in the region. The United States envisioned that Japan would engage in limited rearmament and contribute to providing for its own security. Japan, in this vision, astonishingly a mere five years after the end of World War II, was no longer the United States' enemy, but instead, an important ally during the Cold War fight against communism. All of this was codified in a security treaty the United States signed with Japan in 1952. The treaty allowed the United States to establish military bases in Japan to prevent internal domestic rebellions, to protect Japan from external attacks, and to keep the peace in East Asia. In 1960, this treaty was revised to remove the United States' right to intervene in Japan's domestic affairs, but the military bases remained.

Given the imbalance in the bilateral relationship and Japan's economic state in the immediate postwar years, it was perhaps not surprising that Japan, during its early years of economic recovery, outsourced its own security and defense to the United States, and played a limited role in events like the Korean War. During the war, the Japanese government was concerned about the danger of Cold War politics that could force it to spend its then limited resources on rearmament rather than economic rehabilitation.[126] Thus, despite American encouragement, Japan made only "minimal concessions" of passive cooperation with the United States—allowing the American bases on Japanese territory, upgrading its National Police Reserve to a National Security Force (from 75,000 men 110,000 men), and undertaking very limited rearmament—in return for which the United States would end the occupation early, giving Japan the opportunity to focus on its own economic recovery while guaranteeing its security in the long run.[127] But what was surprising was that, even as the Japanese economy grew, Japan did not play the larger role expected by the United States under the American security umbrella. Japan's reticence in stepping up meant that it constantly took the risk of testing its alliance with the United States; two prominent examples of this were when it limited its participation and backing of the United States in the Vietnam War in the mid-1960s, and in the Gulf War in the early 1990s.

In the first example, other than the provision of bases, Japan helped the United States very minimally, doing just enough (sending medical aid to Saigon in 1964 at US request, for example) to avoid seriously harming the Japan-US alliance.[128] American critics complained that Japan was failing to pull its weight as an ally, and Secretary of State Dean Rusk explicitly called on Japan to expand its armed forces and double its annual expenditure of $100 million on American military equipment.[129] The US government even offered a number of concessions to induce greater Japanese cooperation. The United States proposed selling American military equipment, like air defense missiles, on terms very favorable to Japan, and promised to boost American military procurement from Japanese industry, offering to place orders for vehicles, aircraft parts, and navy vessels with Japanese firms. In return, the United States asked for more Japanese grant aid to Vietnam and any other non-communist country in Southeast Asia, but with little result.[130] Instead, the Japanese government made noises about their approval of American actions and hinted at political and economic alternatives to extensive military help, but made clear that Japan would not play a role in the conflict.[131] By 1966, the American ambassador to Tokyo, U. Alexis Johnson, expressed worry that the security and economic ties between the United States and Japan were badly frayed because, as he put it, Japan took "benefits" from the United States but shunned "responsibility."[132]

A quarter of a century later, during the first Gulf War, Japan had another prominent opportunity to step up to the plate as a full-fledged US ally. Instead, its response to that war displayed its reticence on a very public stage. Under Operation Desert Shield the United States and its allies, as well as many countries in the Arab League, decided to send forces to intervene. Even though the international community almost unilaterally condemned the Iraqi invasion of Kuwait, and intervention took place under the aegis of the United Nations, Japan waffled rather than acting decisively. Despite initially condemning Iraq and imposing sanctions, the Japanese government remained paralyzed in contributing to this multinational force. President Bush had to personally pressure the Japanese government to contribute any financial support and equipment for the United States and its allies.[133] It took much pressure from the United States for Japan to put together a comprehensive aid plan. And it failed to provide even a modest amount of manpower—in striking contrast to neighbors like Korea and the Philippines, which provided 150 medics, and 190 doctors and nurses, respectively.[134] When Japan did agree belatedly to financially contribute, it was not enough, forcing the United States to again request its ally to step up. Moreover, Japan did not contribute any members of its Self-Defense Force to the coalition, and plans to deploy the Air Self-Defense Force to help with transporting refugees, weapons, and personnel were scuttled.[135] Finally, in response to rising international criticism, it provided even more finances as well as, after much debate, minesweepers.[136] As Yoichi Funabashi (then a journalist and now the chairman of the Asia-Pacific Initiative) disgustedly noted at the time:

> A crisis almost always reveals the reality, and the Persian Gulf crisis revealed the real Japan. In the moment of truth, an economic superpower found itself merely an automatic teller machine—one that needed a kick before dispensing the cash. The notion that economic power inevitably translates into geopolitical influence turned out to be a materialist illusion.[137]

Japan faced harsh criticism for its reticence—the fact that Japan had been so reluctant to help the coalition was extremely noticeable,[138] and was highlighted when Kuwait omitted Japan from its expression of thanks to the international community.[139]

Japan's "passive diplomacy" was not confined to its role as a US ally; it also involved hesitancy in decision-making, as well as passivity in negotiating style in international institutions, where it was more likely to accommodate than push back, and often deferred important diplomatic decisions.[140] By the 1980s, Japan had become, as we have seen, one of the largest donors of foreign aid in the world. Yet it was not strategic with that aid. Nor did it take a leading role in times of crisis, as in the example of the 1990 Gulf War, where aid could have enhanced its reputation. Its puzzling reticence even stretched to economic diplomacy. While Japan was clearly an important aid donor, if measured by criteria other than aid volume Japan's contributions were not impressive. In 1988 Japan's overseas aid was only 0.32 percent of GNP, which placed it twelfth of eighteen donor nations within the OECD's Development Assistance Committee (DAC); to place this in context, the average aid from DAC countries was about 0.35 percent. In aid spent per capita Japan again ranked a poor twelfth, while its share of grants to other countries ranked last among the DAC nations.[141]

Despite its wealth, Japan also held back from taking on leadership roles in international economic institutions and multilateral settings. Kent Calder, former special advisor to the US ambassador to Japan and Japan chair at the Center for Strategic and International Studies, famously dubbed it a "reactive state." He argued that Japan, through the 1970s and particularly the 1980s, deployed a foreign economic policy that was a mixture of "hesitancy and pragmatism." It failed to undertake any major independent economic initiatives even though it had the strength to do so, and it reacted (as opposed to *acted*) only in response to outside pressure, as opposed to acting of its own volition. It remained reluctant to take the lead on international initiatives; it consistently gave in to pressure, particularly from the United States; and it was often passive at major financial conferences. For example, in 1971, under some pressure, Japan agreed to a nominal change of 16.88 percent in the parity value of the yen, which was not only the largest realignment imposed on any country, but also the first revaluation of the yen since 1949.[142] Calder argued that Japan was particularly hesitant to take the lead on strategic and trade interests that would have benefited from multilateral leadership.[143] W. W. Rostow agreed, stating that Japan simply did not take on trade responsibility,[144] while Charles Kindleberger declared that Japan had "no appetite for world responsibility."[145] Calder also suggests that while during the 1950s and 1960s Japan's passivity could at times be explained by its postwar relationship with the United States, that became less true in the 1970s. Unlike other reactive states like South Korea, Japan was in a strong economic position. It had no external debt and an expansive domestic market; in addition, it was the world's largest creditor nation, and supplied close to $100 billion annually in capital exports to cover the fiscal deficit of the United States. Yet Japan refused to use this international clout to take a position as an economic leader.[146]

Thus Japan's reticence despite its economic wealth was puzzling. It was claimed that "no responsible decision-maker in postwar Japan" would attempt to "convert accumulated economic wealth into military might."[147] But it also did not shore up its defenses—the defense spending that it did undertake was woefully inadequate. As a result, Japan was not even close to being "a world-class military power"; in fact, by any conventional measure of military strength, it "ranked far behind its major industrial competitors."[148] Some have pointed out that Japan's provision of security should not be seen in traditional terms of defense spending—that, in fact, Japan's security was adequate because it "passed the buck" and relied on the United States for its security[149] or because it engaged in "mercantilist realism" by becoming techno-economically competitive in order to balance the United States.[150] However, it was not just that Japan consistently "under-provided" for its own security, but that it also incurred substantial risks in doing so.[151] Moreover, as we have seen, there were junctures at which Japan could have acted differently and stepped up to support the United States and strengthened its alliance at the same time—but it refrained. Attention to techno-economic competitiveness did not preclude increasing the defense budget. If anything, it should have enhanced Japan's competitiveness against the United States. Japan was considered a bona fide rising power. And if rising powers are challenger states, then they should use all necessary resources to gain an edge over the status quo great power. As Heginbotham and Samuels concede, "Japan had become very rich and could easily have become very strong as well."[152] But yet it resisted—refusing not just entreaties from the United States (before it realized the pace of Japan's economic growth would make it a rival) but also from its own domestic businesses and MITI, which thought that rearmament could be an engine of reconstruction and development.[153]

To understand its reticence, we can turn to a set of beliefs—very different from those of the Meiji era—that existed in Japan in the postwar years. These beliefs were not about Japan becoming a great power as recognized by the current international order. In short, Cold War Japan lacked idea advocacy.

Narratives of Pacifism, Reassurance, and Recovery

As mentioned earlier, Japan's conservative elite were resilient enough to survive into the postwar era. This was partly because during the occupation the Americans left the civilian bureaucracy intact.[154] It was also because, since there had been little effective domestic opposition to the war in Japan, it was difficult after the war to identify who had been an active supporter of the regime and who had not.[155] Thus, the prewar elite were able to take leadership positions in postwar politics. This was to have profound consequences for Japanese foreign policy ideas in the postwar era.

One of the most important conservatives to emerge during that time was Yoshida Shigeru. Not only was Yoshida Shigeru an immensely influential leader, but he also was able to install a powerful group of sympathetic supporters in both the ruling party and in the bureaucracy to continue his policies, even after he left office.[156] Yoshida articulated ideas that would govern Japanese foreign policy for decades after the war. This set of ideas came to be known as the Yoshida Doctrine. To begin with, Yoshida's main concern was to gain Japan's acceptance in international society, and he believed this could be achieved by showing that Japan was committed to peace. This resulted in three intertwined ideas: pacifism, reassurance, and recovery. Japan would associate as closely as possible with one of the great powers of the day, the United States. In his view, just as the United States' close and subordinate association with the United Kingdom had eventually served its long-term interests, so Japan would serve its long-term interests by subordinating itself and aligning closely with the United States.[157] As we've seen, in the Cold War era, the United States saw Japan as an important strategic partner to contain communism; and the Americans came to regret the disarming of Japan. But Yoshida refused to entertain the idea of either rearmament or a regional alliance with Asian neighbors, seeing Japan as culturally and politically distinctive from its Asian neighbors. He also rejected the idea of any war guilt or reparations. He believed instead that commitment to democracy and pacifism by rejecting re-militarization would keep Japan out of Cold War politics and aid in its recovery. Thus, when Secretary of State John Foster Dulles demanded that Japan be part of a regional defense system, Yoshida refused. Instead, he confounded Dulles by invoking Japan's constitution, inspired by "US ideals and the lessons of defeat,"[158] and pointing out the effect that a re-militarized Japan would have on its Asian neighbors.[159] He ended up offering minimal concessions to the United States in exchange for a quick end to the occupation and aid in Japan's economic recovery, believing this would guarantee Japan's security interests in the long run and enable it to concentrate on economic development.[160]

It was not that Yoshida's ideas met with uniform acceptance. Other conservatives as well as liberals disagreed with him. Political scientist Thomas Berger identifies three broad political groups of elites who debated Japan's future—the left idealists, the centrists, and the right idealists. The right idealists were critical of the pre-war militarists who they believed had in the 1930s forced Japan into an undesirable war, and they wished to return to the late Meiji period social and political system with a centralization of authority and strong sense of national pride but with a modern economy. Left idealists were extremely critical of Japan's traditions and past and believed that Japan should proceed as a "peace nation" that opposed war because only it understood the true horrors of an atomic bombing. The centrists such as Yoshida wanted to hew as closely as possible to the American way of doing things and to focus entirely on economic reconstruction.[161] Conservative politicians such as Ashida Hitoshi, for example, thought that the Korean War posed a strong danger to Japan and that Japan should step up and be prepared to defend itself. They believed it would be cowardly for the Japanese to rely on other powers to preserve the nation's security. Leftist liberals demanded, on the other hand, that Japan stay neutral during the Cold War and that US bases be removed from Japanese soil.[162] However, there were many who supported Yoshida's limited engagement with the United States, and thought that Japan should concentrate on building its industries so it could become a powerful trading state. In the words of one, "An army in uniform is not the only sort of army. Scientific technology and fighting spirit under a business suit will be our underground army."[163] This doctrine would narrow Japan's sense of self and national purpose so completely that the US ambassador to Japan stated in the 1950s that "Japan has no basic convictions for or against the free world."[164]

Post-Yoshida, Japanese leaders would take the Yoshida Doctrine, which had been meant as a way to recover from the war, and parlay it into broader beliefs about Japanese interests in the Cold War era. Japan was to play a mercantilist role to gain power. Power was not seen as building a military but as mastering international economic competition. Prime Minister Ikeda Hayato, who was elected in 1960, "deflected attention from the defense question" with a popular plan to double Japanese incomes within a decade. He also undertook a "studied humility" in foreign affairs which he called "low-posture politics."[165] Such low-posture politics meant that during the Vietnam War, Japan provided support in a limited way to the United States, as we've seen. The prime minister at the time, Sato Eisaku, stated that Japan was prevented by the constitution from sending military assistance, but that he would be happy if he could "provide something more than moral support."[166] Fukuda Tokuyasu, director general of the Japan Defense Agency, told American Secretary of Defense Robert S. McNamara that "[Japan] very much appreciate[s] the US efforts in Southeast Asia . . . [but] Japan's constitution and domestic attitude inhibit actions in this regard."[167] And indeed, the "domestic attitude" of Japanese elite was largely vehemently opposed to the Vietnam War, seeing Vietnam as a victim of American bullying. The Sato government often referred to anti-war sentiment as a reason for not doing all that the United States asked.[168]

Rather, Japan continued its policy of concentrating on its economy. As a MITI bureaucrat named Amayo Naohiro wrote, Japan was a cultural state, on the one hand hewing to the principles of liberalism, democracy, and peace, and on the other "pouring its strength" into economic growth.[169] A powerful prime minister, Miyazawa Kiichi, insisted that Japan was "special" and did not have to play a "normal" role in international politics. "The Japanese people have gambled their future in a great experiment, the first of its kind in human history."[170] As a trading state, Japan had to have some defense capability to protect its economic interests, but it would continue to be a "peace nation" which would neither threaten its neighbors nor expand its role in the US-Japan alliance.[171]

The Yoshida Doctrine remained largely unchallenged until the advent of Prime Minister Nakasone Yasuhiro. Nakasone, who held the office of prime minister from 1982 to 1987, decided that Japan needed a sense of national purpose beyond economic growth. It would provide an exemplary model for other countries. Japan needed to take on leadership in international politics and transform the role that it had been playing. He rooted his ideas in a brainstorming session organized in the 1970s by Prime Minister Ohira Masayoshi, who had assembled Japan's intellectual leaders to "remake" Japan. The Ohira research group emphasized neoconservative beliefs that included a conviction that Japan needed to promote Japanese culture by returning to its own values rather than aping the West.

Thus, drawing on such ideas, Nakasone sought a more active era for Japanese foreign policy. He stressed that Japan's capitalist policies had worked in terms of facilitating its recovery but had now outlived their usefulness and were leading the country toward weak and inefficient industries. Japan now needed to move to a leadership role in global economics. But resistance from both the bureaucracy and from political groups—conservatives as well as leftists—meant that Nakasone's agenda did not move forward. Particularly, since Japan enjoyed high economic standards, most were reluctant to tamper with any of the institutions of the postwar order, including national security policy.[172] Japanese foreign policy still remained entrenched in the centrist conservative beliefs of the Yoshida era.[173]

Even more interestingly, the Japanese elite from all sides of the political spectrum came to believe that not only were the Japanese not a martial culture but that they had never even had a martial culture—rather, Japan was "dragged" into World War II, and because they were not good at playing the game of Machiavellian power politics, they lost.[174] For Japan to play the game of world politics, elites believed the country had to rely on its hierarchical dependency on the United States. Thus, despite being one of the "haves," Japan did not see itself as a "rule-maker" in the world.[175] Instead, it thought of itself as a "middle power rather than a great power," without the heft to participate in political decision-making processes in the international realm.[176]

In one respect, we could argue that Cold War Japan did not wholeheartedly accept the norms of great power in the current international order. It rejected the idea, for example, that it needed to re-militarize in conjunction with its economic might in order to attain great power. The idea of security multilateralism was not welcome, and rather Japan relied on the United States for its security. And while Japan did not wholly reject multilateralism and the idea of leadership in international institutions, it often fell short in leadership roles. This lack of responsibility led to international criticism on multiple occasions, such as during the Gulf War crisis, when Japan's entire purpose of power was questioned.[177] In short, Japan's beliefs about its role in the world lacked idea advocacy: it simply did not have the narratives of a great power-to-be.

Conclusion

Meiji Japan and Cold War Japan provide fascinating contrasting snapshots of the same country in two different time periods—a country that was determined to rise by the rules of great power in the late 19th century refused to play by the same in the mid- and late 20th century. In both periods, Japan was considered a rising power by international society. In the first period, it lived up to the role and became an active power. In the other, it stayed reticent. The ideas in both periods were not entirely disconnected from each other; as political scientist Richard Samuels has pointed out, Kato Tomosaburo, who was vice minister of the Meiji Japan navy and one of Japan's most remarkable naval strategists, once stated in an uncanny foreshadow of the Yoshida Doctrine that "no matter how well prepared we may be militarily, this will be of little use unless we develop our civilian industrial power, promote our trade, and develop our natural resources fully."[178] But Meiji Japan was not only prepared to develop both its economic and military might, it was willing to act as a great power-to-be. It upheld the rules of international order and trappings of great power at that time, which included the great power responsibility of owning and operating colonies. Cold War Japan did not. It focused entirely on its economic prowess, hoping to change the rules of the game by becoming a powerful trading state. It lacked both military capability and idea advocacy. Despite international fears that Japan would very soon begin translating its economic might into military strength and revisionism, Japan in fact stayed reticent. And perhaps one can speculate here that Japan in a sense lost its chance in the 1980s. In the 1990s, Japan began to lose its material edge—between July 16 and October 1 in 1990, Japan's economic boom went bust. The Nikkei index dropped by ¥12,951, approximately 40 percent, showing that expectations about the continued strength of the Japanese economy had been artificially inflated.[179] Now, international society's speculation about the next rising power turned instead to two newcomers—China and India.

The Active Rise of China

In 1992, Barber Conable and David M. Lampton published an article in *Foreign Affairs* that carried a stark warning. They argued that the United States was dangerously underestimating China—that Americans comfortably but erroneously assumed the collapse of the Soviet Union meant that China no longer held any strategic value.[1] The following year, *New York Times* journalist Nicholas Kristof, in an article titled "The Rise of China," wrote that the only group in America paying "serious attention" to China was the business community.[2] In today's world, with the 2017 National Security Strategy document of the Trump administration labeling China the United States' number one adversary, these warnings seem prescient. Even Chinese historians have talked of China's rise as inevitable, a part of a longer arc of power transition. The historian Wang Gungwu famously observed that this is China's fourth rise; the sheer size of China and the consequent "political weight" bestowed upon it, he argued, "cannot be wished away."[3] But in the very early 1990s, at the time these warnings were published, any discussion of China's rise was not only unusual, but also superfluous. For the United States, fixated as it had been on Japan as the next challenger, China was neither an adversary nor even a rival.

Instead, China was a developing country with an authoritarian regime, and beyond that, after the Tiananmen Square massacre in June 1989, also a pariah state. Yet a mere two decades later, in 2008, the *New York Times* would be pointing out, "No one worries much about Japan taking over the world today. When we wring our hands, it's China we fear."[4] Thus, somewhere in those years of the 1990s and 2000s, China shifted, in the American mainstream perception, from poor pariah to a "rising economic superpower."[5] By 2002, the journal *Foreign Affairs* had collected all of its pertinent articles on China and republished them as a volume titled *Rising China*. The debate was not *whether* China was rising; rather, it was whether China would be a challenger power or maintain the status quo. And the world, in turn, debated how it should respond: should China be treated as a threat or as an opportunity?[6] Buried in such angst-ridden questions about the rise of a possible threatening power lie bigger questions: What categorized China as a rising power? And was its behavior indeed revisionist?

If we look at China in the 1990s we find a shift in both military and economic power. China's economic reforms, initiated by Deng Xiaoping's politics of opening and reform (*gaige kaifang*) in the 1980s, had resulted in a booming economy. China had also begun to expand its military capabilities, and it already owned that ultimate post–World War II military capability—nuclear weapons. But material power was not the only difference between pre- and post-1990s China. China's behavior on the world stage also began to change. While this behavior was scrutinized as a possible threat to the post–Cold War world, as we will see, much of it was in line with the behavior we have, in this book, come to expect of active rising powers. China shifted from focusing on bilateralism and denouncing American hegemony to accepting multilateralism, the foundation of the post–Cold War international order. Not only did China began integrating itself into global institutions, it, crucially, took on leadership roles. In the 1990s, China began to control, direct, and impact the processes of multilateralism. Its behavior was active—it globalized its authority according to the great power norms of the day, and it began to shape perceptions of its rise. When China participated in the processes of multilateralism it took pains to be *accommodational*, even when being accommodational did not necessarily serve its security and economic interests. And the process of its rise did not just encompass an increase in material power; rather, it was also at this time that its elites began to engage in narratives about what it meant for China to become a great power in the coming decades.

The Rise of China in a Multilateral World

After the end of World War II, the world saw the dramatic proliferation of international regimes and institutions. Whether it was the establishment of overarching political and diplomatic institutions (including the United Nations and later the European Union), the creation of economic and trade institutions (such as the General Agreement on Trade and Tariffs, the World Trade Organization, and the International Monetary Fund), the production of disarmament regimes (the Missile Technology Control Regime, the Chemical Weapons Convention, the Comprehensive Test Ban Treaty [CTBT], and the Nuclear Non-Proliferation Treaty), or the generation of human rights institutions (the International Covenant on Economic Social and Cultural Rights, the Convention against Torture, and the International Criminal Court), international institutions now dominated and changed the way countries interacted and conducted business with each other. By the 1990s, globalization was the word of the day. And the collapse of the Soviet Union meant that these multilateral processes were now dominated by a single superpower, the United States. Thus, even more perhaps than during the Cold War, when dominating regional alliances and winning proxy wars were essential components of power, being able to take a leadership role and control, direct, and impact the processes of globalization through these institutions became crucial for attaining great power. At the same time, the worry about the rise of Japan as the next great power to fear was fading. But discussions about a possible China threat were creating new anxiety.

"China threat" theory, as it was known, became the phrase du jour of the 1990s, a product of those worried about new challengers to the Western liberal order. Journalists, academics, and policy analysts in the West and in Asia now debated the consequences of a resurgent China. Some unequivocally decided that China was the next challenger to the United States and its network of global and regional allies. They saw China as a revisionist state and a threat to the status quo. The American journalist Charles Krauthammer, for example, declared China a "bully" that the United States needed to purposefully contain while also simultaneously taking steps to undermine the Communist Party of China.[7] Others, while implicitly acknowledging China as a threat, envisioned engaging rather than containing China.[8] Policymakers, thus, debated whether the Clinton administration's "strategic engagement" policy underestimated the growing China threat.[9] Behind China threat theories there was an early impetus. The hope of China eventually democratizing had been crushed by the Chinese response to the events of June 4, 1989, in Tiananmen Square. The massacre in Tiananmen Square reminded the world, and in particular the West, not only that China was an authoritarian state, but that democratization and the idea of China eventually becoming "just like us" was a pipe dream. China's evident authoritarianism was to now provide a grim backdrop to its rising capabilities, as the world worried whether China would upend the liberal international order, particularly because the 1990s saw both unprecedented economic growth and rising military investment within China.

The Material Rise of China

The opening up of post-Mao China is a well-known story. Under the visionary leadership of Deng Xiaoping in the 1980s, China undertook extensive reforms to its economy. As a result of the reforms, China radically transformed in the decade of the 1990s. The material circumstances of millions of Chinese briskly improved, China's accumulated capital soared, and urbanization rapidly increased, giving rise to a huge middle class. China also expanded its international financial and trade roles.[10] By 2001, its trade with the rest of the world comprised $500 billion (expanding from $20 billion in the late 1970s), with China becoming the world's sixth largest exporter and sixth largest importer,[11] accounting for almost 24 percent of world GDP growth.[12] Remarkably, it moved from accounting for less than 1 percent of global trade in 1980 to about 6 percent by 2003. By the early 2000s, China's own economy was averaging an astonishing almost 8 percent GDP growth.[13] In a nutshell, China's economic growth was a jaw-dropping phenomenon, uplifting as it did a poor country into the ranks of the world economic powerhouses, and prompting one policy analyst to declare it "one of the most important and far-reaching developments in the last half millennium."[14]

Equally significantly, China began investing in its military, alarming its neighbors and the United States. The official defense budget for China in 1993 was stated as $7.3 billion, but as the *Washington Post* pointed out, "no serious analyst accepts that. . . . The official budget does not include the costs of arms procurement or R&D. Nor does it include profits generated from the vast commercial operations of the People's Liberation Army (PLA). In recent years, the PLA has become by far the largest economic conglomerate in China and one of the biggest in Asia."[15] Absent any official Chinese documents or white papers released during this time, analysts combed Chinese sources and prepared comprehensive reports to build a more accurate picture of Chinese military buildup. The resulting figures did nothing to soothe those fearing the rise of a new challenger.

The International Institute of Strategic Studies (IISS) estimated that in 1992 China's defense expenditures were over $21 billion.[16] RAND, accounting for purchasing power parity, argued that China's defense expenditures by 1994 actually stood at around $140 billion.[17] By 1996, IISS and the Stockholm International Peace Research Institute (SIPRI) were estimating that the PLA's total spending was in the range of $28–$36 billion, four or five times the officially stated figures.[18] Its military modernization included acquiring or building weapons systems that would enable China to project power beyond its shores—Russian SU-27 fighter aircraft, in-flight refueling technology, Russian Kilo class submarines, buying or building aircraft carriers;[19] modernization of its intermediate-range ballistic missile (IRBM) force, and submarine launched ballistic missiles (SLBMs). China also developed the capability to meet a range of threats, including conventional land invasion, nuclear attacks, air-to-air engagement over land and sea, and naval sea battles.[20] For the decade between 1989 and 1999, SIPRI estimated that on average, China's military expenditures hovered steadily around 2 percent of its total GDP.[21]

Although China's military budget and expenditures were indeed increasing, it is also important to understand this increase within some context. Its capabilities were nowhere on par with the United States at the time,[22] and moreover, its defense budget was "a fraction" of the budget of developed countries.[23] However, the concern was that this was merely the "takeoff phase" in the military buildup of a rising power that would eventually challenge the region and the world.[24] Moreover, the fact that the increasing Chinese military investment came in the post–Cold War era—a period of relative peace, when other nuclear powers were reducing their military investments[25]—and at a time when China did not face an immediate national security threat raised misgivings around the world.

All of this must be understood in the context, too, of the ever-present specter of Tiananmen. The *Washington Post,* for example, explicitly invoked the Tiananmen Square incident to emphasize the seriousness of China's arms buildup, pointing out, "The West [was] about to be unpleasantly surprised by the emergence of a non-democratic military superpower in the world arena, armed with the most modern advanced nuclear and conventional arms" and that "since the Tiananmen Square massacre, the official Chinese defense budget [had] increased every year at double the rates. It is now more than double the pre-1989 figure."[26] Similarly, China's neighbors also either viewed China warily, as "an emerging [strategic] player who would eventually replace Japan,"[27] or with open anxiety. As Singapore prime minister Goh Tok Chong remarked in 1995, "It is important to bring into the open this underlying sense of discomfort, even insecurity, about the political and military ambitions of China."[28]

China was not simply on its way to becoming an economic powerhouse and building up its military prowess and power-projection capabilities, it was also changing its behavior on the world stage. This change was noted quite extensively by China experts, but its significance was overlooked in the international arena, focused as the world was on China's altering capabilities and authoritarian regime. China in the 1990s was markedly different from 1980s China, not only in capabilities, but also, and equally importantly, in behavior. This behavior was, moreover, accommodational of the norms of great power at the time.

China Rises: The Active Path to Great Power

Let's take a closer look at the striking transition in China's international behavior from the 1980s to the 1990s. In the 1980s, China's economic reforms had begun to transform its domestic structure and economy. However, China was not yet a player on the world stage. Despite some steps to take part in, for example, educational and scientific knowledge exchanges abroad, China's focus was inward. It was not simply that it *couldn't* be a global player, but also that it *refrained* from attempting to be one. Although Deng Xiaoping was willing to open China up to the world, he was very wary of becoming enmeshed in US-led and created international institutions that could be used against China to constrain it or force it to act against its interests. "Beijing sought many of the rights and privileges of a great power [but] without accepting most of the attendant obligations and responsibilities."[29] This dynamic was evident at many levels. China rarely undertook diplomatic initiatives; it played little role in the United Nations; it was not a member of many international institutions; other than its ongoing commitment to the "Five Principles of Peaceful Coexistence" (conceived by prime ministers Zhou Enlai and Jawaharlal Nehru, this pact affirmed Chinese and Indian commitment to non-interference, equality, and peace), it made little effort to promote neighborly ties, and it remained untethered to any major security regimes. In short, China eschewed any leadership or prominent roles on the global stage.

In the 1990s, however, this behavior began to change, and by the early 2000s the pace had quickened. Setting aside the role of passive player in world politics, China began to take steps not just to integrate into many institutions and regimes in the world order, but also to put forth initiatives in which it assumed the role of leader in various aspects of international issues. There were multiple new and overlapping kinds of behavior—from bilateral cooperation and participation to the expansion and initiation of economic, diplomatic, and security ties. The fact that this behavior was different from the past decade was noted and commented upon by many China experts. David Shambaugh dubbed it China "going global."[30] Evan Medeiros and M. Taylor Fravel called it a "stark departure from more than a decade of Chinese passivity."[31]

One of the most important steps China took was to expand and deepen its bilateral relationships and establish multilateral networks. In the years 1988 to 1994, China established or normalized bilateral ties with eighteen countries, as well as with the new countries that emerged from the disintegrated Soviet Union.[32] Some of the transformation of its bilateral relationships occurred through the settlement of border disputes, including with Kazakhstan, Kyrgyzstan, Laos, Russia, Tajikistan, and Vietnam.

From the mid-1990s onward, China also began to deepen these bilateral relationships, by establishing what it called "partnerships" at different levels of engagement with various countries.[33] The partnerships involved both economic and security collaborations, and reflected China's anxiety about the United States' network of regional alliances. The China-Russia relationship which began in the mid-1990s is a case in point. Between 1992 and 1996 the Sino-Russian relationship undertook a dramatic transformation. It changed from a "friendly" relationship to a "constructive partnership" to a "strategic partnership."[34] Since China and its relationship with the Soviet Union had soured and split in the 1960s, many issues, both broad and specific—including differing interpretations of history, opposing ideologies, mutual insecurity, Chinese illegal immigrants, and border disputes—had made strong bilateral ties unthinkable. Thus, rapprochement involved several steps including, importantly, the settling of several contested border territories. Determined to improve ties, the Chinese stayed flexible on the settlements, resulting eventually in treaties in 1997 and 1998, and a final border deal in 2004.[35] At the same time, Russian arms sales and technology transfers to China rapidly increased, and by 2005 the Chinese and Russians were conducting joint military exercises, code-named "peace mission," in Vladivostok and the Shandong Peninsula. According to the *Beijing Review*, they were "the largest scale military exercises the PLA [had] ever launched with foreign Armed Forces."[36] Improving Sino-Russian bilateral ties were highlighted by a twenty-year renewable friendship treaty signed in 2001 by both President Jiang Zemin and President Vladimir Putin—an unthinkable occurrence a decade prior.

In addition to improving bilateral ties with neighbors, China also reached out to the European Union and even NATO, initiating political dialogues and formal conversations. By 2003, China and the European Union were committed to building an "all around strategic partnership," undercutting the arms embargo that the EU had placed on China after the Tiananmen Square massacre in 1989. Trade with the EU rapidly climbed, and China soon became second only to the United States in terms of the European Union's foreign trade. China also embarked upon a number of projects with the EU including, importantly, participation in Galileo, the EU civilian global navigation satellite system.[37]

Most significantly of all, China began to actively integrate itself into the existing international regimes in compelling ways. Economically, diplomatically, and politically, it took steps to enmesh itself in existing global trade, diplomatic, and security regimes by joining various treaties, increasing its participation in multilateral organizations, and spearheading the creation of new institutions. At the end of 1989, China was a member of 12 percent of all intergovernmental organizations. By 1997 this had increased to 20 percent.[38] By the end of the 1990s, China was a member of several hundred international organizations and regimes, including the Nonproliferation Treaty (1992), the United Nations Convention on the Law of the Sea (1996), the International Covenant on Economic Social and Cultural Rights, and International Covenant on Civil and Political Rights, the Asia-Pacific Economic Cooperation forum (APEC, 1989), and the ASEAN Regional Forum (ARF). (ASEAN stands for the Association of Southeast Asian Nations.) But China was by no means content during this time to be a passive player in these institutions. Its changing relations with ASEAN in the 1990s present a case of how China not only deepened relationships with regional neighbors, but also became an active member of international institutions and took on leadership responsibilities.

In 1994 ASEAN established the ARF for its members and invited partners. The ARF was the first regional Asia-Pacific multilateral institution for dialogues on peace and security in the Indo-Pacific that could lead to cooperation between countries that had a stake in the region. China was initially suspicious of the ARF as a tool of American influence, but by 1997 it had become an active participant in the institution as well as the Track II (unofficial) dialogues that complemented official proceedings.[39] In 1997 China helped to initiate the ASEAN + 3 forum, which comprised annual meetings between China, Japan, South Korea, and the ten members of ASEAN. In 2001 China initiated ASEAN + 1, which resulted in a groundbreaking agreement in 2002, the China-ASEAN Free Trade Agreement (CAFTA). CAFTA, which was formalized in 2004, was the world's largest free trade agreement, covering 1.7 billion people in China and Southeast Asia.[40] China pushed for the launch of the annual Boao Forum, which held its first meeting in 2001 on Hainan Island, bringing together business leaders and government officials for a regional dialogue. By 2003 more than 1,000 delegates from around the region were attending the meetings. China also initiated the idea of using the ARF to increase communication among the militaries of Asian countries. And in 2002, China espoused the idea of a defense ministers' dialogue within the framework of the ARF, an idea that had originally been suggested by US diplomats.[41] As a result of this participation and these initiatives, economically China became "the new game in town,"[42] nudging Japan away from its financial role. There were now both increasing investment in China and increasing Chinese investment in Asia; China's investment in ASEAN grew from $400 million in the 1980s to $2.9 billion in 2002, while 61 percent of China's foreign direct investment (FDI) came from Asia. Moreover, China's decision to tolerate trade deficits with countries in the region ($23 billion deficit with South Korea, $16.4 billion deficit with ASEAN) increased the growing economic interdependence with China at the core.[43]

In central Asia, China spearheaded the creation of the Shanghai Cooperation Organization (SCO) in 2001. It included Russia, Kyrgyzstan, Kazakhstan, Tajikistan, and Uzbekistan. (The first four of these had met in Shanghai in 1996 and 1997 to reach agreements with regard to border security and confidence-building measures. But China then took a leading role to expand this forum—including Uzbekistan—into the SCO.) The SCO became the world's first security forum that did not include the United States.[44] Together, the SCO members vowed to "combat terrorism, separatism, and religious extremism." While the Sino-Russian relationship was the core of the SCO, the SCO also served to expand China's energy and economic trade with other Central Asian countries.

The 1990s also saw China significantly alter its behavior when it came to security institutions and regimes. China continued to remain non-aligned and did not embrace multilateral security alliances, but it began to indicate that it accepted the underlying norms of existing security institutions. While this behavior had begun in the 1980s, when China shifted from completely rejecting any arms control measures to endorsing some arms control positions and institutions such as the Conference on Disarmament and the International Atomic Energy

Agency (IAEA), by the very early 1990s China had still not joined most major international non-proliferation regimes and negotiations. During the decade of the 1990s, however, China's participation both increased and deepened. It joined many major international arms control and non-proliferation treaties, and introduced a variety of domestic regulations that governed the exports of nuclear, chemical, and dual-use materials and technologies. It signed the Non-Proliferation Treaty (1992) and the CTBT (1996), signed and ratified the Chemical Weapons Convention (1993, 1997), and joined the Nuclear Suppliers Group (2004). In 1996 it also pledged not to provide assistance to unsafeguarded nuclear facilities and began dialogue with other multilateral export control regimes like the Missile Technology Control Regime, the Australia Group, and the Wassenaar Arrangement.[45]

But again, as in the case of trade regimes, China did not simply assume the role of a passive member. Between the late 1990s and 2002, it also undertook various diplomatic initiatives through these treaties and conventions to push for a consensus that US missile defense plans were a threat to the already existing global arms control and non-proliferation regimes. At the United Nations, China rallied many Global South countries to push through a non-binding resolution that would sustain the 1972 Anti-Ballistic Missile Treaty and prevent the weaponization of outer space.[46] In 1997, it established a new Department of Arms Control and Disarmament within its Ministry of Foreign Affairs, showing its commitment to instituting an export control system. It also created a China Arms Control and Disarmament Association in 2001 to coordinate China's emerging NGO arms-control research programs.[47]

With its participation in current institutions and assumption of leadership roles, China also upped its game diplomatically. China's top leaders began taking a more active role in international summits, forums, and meetings. In the 1990s, Jiang Zemin, Zhu Rongji, and Li Peng increased their travel tremendously within Asia and outside of the continent. The launch of the Asian European Meeting (ASEM) by ASEAN in 1996 in Thailand (to bring together the European Union, European Commission, ASEAN countries, and China, Japan, and South Korea) was first attended by Chinese prime minister Li Peng, and subsequent meetings were consistently attended by official Chinese representatives. This diplomatic commitment increased even more in the 2000s. In 2001, China offered to host the ASEM Foreign Ministers meeting in Beijing. In 2003, President Hu Jintao and Prime Minister Wen Jiabao traveled to Indonesia for ASEAN talks. Within forty-four hours, Wen attended twenty meetings, proposed twenty-nine collaborative proposals, and signed a wide variety of diplomatic agreements.[48] The international diplomacy by top Chinese leaders stood in contrast to the style of Mao, who went abroad only twice in his life, to the Soviet Union, and of Deng, who also traveled abroad very rarely.

Toward the late 1990s and early 2000s, China also began to try its hand at peacemaking. During the 1993–1994 nuclear crisis with North Korea, it was a passive onlooker. But this was to change. China began by participating during the Four-Party Talks (the multilateral dialogue effort with North Korea, South Korea, and the United States to negotiate a lasting peace) in 1997 and 1998. By 1999, China was hosting. In January 2003, when North Korea initiated another crisis by withdrawing from the Non-Proliferation Treaty (NPT) and beginning again to operate its nuclear facilities, China took on a more noticeably active role to rein in North Korea. China shuffled troops around the Sino-Korean border; it suspended vital oil shipments to North Korea; and it sent high-level envoys to the country. And, crucially, it decided to broker direct talks between the United States and North Korea. By April 2003, China had held more than sixty meetings with North Korean officials and had transmitted over fifty messages between Beijing and Pyongyang and between Beijing and Washington. It is also rumored that China secretly sent Vice Premier Qian Qichen to North Korea to discuss a way out of the crisis with Kim Jong-Il.[49] The failure of tripartite talks between China, North Korea, and the United States led China to initiate and host the Six-Party Talks (involving China, Russia, Japan, the United States, South Korea, and North Korea). Between 2003 and 2006, the Chinese government "remained a central driving force" for the Six-Party Talks, and hosted all four rounds of the forum, helping Sino-US relations reach a "mini-climax."[50]

In another example of the switch to active peacemaking diplomacy, China also reversed its attitude toward peacekeeping. When China assumed its seat at the United Nations in 1971, it completely rejected the idea of involvement with UN peacekeeping. But, two decades later, in 1992, China sent its first peacekeeping troops to the United Nations Transitional Authority in Cambodia (UNTAC). By 1999, China had increased its troop commitments to peace-keeping, as evidenced by the size of the contingent it sent to East Timor. It also changed the quality of its participation, dispatching "highly trained and sought after enabler troops—the logisticians, engineers, and medical teams that pro-vide the backbone for peacekeeping missions in the field."[51] By the early 2000s, China was deploying combat troops, representing a "major breakthrough" from previous patterns of deployment.[52]

Active and Accommodational of Great Power Norms

All in all, it was clear that from the 1990s onward China had begun to completely redefine its role in the international system. As political scientist Andrew Nathan has pointed out, "[China] moved from a position of almost no participation in international regimes" to one where it "participates in almost all of the major in-ternational regimes in which it is eligible to participate."[53] But it was not simply that its behavior changed. Rather, its behavior changed in very specific ways. China was beginning to acquire global authority and to shape both internal and external perceptions of its rise. If we look at the kinds of behavior that China undertook in the 1990s (and accelerated in the early 2000s), what we find is that the behavior was accommodational of the great power norms of the day. Great power by the late 20th century meant the exercise of power through multilateralism and international institutions. Great power was not simply a recognition of a country's capabilities, but also a recognition of a country's ability to set the global agenda through institutions. And with its new behavior, China was making its first attempts to control, direct, and impact the processes of globalization.

Some of the behavior China undertook was expected, that is, it was behavior that benefited it not only in terms of security,[54] but also economically (regional integration with ASEAN or creating the SCO, for example). But China also undertook important actions that were quite puzzling and difficult to understand if seen only from the point of view of increasing material power and fortifying its security and economic interests. However, these actions can be understood if seen as efforts to be accommodational of established international norms.

To begin with, there were no international institutions that China joined, only to violate the rules thereof. [55] Nor was it the case that China only took part in international regimes and agreements that it perceived, as some have argued, as yielding concrete material and security benefits.[56] Consider, for example, China's efforts to settle border disputes; the terms reached on a number of these settlements were not necessarily favorable to China—in some cases it even lost up to half the territory at stake.[57] Thus, these settlements did not necessarily benefit China materially, but they increased its global authority by showcasing its willingness to behave "responsibly," contrasting with perceptions of it as a threatening actor in bilateral and multilateral settings. In other important cases, China committed itself to settling disputes peacefully—one example is the contestation over the Paracel, Spratly, and Senkaku islands—by drawing on international law. To this end, it even signed a code of conduct with ASEAN in 2002 that was based mostly on language drafted by ASEAN rather than China, which again showed its willingness to be accommodational of international order.[58]

In one of the biggest and most dramatic about-faces[59] in its behavior, China also signed onto many arms-control regimes in the 1990s, as mentioned earlier. From once condemning the arms-control institutions as serving to consolidate the hegemony of two superpowers, it now began cooperating with international efforts to curtail the proliferation of nuclear weapons, including in friendly governments like North Korea and Iran.[60] It participated in and even took the lead on curtailing arms exports with the result that the "scope, content, and frequency of its export of sensitive weapons-related items declined."[61] In the area of nuclear arms control, it aligned its views on arms control with that of the United

Kingdom and France, declared open support for the norm of non-proliferation, and importantly, as noted earlier, it signed the Non-Proliferation Treaty in 1992, signed and ratified the Chemical Weapons Convention in 1993, and signed the CTBT in 1996.[62] As Nicola Leveringhaus and Kate Sullivan de Estrada point out, this behavior was surprisingly "conformist"; before the 1990s, China had not just stayed away from the arms control regimes but had been a "vocal outsider," even supplying nuclear assistance to other socialist countries.[63] Signing onto arms control treaties like the CTBT thus came at a price. Such arms control measures not only placed limits on testing, but also risked domestic stability, as military hardliners in the Chinese government were against it.[64] Similarly, China displayed surprising cooperation with and commitment to space regimes that governed the "peaceful and orderly use of outer space," even when geopolitical rivalry was at stake.[65]

China displayed surprising cooperation in terms of economics, trade, and diplomacy as well. As China's investment in Southeast Asia grew, it tolerated huge trade deficits with Asian countries, and it made political compromises with ASEAN—for example, Beijing signed political agreements with ASEAN, such as the Declaration on the Conduct of Parties in the South China Sea, where it pledged self-restraint.[66] During the Asian financial crisis of 1997–1998, despite being protected by its own currency control and large foreign exchange reserves which helped buffer its economy, China took steps to assist Southeast Asian countries by not devaluing its currency and by offering aid packages and loans at low interest rates.[67] Even China's hosting of the Four Party talks was noteworthy—NATO had just mistakenly bombed the Chinese Embassy in Belgrade, leading to immense Chinese hostility toward the United States. Yet, China refrained from using the international platform afforded by the talks to condemn the United States.[68] Moreover, it found a voice to protest actions through the established norms of international institutions and rules (for example, when it protested US missile defense) rather than outside of them.

Thus, in many aspects, China began to play *by* the post–Cold War rules of great power rather than *resist* them. Its behavior changed in the 1990s when it moved to join, comply with, and lead international institutions and regimes. In short, it was an active rising power. And like the United States before it, the process of its active rise was accompanied not only by increasing military and economic power, but also by narratives about how to become a great power.

Narratives of Attaining Great Power

It was not that 1980s China did not have a conception about China's place in the international system. Nor was it that China did not think of itself as a great civilization. On the contrary, China had always been acutely aware of its great power past. But, even within China, discourse on China's rise was uncommon until the mid-1990s. A simple search of the CNKI archives, the database of Chinese-language journals and newspapers, reveals that the earliest explicit reference to China's modern rise (*jueqi*) does not appear until 1994.[69] But once such discourse appeared, narratives also proliferated on what it meant for China to be on the path to great power. The narratives were about China *regaining* great power, the notion that China needed to recalibrate its role globally, and about conceiving what the current international system itself held for China. Aptly perhaps, in 1994, the Chinese scholar Ye Zicheng offered the phrase "China's great power consciousness" (*daguo yishi*), which he said China was just beginning to develop, even while he cautioned that it was not really yet a great power.[70]

During the Cold War, China had viewed the distribution of power in the world in very stark terms. China saw the Cold War world as divided by the domination of hegemonic powers. These hegemonic powers strove for global domination by constraining others. Thus, one important guiding principle in the 1980s was the idea that China needed to aggressively counter "hegemonism" (*baquan zhuyi*). Anti-hegemonism (*fanba*), the successor to the Maoist principle of anti-imperialism, primarily meant guiding Chinese foreign policy opposition to the superpower status of the United States. But in the 1990s, Chinese government statements dropped anti-hegemonism as a prominent idea in Chinese foreign policy, indicating that its most foundational foreign policy goals had shifted.[71] What did this shift in ideas mean, and which ideas replaced it?

Most importantly, there was an increasing recognition among Chinese elites of the forces of global interdependence (*xianghu yicun*). Interdependence was hardly mentioned as a concept or considered important prior to the 1990s. Indeed, China had, in the past, even belittled the liberal international order and its institutions.[72] Writing in *Foreign Affairs*, American academic and noted China scholar Michael Oksenberg noted of the 1980s, "The prevalent stated Chinese conceptual framework leaves little room for notions of interdependence and subordination of national independence to international norms and regimes—ideas likely to be central to the American search in the 1990s for a new international order."[73] Chinese academics began flagging the significance of global interdependence in the early 1990s, pointing out, for example, that countries were facing many common problems and challenges,[74] and that it was important to address global interdependence with foresight because participation would make China a truly global partner.[75] By the mid-1990s, such beliefs had picked up steam. Prominent Chinese academics such as Wang Yizhou (Peking University) were emphasizing that China needed to start thinking globally in order to transform itself in accordance with the processes of globalization.[76] Liu Jingbo (PLA National Defense University) argued that China's development simply could not occur in isolation.[77] Wang Jisi (Peking University) offered that Chinese officials were now exploring ideas of the "Asian path of moderniza-tion"—that modernization was not equivalent to Westernization, and that inter-national interaction would benefit China.[78]

At the same time, Chinese elites remained wary, asserting that interdepend-ence did not imply that "the economic security of sovereign states" should be undermined, nor that there "should be discrimination in international trade or attempts to use currency and financial levers to impose political and economic conditions which violate the legitimate national interests of any particular country."[79] Yet while beliefs differed on the exact nature of interdependence and how it could constrain China, there is no doubt that Chinese elites increasingly understood that interdependence was crucial to China's rise. General beliefs about the importance of interdependence in terms of China's approach can be divided into two broad types of narratives.

The first category of narratives was a response to how China perceived its ex-ternal situation and threats to its changing position: these narratives attempted to underline how China was not a threat to the United States, its neighbors, or the international order. The second category of narratives framed what China's role could be, given external realities. Underlying both of these two categories was the belief that a stable external environment would enable China to focus on its economic development, would serve as a way to create an image of China as a rising power promoting peace and cooperation,[80] and importantly, would bolster recognition of China's position as a major power operating *within* rather than *outside* the parameters of the current international order. In short, China's apparent willingness to integrate into the international order became an explicit way of communicating that China could and would behave like a great power-to-be. These narratives together assured the world, and the United States and its neighbors, in particular, that a rising China would not be a challenger to fear; showed how China could gain influence in the world; and defined its image in the international system.

Responding to the international situation in the 1990s, and the proliferation of "China threat theories (*zhongguo weixielun*) in the United States, narratives began to percolate in China about its benign path to great power. Elites began to emphasize that it was not a threat to the current international order, and that indeed it accepted many aspects of it. Shortly after the disintegration of the Soviet Union, speaking at the Fourteenth Party Congress, Jiang Zemin stated that "China abides strictly by the charter of the United Nations and the acknowl-edged norms of international relations. . . . Differences and disputes between nations should be resolved peacefully through negotiation, in compliance with the United Nations charter and the norms of international law, and force or the threat of force should not be used."[81] The Five Principles of Peaceful Coexistence, always a tenet of Chinese foreign policy, were given renewed emphasis in the 1990s. Reassuring the United States that a rising China would not be a threat became key.

China had long adhered to the inevitability of multipolarity (*duojihua*), arguing that eventually the world would become a multipolar one. But now, Chinese elites also asked what the nature of that multipolarity would be: whether regional powers would be able to form a pole or whether a pole would consist of just the United States, Russia, and China. By the late 1990s, there was a consensus that the world was both unipolar and multipolar (*yi chao duo qiang*).[82] In such a world, where China was gaining a voice but the United States remained a crucial deterrent to it gaining great power, it became important to ensure China's path to great power *within* the constraints of the current order while limiting American antagonism. Thus, China was still often harshly critical of United States' policies and remained wary of attempts to "Westernize" China and turn it into a "Western dependency"; it also often emphasized a "consciousness of suffering"[83] and memories of victimization at the hands of imperialism[84] as a key part of Chinese identity. But China also now began to combine this with other narratives: rather than promoting "anti-hegemonism," China began to emphasize that engagement with the United States was critical to its growing influence. In 1992, Chinese foreign minister Qian Qichen declared that China and the United States should not antagonize each other, and that China, in fact, represented an opportunity for Americans.[85] The ideas about normalizing the relationship and engaging the United States after the low point of Tiananmen were so important that they survived despite serious bilateral friction over events such as the Taiwan crisis in 1995–1996[86] and the US bombing of the Chinese Embassy in Belgrade in 1999.

China was also very eager to reassure its neighbors that it did not pose a threat to the region. Accordingly, it re-emphasized its "good neighbor" policy (*mulin zhengce*). The "good neighbor" policy was begun in the 1980s alongside China's economic reform to help it develop friendly relations with the surrounding countries and create a supportive regional environment for its economic modernization.[87] In the 1990s, in addition to promoting cooperation, the "good neighbor" policy also now meant explicitly reassuring its neighbors that China would support the current norms of the international system. The "good neighbor" policy both harkened back to the Five Principles of Peaceful Coexistence and put forth new ideas. Broadly, the policy had four ideas: sovereign equality, peaceful coexistence, seeking common ground while resolving differences, and seeking a peaceful settlement of territorial border disputes.[88] While the former two ideas originated in the Five Principles, the latter two promoted a new approach to the region. This approach meant an emphasis on frequent high-level communications and active bilateral relationships, participation in and promotion of regional security dialogues and economic cooperation, a calm response to changes in neighboring countries, and maintenance of peace and stability in the region.[89] From 1997, China also offered the idea of a "new type of security relations" (*xin anquan guan*). The "new security concept" emphasized that countries could ensure collective security by cooperating with each other.[90] Some elites saw it in even more ambitious terms. They saw this concept as a rejection of the narrative that threats to security (*anquan weixie*) were the result of differences in the military strength (*junshili de chaju*) of countries.[91] Under this new concept, common interests (*gongtong de anquan liyi*), mutual trust (*xianghu xinren*), and economic development (*jingji fazhan*) were the foundations of international security (*guoji anquan de jichu*).[92] Moreover, "a new type of security relations" was put forth as a *Chinese* concept, even while cautioning that in taking such a lead, China should beware of inciting suspicions (*yixin*) and wariness (*jiexin*) of itself.[93] At the same time, along with the narrative that China was not a threat to the current international order and was rather a peaceful and cooperative large nation, there was also now a proliferation of narratives about how China could adapt and leverage influence in the international system.

China began to endorse the idea of multilateralism (*duobian zhuyi*)— another shift, as previous Chinese Communist Party policy had been to promote bilateralism over multilateralism. But Jiang Zemin now explicitly embraced multilateralism in Chinese foreign policy.[94] This was compatible with previous Chinese beliefs about great power and the acquisition of power and influence. The Chinese conception of hegemony, at its core, included the belief that the hegemons use their resources to direct and control the behavior of other countries.[95] Thus, multilateralism and the use and control of international institutions were now cast as an important way for China to play a leading role in the international system.

In 1991, an article by academic Zhang Wu noted how ASEAN countries had begun to develop multilateral military ties to strengthen regional security cooperation.[96] A few years later, in March 1994, Prime Minister Li Peng declared China's support for dialogues on security and cooperation in the Asia-Pacific region, and in May of that year, Foreign Minister Qian Qichen promised for the first time that China would play an active role in the ARF.[97] Later that year, Qian went on to outline China's ideas on regional multilateralism. He reiterated that China was committed to dialogues and consultation on the basis of some foundational principles: that all countries would be equal and respectful of each other's sovereignty as per the Five Principles of Peaceful Coexistence; that no country would aim to become a hegemon, organize into military blocs, or seek spheres of influence; that countries would adopt a fair approach to disarmament and arms control, would prevent nuclear proliferation, and would settle territorial and border disputes and other differences peacefully without the use of force.[98] There were also voices of caution on multilateralism, particularly multilateral security efforts: multilateral security, some suggested, could only be built once cooperative relations between major powers had been established. Others believed that efforts to promote multilateral security were not the answer to solving major disputes in the region.[99] Yet the contesting ideas on multilateralism leaned toward accepting rather than rejecting multilateralism. Accepting multilateralism would be linked by the late 1990s and early 2000s to another related narrative: how China could be a *responsible* great power.

China conceiving of itself as a responsible great power is often attributed in the West to US deputy secretary of state Robert Zoellick.[100] In 2005, Zoellick had famously called for China to become a "responsible international stakeholder" in the international system. But, in fact, Chinese elites were discussing the idea of China's responsibility as a great power in the international system many years prior to Zoellick's urging. As early as 1992, in a speech to the US Foreign Policy Association, Qian Qichen characterized China as a "responsible great power" (*fuzeren de daguo*).[101] This was the first time that any senior Chinese leader had explicitly tied together the concept of "responsibility" and "great power."[102] As an article in the Chinese journal *World Economics and Politics* explicitly titled "China's Responsibility as a Great Power and Its Regional Strategy" pointed out in 2003, Chinese academics had been discussing the objectives of China as a responsible great power since the 1990s.[103] But ideas about how China could be a responsible great power would multiply by the middle of the first decade of the 2000s. Responsibility as a great power was discussed with reference to three connected elements: great power responsibility as a whole, China's responsibility as a great power in particular, and the importance of multilateralism in showcasing China's willingness to act responsibly.

One argument strand was that modern-day great powers who took on responsibility were different from traditional great powers precisely because they recognized that today's international community is characterized by pluralism, coexistence, and interdependence.[104] And since China was an influential power in the world, a great power that needed to step up to its responsibilities and obligations, it could play a crucial role in maintaining peace and stability through participating in multilateral cooperation.[105] Thus, responsibility was explicitly tied to China's own role in multilateralism.

Given China's authoritarian regime, some may argue that these beliefs about great power did not represent idea advocacy (elite narratives debating and discussing the path to great power), but rather were simply imposed from the top. This would be a mistake. It is true that unlike the United States in the late nineteenth century, China was not and is not a democratic rising power. Domestic ideas in China were and continue to be subject to state approval. This does not mean, however, that these narratives were indistinguishable from state propaganda, but rather that they had to exist with the blessing of the Chinese Communist Party.[106] The passionate and public debates that existed within the United States when it was rising would be hard to duplicate in China today, and were hard to duplicate in the 1990s. And some of these narratives could also have been solicited by the Chinese government. But this also does not imply elite consensus in China. Rather, just as in the United States as an active rising power, there were divisions among Chinese elites about China's path to great power.

The emergence and demise of the "peaceful rise" theory under President Hu Jintao in the early 2000s illustrates not only some of the narratives that had crystallized in China in the 1990s about the path to great power, but also how these narratives built upon preexisting foundations, and could be interpreted in varying ways. Hu Jintao took office at a time when China's rise was, like that of the United States in 1898, undisputed. In 2002, shortly after Hu Jintao came to power, one of his confidants, Zheng Bijian, visited the United States and became concerned about the pervasive "China threat" theories. On Zheng's return, he put forth the concept for the "development path of China's peaceful rise" (*zhongguo heping jueqi fazhan de daolu*). His idea was approved by Hu Jintao, and the theory of China's "peaceful rise" (*heping jueqi*) was advanced. Some contend that the idea predated Zheng and Hu and had already been prevalent in academic and think tank circles, particularly in Shanghai. Whatever the origin of the idea, it was clear that it was a new type of belief about China's changing status, and it led to diverging elite ideas about its implications.

At its most basic, the idea of a peaceful rise was meant to convey that China would avoid the path of previous colonialists and imperialists, because it would not pursue expansion and instead would promote peace, cooperation, and development. Thus, unlike historical power transitions, the coming power transition would not be conflictual. The idea had three concepts that emanated from the leadership: developing socialist economic and political institutions, fostering Chinese civilization, and creating an appropriate social environment to guarantee that China would rise peacefully without seeking hegemony. These elements of "peaceful rise" were not simply accepted as a given by the Chinese epistemic community. Rather, there was much discussion and a range of different narratives among elite scholars and policy analysts about what exactly "peaceful rise" meant, what China's behavior in the international system should be, and whether China's "peaceful rise" was even possible. But all of this happened under the governmental umbrella of permissible discussion.

A survey of the flagship journal of the China Institutes of Contemporary International Relations (CICIR),[107] one of China's most powerful think tanks affiliated with the government, for the years 2004–2005, as well as interviews conducted by the author, reveal a range of narratives on the concept. For example, some writers emphasized that a "peaceful rise" was dependent on China's external environment and that China had a responsibility to shape that environ-ment. Some located responsibility in reputation—in order to effect a peaceful rise, China needed to increase its national power yet maintain the image of a re-sponsible great power for the international community. Others emphasized that China needed to go beyond a mere projection of image, and not only maintain a commitment to peace, but create a framework to do so within the constraints and rules of the international system. But there were also skeptics who deviated from these narratives. They were not only more pessimistic about China's ability to control its rise, but also skeptical of even the possibility of a peaceful power transition. Still others believed a peaceful rise to be conditional not on China's policies as much as on the existence of an opportune geopolitical structure. Other naysayers believed that the United States would never tolerate the rise of China, making the question of a peaceful rise moot.[108]

However, within a few years, the theory of "peaceful rise" fell out of favor and was replaced by discussions of "peaceful development" (heping fazhan). The first wind of this came when Hu Jintao in a speech in April 2004 mentioned "peace and stability" and "peaceful coexistence" but not "peaceful rise." Rather, he emphasized that China would follow the road of "peaceful development." The consensus was that the leadership made the decision to allow the discussion of "peaceful rise" in academic circles but no longer use it in "leadership speeches, or government and Party documents."[109] The opacity of decision-making means that we do not know exactly what transpired and exactly why "peaceful rise" was replaced. An interviewee said in conversation with the author that he believes it was a deliberate decision reached at the highest levels. (Others, including China policy analysts Bonnie Glaser and Evan Medeiros, have suggested that the "de-mise" of peaceful rise was due to passivity more than anything else.) Other interviewees suggested that the reasons could have been prosaic (for instance, Zheng Bijian falling out of favor) but were most likely related to domestic belief disputes about the appropriateness of the concept.

Some believed the word "rise" in "peaceful rise" unsettled China's neighbors. Others thought that "rise" (jueqi) itself was an immodest term—it was accept-able for foreigners to talk of China's rise, but immodest for the Chinese them-selves to do so. Some suggested that there should be more focus on the idea of China as "a responsible stakeholder." Peaceful development as a concept did not generate as much of a divergence of narratives as peaceful rise. Some did at-tempt to root out specific differences between the two concepts of peaceful rise and peaceful development, tying each concept to the relative pace of change of China's status—whether it was or was not rising quickly. A search of the articles in the Contemporary International Relations journal for 2005 reveals more usage of "peaceful development," but also shows that the two terms were often used almost interchangeably.[110]

The narratives that proliferated and were debated in China in the 1990s showcased very particular kinds of beliefs. They reconciled China's capabilities with the constraints of the international order, focusing particular attention on those goals perceived to be materially attainable within such constraints. Crucially, they acknowledged the current norms of great power by outlining China's acquisition of global authority within the framework of these norms and defining its relationship with the status quo great power (the United States) and the current international order. The narratives tried to shape perceptions of China's role in the international system, presenting China as a great power-to-be in order to expand its influence. And finally, these narratives explained the purpose and goals of China's increasing international involvement for its domestic public.

These narratives were accommodational of the great power norms of the current international order—the ability to set the global agenda through multilateralism and the dominance of institutions—and an acknowledgment that, to actively rise to be a great power and be recognized as such, China needed to first behave in accordance with these norms. Thus, behavior such as Chinese peacemaking actions in North Korea in the 1990s, for example, should also be understood in the light of narratives that emphasized the need for China to build and prioritize a multilateral security cooperation mechanism (*duobian anquan hezuo jizhi*) over bilateral ties in Northeast Asia to tackle the security crisis.[111] And China's leadership behavior within international institutions can be seen in the context of its understanding that international regimes, laws, and institutions were an important "new element" (*xin de yaosu*) in international politics. Thus, to act like the "great powers" (*daguo*), China had to use multilateral mechanisms over unilateral action.[112] Even Chinese assistance to Southeast Asia during the financial crisis of 1997–1998 can be understood in the context of these narratives about great power; American academic David Shambaugh argues that acting responsibly (not devaluing its currency and offering aid packages and low-interest loans) helped China begin to reshape its image in Asia as a responsible great power rather than an aloof country.[113]

Conclusion

Just as in the case of the United States over a century ago, Chinese narratives about attaining great power were not organic, and had historical roots; nor, despite China's authoritarian political system, were they homogenous. There were avid discussions of China's role in the post–Cold War world that built upon and refined preexisting ideas. To take one example, the collapse of the Soviet Union made China feel insecure and vulnerable,[114] uncertain as it was about the United

States' long-term strategy with regard to China. Some feared the United States wanted "to eliminate communism from the face of the earth" [115] and have the entire world follow the Western model of democracy and freedom,[116] while others believed that it was the United States' comprehensive national power (*zonghe guoli*) and international dominance that would probably lead to a post–Cold War expansionist strategy.[117] Underlying these fears was the belief that the United States would be a superpower enmeshed in Asia for some time to come and that it needed to be "managed." Thus, China's perception that the United States is out to "curtail" China's political interests and "harm" it continued to play a strong role in China's foreign policy.[118] The famous maxim attributed to Deng Xiaoping, "*taoguang yanghui*" or "conceal one's strengths and bide time," was an outcome of how China perceived its external threat environment, and it was explicitly adopted by Jiang Zemin as a guiding principle. But the narratives in China in the 1990s both encompassed more than mere threat perception vis-à-vis the United States and its neighbors and offered varying ideas on China's response.

The United States needed to be engaged, and China needed to show that it accepted the US-led international order with its ideas of interdependence and multilateralism. It was the promotion of regionalism and multilateral action that could establish China's image as a "responsible regional great power" (*fuzeren de diqu daguo*), and the strategic use of multilateral mechanisms in Asia would help China gain this recognition from other countries.[119] Whether some saw such ideas as an important tactic for China to gain power in other arenas or as connected to soft power, whether they believed they needed to pay lip service to great power norms or whether they truly believed that only by accepting such norms could China regain great power, accommodating the great power norms of multilateralism and independence was underlined either implicitly or explicitly as a necessary part of great power behavior. Thus, the narratives were not simply reactive but also proactive, and even an entrenched maxim like "conceal one's strength and bide one's time" or "peaceful rise" versus "peaceful development" generated many differing interpretations. China's active behavior in the early 1990s foreshadowed, as we will see in this book's conclusion, its tentative steps toward activism almost three decades later. The move to active behavior in the 1990s was not the natural product of China's increasing material power. If we turn now to another country hailed as a rising power during these years of the 1990s, we find a different story. India was a *reticent* power, reluctant to embrace multilateralism, and often reluctant to buy into the norms of great power. In the process, it frustrated even those countries who were eager to cooperate with it and help it rise to counter China.

The Reticence of India

The post–Cold War world saw the material emergence of not one but two possible great powers-to-be. China, as we have discussed in the previous chapter, was one of them. With China marked as a challenger to this new post–Cold War world, international society fretted about whether this rising power would maintain or upend the status quo. At the same time, another country was also beginning to be acclaimed as a rising power. That country was India. But unlike the reaction to China's rise, the reaction to India's rise was more circumspect—while some said India should not be underestimated,[1] others feted it as a welcome "counterweight" to the China threat. While India had always been seen as a regional heavyweight and as a leading voice among developing countries, perceptions of it in the 1990s began to shift.

Like China, India had begun policies of economic reform that led to substantial economic growth in the 1990s. It, too, had increased its military spending substantially. And crucially, in 1998, India conducted five nuclear tests, including a thermonuclear hydrogen bomb of 43 kilotons. To put that in context, this bomb was almost three times more powerful than the bomb that was detonated in Hiroshima.[2] With Operation Shakti ("strength"), as the nuclear tests were dubbed, India was now a bona fide nuclear weapons state, a part of the exclusive nuclear club of which China also was a member. Thus, pointing to its armed forces, military potential, and changing economy, combined with its large population and geographical size, international society predicted that India too would begin to achieve great power.

Yet curiously, India behaved quite differently from China. Although conscious of its great civilization, it seemed not to seize opportunities that would be consistent with great power behavior in the post–Cold War era. Nor did it even pay lip service to notions of multilateralism and great power responsibility and leadership in international institutions that China embraced. India, in short, was reticent. And if we look at the foreign policy ideas in India at that time, rather than narratives about how to attain great power, we find much continuity from

Why Nations Rise. Manjari Chatterjee Miller, Oxford University Press (2021). © Oxford University Press.
DOI: 10.1093/oso/9780190639938.003.0006

the Cold War era—ideas that spoke to India's past as a non-aligned country and that didn't conform to what were seen as Western-imposed expectations about great power.

The Material Rise of India

After gaining independence in 1947, following 200 years of British rule, India emerged as the world's largest democracy, with leaders at its helm who had gained global recognition for their anti-colonial credentials. It was expected that India would quickly grow out of poverty. But in the years following 1947, India decided to pursue a Soviet-style economic model of central planning under the leadership of its first prime minister, Jawaharlal Nehru, who was sympathetic to socialism. Taking advice from Soviet experts, India set up a planning strategy, with regular Five-Year Plans commencing in 1951. It expanded its public sector and subjected its private sector to very strict quotas and licenses. As a result, particularly compared to the East Asian countries, India fared badly. In the 1950s and 1960s its GDP grew at just 3.5% per year, while its GDP per capita grew at 1% per year—such a growth rate for an emerging economy, as India was at that time, was abysmally low by most measures, especially considering that its population was increasing at the same time at 2.5% per year.[3] Consequently, India began to be seen as a basket case of poverty and economic dysfunction.[4] By the late 1980s, Ramesh Thakur, a former assistant secretary-general of the United Nations, points out, "India cut a sorry figure... wracked by economic stagnation, political turmoil, and social ferment."[5]

Yet at the same time there were starting to be glimmers of change. Between 1985 and 1990, India underwent substantial economic liberalization. This included a massive depreciation of the rupee, expansive fiscal policies, and borrowing abroad. As a result, exports increased substantially, and the growth rate increased to 4.8% between 1987 and 1988, and to 7.6% per year between 1988 and 1991.[6]

In 1991, the government of Prime Minister P. V. Narasimha Rao decided to implement "historic" economic reforms that would decisively move the country away from central planning and socialism, and "change [India] and the world."[7] An important first step was to appoint as his finance minister Dr. Manmohan Singh, an economist. Together, Rao and Singh ushered in "an era of more systematic reforms."[8] As Singh commented, paraphrasing Victor Hugo while presenting his transformational budget to parliament in 1991, "No power on earth can stop an idea whose time has come."[9]

With changes of government during the 1990s, and particularly the election of coalition governments, the reform process was affected, and growth slowed slightly. But the economy and reforms picked up again in 1996, when Prime Minister Atal Behari Vajpayee came to power. Vajpayee implemented further reforms that would open the Indian economy to both foreign and domestic competition and build up its infrastructure.[10]

These economic reforms transformed India, radically changing the economic system that had been in place for decades.[11] Consequently, between 1993 and 1997, India enjoyed "a handsome growth rate of 7.1 per cent ... [which] placed the economy on a long-term growth trajectory of 6 per cent."[12] Even during the Asian financial crisis of 1997–1999, the Indian economy was more resilient than other Asian nations. Average GDP growth slowed down slightly to 5.7% during the years 1997–2003. But it picked up again, and between 2005 and 2008, it grew at a whopping rate of almost 9%.[13] In effect, India's economy almost quadrupled in size, and by the early 2000s it was projected that India would become one of the fastest growing economies in the world.

India's military reforms began decades before the economic reforms. The watershed moment for India's military came when it was overwhelmingly defeated in 1962 in its border war with China. Prior to 1962, the Indian military had been "in shambles." The former British Indian colonial army had been divided between India and Pakistan. After independence in 1947, the finances that the Indian government diverted to the military were "minimal." The army was also stretched thin with commitments to the United Nations in both Gaza and the Congo, as well as with dealing with insurgencies in India's Northeast.[14] After the humiliating defeat by China, India not only changed its threat perception, but also began rapidly increasing its military power. It formulated a strategic doctrine, reorganized and equipped its armed forces, improved its R&D sector, and built a base for its military nuclear program. Moreover, it began cooperating with Western countries in joint exercises, defense planning, and modernizing its services. By 1971, India had completely reconstructed its military, which was obvious when it intervened in Pakistan's civil war. Pakistani Bengalis were located in the non-contiguous territory of East Pakistan, which declared independence from West Pakistan. India's intervention on the behalf of the East Pakistani Bengalis tipped the balance in their favor. India won a formidable victory: Pakistan lost the territory of East Pakistan, which now became a new country, Bangladesh.

Indian military spending substantially increased again in the 1980s under Prime Minister Indira Gandhi, whose hawkish policies led to Indian military activism at home and in the region. The defense budget more than doubled, from $4.09 billion in 1982 to $9.89 billion in 1988–1989.[15] Between 1986 and 1990 defense expenditures reached a high of between 2.97% and 3.37% of the GDP.[16] The spending on war-fighting capability grew at a rate of 12% every single year from about the mid-1980s to 1993.[17] In the 1990s and early 2000s defense expenditure as a percentage of the GDP fell and hovered between 2.54% and

2.39%, while defense expenditure as a proportion of government expenditure fell from about 9.68% in the 1980s to about 7.99% in the 1990s.[18] Despite this dip, there were three important developments. First, India massively expanded its R&D. Second, it focused on modernization. Finally, as mentioned earlier, India tested thermonuclear devices to become a declared nuclear weapons state.

India's defense industries and the associated research organizations became, in the 1990s, the largest in the developing world, along with China's. Spending on R&D by the Indian government's Defense Research and Development Organization (DRDO) increased throughout the decade.[19] Moreover, R&D spending by the Defense Public Sector Undertakings (DPSUs), which produced sophisticated weapon systems and platforms, also increased rapidly. Companies such as Hindustan Aeronautics Limited (HAL), one of the largest of the DPSUs, increased their spending to a level that was almost one-fifth of the cost of the work undertaken by the government DRDO.[20] Despite the absence of a formal military-industrial complex, India's military and its associated bureaucracies constituted one of the largest single sectors of the Indian economy; the military accounted for almost 10% of the organized sector of the labor force.[21]

As the Indian government liberalized the economy and drew away from socialism, it also enabled reforms in the defense industry, outlining codes of conduct and methods of inviting private participation. Whereas private industries in India had previously been all but barred from entering into defense production, their roles limited to producing spare parts and similar minor contributions, now they started to become an integral part of the defense industry. By 2001 the government had allowed, subject to issuance of licenses, 100% participation by the private sector in defense production and foreign direct investment of up to 26% in the defense industry. Moreover, the government began awarding licenses to domestic companies to produce military vehicles and weapon systems.[22]

Unlike China's People's Liberation Army, which had to undertake a comprehensive modernization program, the Indian Army already had relatively modern equipment. And it doubled in strength from 1.2 million soldiers in 1990 to 2.3 million in 2000.[23] During the 1990s, the government was focused on the modernization of India's navy and its ballistic missile program, and, to a lesser extent, its air force. Modernizing its air force involved upgrading existing aircraft, spurring indigenous domestic aircraft production, and buying aircraft from other countries. In terms of its navy, India's plans were clearly more ambitious. In addition to upgrading its two aircraft carriers, India vastly expanded its undersea capabilities, including drawing up plans to add nuclear-powered boats and to procure nuclear-powered attack submarines and cruise missile submarines. This naval modernization plan was a clear indication that India was developing a blue water navy that would be able to operate far from home and project significant power in the region.[24]

Finally, India had begun by the late 1980s and early 1990s to develop short- and intermediate-range ballistic missiles (Prithvi and Agni) and satellite-launch vehicles which seemed to indicate that a change in India's nuclear policy was imminent.[25] In 1998, on May 11 and 13, India shocked the world and embarrassed US intelligence agencies when it detonated five nuclear devices. While India's nuclear program predated 1998, its earlier test, in 1974, had been of a small 5-kiloton device which Prime Minister Indira Gandhi referred to as a PNE, or "peaceful nuclear explosion." India had then halted all testing for over two decades, until the May 11 tests, when Prime Minister Vajpayee released a terse statement:

> I have a brief announcement to make. Today at 1545 hours, India conducted three underground nuclear tests in the Pokhran range. The tests conducted today were with a fission device, a low yield device, and a thermonuclear device. The measured yields are in line with expected values. Measurements have confirmed that there was no release of radioactivity into the atmosphere. These were contained explosions like in the experiment conducted in May 1974. I warmly congratulate the scientists and engineers who have carried out the successful tests.[26]

Two more tests followed, two days later. Together, the five tests heralded India's entry into the club of nuclear weapons states. Already the dominant military power in South Asia, with Operation Shakti, India was now also an overtly nuclear power. By the spring of 1998, therefore, shifting global perceptions of India had been cemented. India was no longer a beggar state, an economic basket case, or simply just a regional power, and the nuclear tests seemed the crowning glory of the country's rapid ascent as a rising power.

The Acknowledgment of India's Rise

It is important to mention here that China and India were viewed in different ways by the world around them. Thanks to Indian leaders such as Nehru (who had forged an international reputation as a renowned anti-colonial nationalist and diplomat) and India's robust democratic system, India had the advantage of a certain status in international society that China lacked. Rather than being seen as a pariah state with a dictatorial and belligerent leader, India was hailed as a moral force to be reckoned with in the developing world. Subsequently, during the Cold War, India spearheaded the non-aligned movement (NAM) which brought together many of the newly decolonized countries and offered them an alternative to joining either of the Cold War superpower blocs. India's leadership in NAM established it as fiercely independent from both superpowers and the squabbles of Cold War politics. Even when it eventually leaned toward the Soviet Union, India's frosty relationship with the United States never turned hostile.[27] Situationally, India's position in international society had been diplomatically powerful for many decades. Yet, despite being too large and too visible among developing world countries to ignore, in the decades following independence two important factors had held it back from being counted as a rising power. The first was its economy, and the second was its military capabilities.

But by the end of the 1980s, there was the beginning of an international acknowledgment of a difference in this material power. India was starting to matter well beyond its region, and even beyond its company of developing countries. The change in power capability first had immediate consequences in India's neighborhood. Thus, South Asian countries began referring to its rise even before the West. In 1987, Sri Lankan president J. R. Jayewardene, for example, called India "a great power in the region."[28] But within a couple of years, countries beyond South Asia, particularly Western countries, also began to acknowledge the coming power transition. In 1989, for example, *The Sydney Morning Herald* declared that India was "the third rising power" after Japan and China.[29] *The Christian Science Monitor* predicted in 1991, "India is the world's most populous democracy and a rising power in world affairs.... With a wealthy and highly skilled middle-class.... [It] has been engaged in a steady military buildup, which has greatly strengthened its land and air forces and created the most powerful navy in the Third World. In addition, India is widely believed to possess the capability to produce and deploy nuclear weapons.... [Its] future course ... will have vital consequences for the United States and the world."[30]

Such references to India's rising power took off in the 1990s, spurred by the country's economic transformation, its boosted defense capabilities, and particularly, its nuclear tests. By the early 2000s, despite its domestic troubles, despite the fact that it lagged behind China on many metrics, India had arrived as a rising power, and was repeatedly heralded as a counterweight to China. Teresita Schaffer, former US deputy assistant secretary of state for the Near East and South Asia, pointed out in 2002 that the United States' increased interest in and attention to India since the late 1990s was a reflection of "its economic expansion and position as Asia's newest rising power."[31] But it was also more than that. India was a robust, diverse democracy, the only other country that could rival China in both size and population in Asia, while maintaining a commitment to liberal democratic norms. It seemed in many ways that India was a "natural" partner for those committed to the current liberal international order, and the United States, as the upholder of that liberal international order, would of course have a vested interest in India: "It was time," as one US expert asserted, "to play the India card" and use it to "counter the adverse effects of China's rise."[32]

Thus, unlike China, India's heralded rise was not accompanied by international chatter about India's threat to the status quo. Rather, other than its immediate neighbors who had always eyed it with suspicion, India enjoyed the somewhat oxymoronic reputation of being a benign rising power,[33] and its arrival on the global scene was largely welcomed, especially by the United States. Yet, despite the capabilities, both economic and military, and despite the presence of a superpower that was eager to welcome it as a partner, India's rise often seemed stymied. US-Indian relations, which had always followed a pattern of attraction and repellence since Indian independence in 1947, continued to develop painfully slowly. Many Asian countries, particularly those in ASEAN[34] and Japan, while on the one hand welcoming the thought of a counterbalancing power in Asia, also found the effort to build a relationship with India particularly slow. India's bilateral relationships in its neighborhood continued to be fractious and contentious. Although India participated in multilateral institutions and the multilateral order, and had always done so, it did not display the same desire as China did to take on leadership roles, even though it had substantially increased its economic clout. And even when participating in multilateral settings such as those offered by ASEAN institutions or the United Nations, Indian continued to emphasize and prioritize bilateral over multilateral relationships. There was little attempt to parlay its bilateral relationships into strength in multilateral settings, such as China did, for example, when it set up the Shanghai Cooperation Organization. Nor did Indian officials embrace the idea of taking on leadership responsibility through institutions. Rather, many vehemently rejected it.

Why was India different? To understand this, we need to first turn to some of India's foreign policy behavior in the 1990s to understand how this behavior was reticent rather than active.

The Reticence of India

As we have seen in previous chapters, active rising powers have engaged in three kinds of behavior: they have increased their economic and military power, they have globalized authority, and they have attempted to shape perceptions of their changing status. By the 1990s, India had certainly engaged in the first kind of behavior. It had increased its economic and military power significantly compared to the previous decades and had also taken the momentous step of becoming a nuclear weapons state. But it displayed curious reticence when it came to the second and third kinds of behavior. China engaged in all of these behaviors in the 1990s. So did the United States in the late 19th century. And so did Meiji Japan. Particularly, we should expect, as we saw with China, that a rising power in the 1990s would attempt to take on roles and display behavior that would enable it to control, direct, and impact the processes of globalization, particularly through multilateralism and international institutions, the bywords of great power in the post–Cold War world. India was different. It is not that India's foreign policy behavior did not change. It did. However, other than increasing its capabilities, it did not fully embrace the behaviors of a great power to be. It was *reticent*.

In order to understand its reticent behavior, we need to first understand India's complex approach to multilateralism. On the one hand, India's participation in international institutions long predated China's. Unlike China, during the Cold War, India embraced multilateralism in some ways. Multilateral institutions like the United Nations were particularly key to Indian foreign policy. For example, after the first war with Pakistan, Nehru approached the United Nations to resolve the Kashmir conflict (which backfired on him when the UN Security Council called for a ceasefire to be followed by a plebiscite in the territory—a plebiscite which India would reject). India was also one of the biggest contributors to UN peacekeeping. NAM was a multilateral institution, which India had been instrumental in building, and through which India had pushed for cooperation among developing countries to resist superpower politics. On the other hand, India, despite its participation in international institutions, was reluctant to engage in economic, security, or diplomatic multilateralism with respect to its own relationships with other countries: where its own relationships were concerned, India consistently preferred bilateral negotiations. Vehemently opposed to hegemonic interference and any suggestion of superpower involvement, India viewed the norm of multilateralism suspiciously.

When the Cold War ended, the relevance of NAM declined. NAM was premised on the existence of superpowers. Now, not only was the world unipolar, but in this unipolar world India would significantly increase its material strength, changing its bargaining power on the world stage. A logical step would have been for India to adapt NAM to the changed geopolitical context. But India did not evolve and develop a new approach for NAM; neither did it adjust its attitude toward multilateralism, in terms of security or economics. By contrast, China was carving out a role where it would lead and where it would act—not simply react—in its relationships. Particularly given the geopolitical constraints and tense relationships in its immediate neighborhood, it was important for India to globalize its authority and shape perceptions of its rise by forging relationships outside the region, with willing actors that would enable it to integrate into multilateral institutions and assume leadership. For a country that had, often to its annoyance, been defined internationally by its warring relationship with Pakistan and economically as a basket case, these outside relationships, along with its changing economic and military capabilities, offered a way to reset its foreign policy behavior and its reputation in the post–Cold War world.

Two of these relationships were particularly crucial—its relationship with the sole remaining superpower, and with the Southeast Asian region, particularly ASEAN. The United States and the ASEAN countries were eager to transform their relationship with a materially rising power, and they offered India the opportunity to signal its acceptance of the post–Cold War international order and of norms of great power, and particularly to take part in multilateral relationships and agenda setting. These relationships had been fractious throughout the Cold War era and needed to now be reconfigured to display India's leadership and clout in the current system of great powers. And indeed some shifts did occur. Nevertheless, despite some change, these relationships did not develop in the 1990s and early 2000s as one would have expected. As we will see, there was significant frustration on the part of India's partners, and constant attempts at and references to "resetting" the relationships.

Seesawing Relations with the United States

The trajectory of Indo-US relations has always puzzled observers in both countries. Despite India's bona fide credentials as a democracy, Washington's supply of both aid (after independence in 1947) and arms (during India's 1962 war with China), and the lack of ideological or historical enmity between the two, the two countries never drew close during the Cold War. Indeed, after 1947, despite the commitment to non-alignment and overtures from the United States, India ended up leaning toward the Soviet Union, a superpower its leaders both admired and courted from almost immediately after independence. US diplomat Dennis Kux, in his seminal 1994 book *Estranged Democracies*, placed the blame on India's and the US's conflicting views on non-alignment: India's ostensible commitment to non-alignment, combined with the United States' suspicion of that view, resulted in a testy bilateral relationship.[35]

In the 1980s, some scholars saw hopeful signs of an improving relationship between the two countries. The United States surpassed the Soviet Union to become India's largest trading partner between 1983 and 1984. In the fall of 1984, the two countries signed a Memorandum of Understanding that was touted as the path to deepening bilateral cooperation through increased economic exchanges, transfers of US technology, and defense cooperation.[36]

With the end of the Cold War, the United States and India shared deep mutual interests, spurred by the loss, for India, of a valuable and powerful partner (the Soviet Union); the rise of China, a country that India considered its number one adversary; India's ongoing commitment to democratic ideals; and the economic liberalization that would make India a huge and attractive market. Yet the Indo-US relationship did not follow a steady and deepening upward trajectory. This is particularly important if we consider that given these interests India, arguably, needed the United States more than the other way around. In India's case, not only could many of its post–Cold War interests be served by the United States, but the United States as the sole remaining superpower was eager to both counterbalance China and to welcome India's rise.

Yet the relationship proceeded in fits and starts, seesawing back and forth. In key instances, where opportunities for taking steps to engage in or support security or economic multilateralism opened up, India proved reluctant and slow to change traditional positions in order to accommodate the United States. In 1991, for example, India's response to the Gulf crisis was openly unsupportive of the United States. The Gulf crisis unfolded in the summer of 1990 when Iraqi president Saddam Hussein ordered the invasion of neighboring Kuwait. It was a key moment in the new post–Cold War world and defined what US president George H. W. Bush referred to as the "new world order"—the United States took the initiative to lead a multilateral intervention, legitimized by the UN Security Council.[37] While being "less than forthright" in its condemnation of the Iraqi invasion, India was quick to condemn US actions.[38] Indian foreign minister I. K. Gujral expressed displeasure that "the great issues of the day" were being "decided in the capitals of a few major powers."[39] When the United States pushed for the authorization of force through the UN Security Council, India refused to join the American-led forces, arguing that the US-led multinational force was "neither a UN force nor a peacekeeping one."[40] When it emerged that the Indian government had allowed US warplanes to refuel on Indian soil en route from the Philippines to the Gulf, political opposition in India was so intense that it nearly toppled the ruling minority party, and Prime Minister Chandra Shekhar had to cease all assistance—infuriating the United States, which saw support from developing countries as crucial to the war.[41] In comparison, China, which had spent all of the 1980s vociferously opposing multilateral interventions, acted differently. China was still in the early stages of shifting its position on multilateralism. Prior to the beginning of the Gulf War, China, a permanent member of the Security Council, supported UNSC660, the Security Council resolution which condemned Iraq and demanded that it withdraw from Kuwait. Once the intervention began, China abstained on UNSC678, which authorized the use of force against Iraq. As Chinese foreign minister Qian Qichen explained, China wanted the United Nations to avoid acting hastily where military action against a member state was concerned, but it would not cast a negative vote and scuttle the multilateral action.[42] In effect, in an important post–Cold War crisis that utilized multilateral norms, the Chinese government, in contrast to India, stayed neutral, and much of the Chinese public rooted for the United States.[43]

In 1992, in a step forward, India and the United States undertook joint naval exercises for the first time. But this, in turn, led to a backlash from many Indian parliamentarians.[44] By 1994, in a flashback to the historically tense relationship, Bill Clinton had referred more than once to the "bad relations" between India and the United States.[45] But over the next four years, the two governments took a series of small diplomatic steps to interact with each other. Still, there was such opposition in India to a close relationship with the United States that these initiatives were rarely made public. In an unusual step, in 1997 Joseph Ralston, then vice chairman of the US Joint Chiefs of Staff, made a visit to India, the first by such an official since 1953. Yet despite the Pentagon's eagerness to build a relationship with India, its enthusiasm, Ralston stated, ended up being "glazed over" by Indian officials.[46]

With the 1998 nuclear tests, India-US relations took another nosedive. US intelligence agencies had utterly failed to detect India's plans for the tests. Clinton publicly denounced the tests in strong terms, stating that for India to engage in behavior that "recalls the very worst events of the 20th century on the edge of the 21st century, when everybody else is trying to leave the nuclear age behind, is just wrong. It is just wrong."[47] India, for its part, had never accepted the non-proliferation regime dictated by the United States, deeming it exclusionary, and so such condemnation fell on deaf ears. Still, the relationship again crept forward because, despite the sanctions imposed by the United States after the nuclear tests, back-channel communications continued between the two countries,[48] as the Clinton administration slowly seemed to reconcile itself to the tests.

A year later, when war broke out between India and Pakistan in the Kargil district of Kashmir, the US government took the unusual step of strongly siding with India. India was "flabbergasted" by this unconditional support.[49] India-US relations again seemed on the upswing. The US government's "unambiguous and uncomplicated" response to Kargil was seen as a "game changer."[50] In a sense, the Americans re-prioritized their interests simply to inculcate a better relationship with India—the commitment to non-proliferation became less important than the bilateral relationship.[51] Ashley Tellis, who was a senior advisor to the undersecretary of state for political affairs during this time, points out the "often remarkable generosity of the United States towards India [during this period] . . . a largess rooted as much in its own interests as in its disproportionate advantage in relative power vis-à-vis India."[52] While "generosity," whether rooted in self-interest or otherwise, may be a loaded word, there is no doubt that the United States made strong attempts during the 1990s to rectify its past coolness toward India and to reshape the history of estrangement.

In return, India did make some concessions to the United States—agreeing, for example, to regular back-channel meetings between US deputy secretary of state Strobe Talbott and Indian minister of external affairs Jaswant Singh. But it was apparent that the United States was a more eager partner than India. Indian experts, for their part, continued to suspect that the US government did not

have an empathetic understanding of India's security interests and that its ultimate goal was to deprive India of its right to leave its nuclear option open, an
option which was "one of the least expensive security guarantees."[53]

With the advent of the George W. Bush administration, a government both
politically and ideologically different from the Clinton administration, the
United States' push to improve the relationship with India continued, and was
centered more predominantly with the Americans than with the Indians. Senior
Bush administration officials like Condoleezza Rice, Donald Rumsfeld, Douglas
Feith, and Robert Blackwill were committed to cementing India's status as a "natural ally," a phrase that would be increasingly used to describe it. When the Bush
administration began its intervention in Afghanistan post–9/11, it allied itself
with Pakistan and accepted that country's support. However, to assuage India,
Donald Rumsfeld traveled there to personally reassure the Indian government
that the Pakistan alliance was not a snub and did not mean that India would be
marginalized to its rival's advantage.[54] In other words, the United States worked
to show India its continued commitment to the bilateral relationship.[55]

But then another crisis for this renewed relationship occurred during the
2003 US invasion of Iraq. India maintained consistent official opposition to
the US intervention, citing its general reluctance to back any unilateral action
without the approval of the United Nations. Even the eventual UN authorization
of a multinational force did not change this position.[56] (Later, India also chose
to remain uninvolved in reconstruction.) The Indian Parliament "deplored" (or
"condemned"—the Hindi word *ninda* can be translated as either) the invasion,
and many in the Indian opposition parties called it naked aggression.

India's decision not to support the US-led intervention in Iraq deeply disappointed the Americans. Paul Wolfowitz, the US deputy secretary of defense,
allegedly called India's behavior "devious" and yet "ingenious."[57] India made it
clear that, UN mandate or no UN mandate, it was not sending troops to Iraq,
a refusal that seemed to point, for US officials, to its old reputation as "a won't-
do country" that "never missed an opportunity to miss an opportunity."[58] Post-
invasion, India objected when the UN Security Council, through Resolution
1483, asked member states to "contribute to stability and security in Iraq by
contributing personnel, equipment and other resources under the Authority."[59]
Since "the Authority" referred to the joint command of the United States and
the United Kingdom, India balked. Jaswant Singh argued forcefully that India
could not "and must not be in Iraq as part of an occupying force."[60] With India's
refusal to take part in both the intervention and the reconstruction of Iraq,
Prime Minister Vajpayee signaled that India was no lackey of a superpower.[61]
The relationship would only publicly seesaw back up in 2008, when the Bush administration offered India a groundbreaking nuclear deal. The 123 Agreement,
as it was known, bound the United States and India in a civil nuclear agreement.

Even though India was not a signatory to the Nuclear Non-Proliferation Treaty (NPT), it was offered the same benefits as other leading nuclear weapons states. This essentially bestowed upon India legitimacy as a nuclear weapons state. The Americans approached India, stated Tellis, who was intimately involved in negotiating the deal, as a "part of the solution to nuclear proliferation rather than as part of the problem."[62] Historian Rudra Chaudhuri points out that the "determination" of senior US officials like Blackwill and Rice, as well as Nicholas Burns (the undersecretary of state for political affairs), Philip Zelikow (executive director of the 9/11 Commission), and Tellis, proved "vital" to the success of the deal.[63] In what Indian commentators called "the deal of the century,"[64] the Bush administration was ultimately able to provide the waivers that India would need to engage in international nuclear commerce. But even the nuclear deal, a watershed in the relationship and in a sense the ultimate proof of American responsiveness to India's security interests, did not result in a close relationship.

If we turn to India's relationship with Southeast Asian countries, and ASEAN, we see some similar patterns.

Looking East . . . Sometimes

In an apparent shift away from the policies of the Cold War era, India reached out to Southeast Asia, particularly ASEAN, in the early 1990s. However, despite India's ample economic, political, and security interests in the region, it remained reticent in fully developing the relationship. This was in spite of the eagerness of Southeast Asian countries to ally with India as a way to balance out China's growing presence in the region. As Indian ambassador Rajiv Sikri, former secretary (east), later acknowledged in an interview, "ASEAN wanted closer ties with India to balance the influence of China. Singapore [as a prominent ASEAN country] played a particularly important role in creating awareness of India's strategic importance."[65]

In 1991, Prime Minister Narasimha Rao initiated India's "Look East" policy (LEP), and in 1994, emphasized its importance with a speech in Singapore.[66] The policy was meant to be a new strategic vision for the post–Cold War world and to move India's priorities beyond its neighborhood to the greater Southeast Asian region. The plan was to make India, particularly its Northeast region, politically and commercially attractive to the Southeast Asian countries, especially ASEAN, and also to reach out to Japan and Korea, thus embedding India as a vital partner for the region. At the same time, with its economic reforms, India meant to emulate the Southeast Asian miracle model of growth. Prime Minister Manmohan Singh pointed out that Korea and India had the same GDP per capita in the 1950s, but that India had been left behind. "The dynamism of the [Asia-Pacific] . . . shall [lead it to] soon be the tiger economy of the world. We want to be participants in this process."[67] India, in other words, needed to emulate South Korea. The announcement of the LEP was indeed a significant foreign policy outreach on India's part; during the Cold War, India had, somewhat snootily, looked upon the Southeast Asian countries as American stooges with propped-up authoritarian regimes.[68]

In the beginning, LEP did garner India some important policy successes. India began as a dialogue partner of ASEAN, but was soon upgraded to a summit level partner, a closer relationship. India was able to increase its strategic and security cooperation in the Southeast Asian region to protect sea lanes and pool resources in the war against terrorism. Indian and ASEAN navies also began conducting naval exercises together starting in 1991, while India began hosting the navies from Bangladesh, Sri Lanka, and the ASEAN countries of Indonesia, Malaysia, Singapore, and Thailand in a joint exercise called Milan. India and Singapore also began the first joint exercises in Singaporean waters in 2003; India and Indonesia conducted joint exercises in 2004. Since 2000 the Indian navy has deployed warships, tankers, and submarines to conduct bilateral exercises with Japan, South Korea, Thailand, Indonesia, and Vietnam through mechanisms like the ASEAN Regional Forum (ARF) and the Regional Cooperation Agreement on Combating Piracy and Armed Robbery against Ships in Asia (ReCAAP). India and ASEAN members also worked together to tackle insurgency, pollution, drug trafficking, and safety of the sea lanes of communication (SLOC).

Through LEP, India was also able to develop better economic ties with Thailand, Indonesia, and the Philippines. In 1997, India and Thailand launched the Bangladesh-India-Sri Lanka-Thailand economic cooperation (BIMSTEC) to increase trade and tourism in the Bay of Bengal region.[69] While the ASEAN countries received only 3.6% of India's exports to the world in 1980, by 1992 this had increased to nearly 6%. Particularly, trade with Malaysia and Singapore increased rapidly.[70] In 2002 ASEAN leaders held the first separate ASEAN-India summit, showcasing the importance they gave to the relationship with India.[71] In 2005 India attended the first annual regional forum of the East Asia Summit (EAS), where it endorsed an enlarged ASEAN free trade agreement. India also negotiated a number of bilateral free trade agreements.

Yet, despite these achievements, India's supposed turn toward Southeast Asia was, in the words of one observer, "clogged."[72] From optimism at its inception, progress was frustratingly slow. ASEAN was consistently frustrated with what it felt was India's fluctuating commitment to the relationship[73] and its passivity in multilateral settings and institutions. For example, India accepted an invitation to join the ARF, but then, other than "[its] initial enthusiasm to join the multilateral process so that it would not be left out of developments of this important region, there [did not seem to be] much deliberation or thinking that [went] into the whole process of multilateral institutionalism and its role in the future."[74]

India seemed to be unsure of what its role "should be in the ARF and how it should approach [it] as a forum."[75] One question that came up repeatedly in the annual forums was each country's responsibility in protecting the Straits of Malacca from piracy. Yet on this important question of securing a vital sea lane between India and ASEAN, India remained "inactive and noncommittal. . . . It took India 9 annual meetings before it could finally offer, in July 2004, 'any help in principle' in securing the Straits of Malacca."[76] While bilateral relationships improved with certain countries, multilateral initiatives such as BIMSTEC "fell flat" and were considered "less than a grand success."[77] Agreeing to a road map for an ASEAN-India free trade agreement took over twenty meetings over the course of five years, with regular political interventions.[78] In 2003 one expert pointed out, in his analysis of the ninth ASEAN summit, that "aside from the ancient cultural linkages and a modern demand for South Asian labor, ASEAN and India have little to offer each other in terms of trade."[79] This was because, although trade between India and ASEAN continued to increase ($10 billion by 2001), it "paled by comparison" with ASEAN-China trade ($55 billion in 2001). ASEAN countries continued to perceive India, unlike China, as not being serious about implementing economic reforms.[80] Others pointed out that although ASEAN lay at the "core" of India's LEP, India continued to "remain a rudimentary power in terms of defense and security engagements" with ASEAN countries.[81] And since India also remained wholly uninvolved in the "Northeast Asian security matrix" (the crises with North Korea being an issue of great importance for stability in the ASEAN region), its position in Southeast Asia as a security actor or provider was limited.[82]

Importantly, India also failed to develop its own Northeast region into a node of connection with Southeast Asia, as originally envisioned in the LEP. Ninety-eight percent of the region of India's Northeast shares its borders with Bangladesh, Myanmar, Bhutan, and Tibet, while its only land link with the rest of India is through a very narrow corridor of territory that runs through Bangladesh.[83] Yet, despite consistently emphasizing that the government was eager to develop better connectivity with the Southeast Asian countries, particularly through the Northeast region and Myanmar (which connects India with the Southeast Asian nations), India took very few initiatives to do so. In 2014, over two decades after the initiation of LEP, Skand Tayal, former Indian ambassador to South Korea, was left lamenting that the LEP was "incomplete without [the] physical connectivity" that would develop the Indian Northeast through Myanmar even though it was a "win-win" proposition for all parties."[84]

India's LEP certainly suffered from some factors that were geopolitical— ASEAN condemned (although weakly) India's nuclear tests, for example, while, more significantly, the Asian financial crisis also took a big toll on trade in the region. [85] But at the same time, there was a sense both among Southeast Asian nations and in India that the onus for deepening the relationship really rested on ASEAN—that ASEAN viewed the relationship as more important than India did. In a tacit acknowledgment of this, Ambassador Sanjay Singh, another former secretary (east), in a discussion on India-ASEAN relations, interestingly referred only to ASEAN, not India, as "the glue" that brings together countries to build a common understanding.[86]

Observers also argued that while ASEAN members, particularly Vietnam, the Philippines, and Singapore, consistently expected India to take a leadership role in the region,[87] India lacked big power diplomacy, leadership vision, and a strong reciprocal presence with its neighbors.[88] Instead, India continued to push a bilateral-centric strategic partnership with ASEAN, preferring to engage one-on-one with individual ASEAN countries—by conducting dialogues, high-level visits of defense personnel, training, and education, joint military exercises, and coordinated patrols—rather than with ASEAN as a whole. Its defense engagement in the region "lacked comprehensiveness,"[89] due to its "cautious posture" on maritime disputes, its limited outreach in Northeast Asia, and its lack of depth in strategic partnerships with East Asian countries.[90] Its "inert" LEP left these countries with the perception that India was far less proactive than China in wanting to engage with the region.[91] Even though India was invited to become a member of the East Asia Summit on an equal footing with China, Japan, South Korea, Australia, and New Zealand, Southeast Asian nations ended up deeply "unhappy" with India—India agreed to many pacts, agreements, and free trade agreements, but failed to implement them. They were also disappointed by India's "slow pace of integration" with the region.[92]

For all these reasons, the LEP, with its goal of positioning India as centrally important to Southeast Asia in terms of trade, security, and diplomatic regimes, was stymied even though India made progress on some bilateral relationships. And this was the case even though the region's countries were actively rooting for India's success, eager for it to assume a leadership role and act as a balance to China. "Look East," in short, turned out to be reactive rather than active. India remained more comfortable with bilateral relationships than with crafting and taking the lead on multilateral initiatives. And it eschewed the idea of great power responsibility and leadership in existing or new settings.

A Continuity of Ideas

While some of the obstacles that impeded these relationships were a matter of opportunity, there were also key instances where India's perception of its interests was very much impacted by institutionalized foreign policy ideas it had held since 1947, rather than by ideas of great power. Thus India remained reluctant in the post–Cold War era to embrace multilateral norms and respond fully to opportunities for leadership. In short, its behavior was reticent in the 1990s, particularly as compared to China, which shifted much more rapidly.

The elite narratives that accompanied India's economic and military rise in the 1990s and early 2000s showed certain patterns. The ideas in these narratives were not about how to reconcile India's newly acquired capabilities and achieve its goals within the constraints of the international order, nor were they about the current norms of great power, nor did they pertain to explaining increasing international involvement for a domestic and international audience. Rather, Indian foreign policy ideas in the 1990s demonstrated strong continuity from the Cold War era. Like China, India had always thought of itself as a major power and great civilization. But unlike China, these ideas were not reframed in the context of current norms of great power. Instead, the ideas continued to hold India up as an exemplary country in global politics. In addition, newer ideas that were introduced with the changed geopolitics and increasing capabilities were inward-facing, focusing very emphatically on domestic constraints and goals. Consequently, Indian ideas on foreign policy were reactive, and subsequent behavior often *reticent*.

For many decades, non-alignment had been the driver of Indian foreign policy. India's historical legacy of colonialism, and the fact that its post-independence leaders were vehemently anti-colonialist and anti-imperialist, resulted in India's adamant opposition, after independence, to any kind of intervention by the two superpowers. India prized its autonomy in international society. In general, Indian foreign policy theorists agree on the broad Nehruvian ideas that permeated Cold War–era foreign policy decision-making, and impacted its decision to remain non-aligned in international politics: liberal internationalism, eliminating colonialism and racism from international relations, a dedication to supporting developing countries, and a suspicion of great power intervention.[93]

In the 1990s, however, with the end of the Cold War, and India's newly emerging capabilities, many scholars argued that India had moved away from such old ideas and had realized that Nehruvian idealism had been an abject failure. Such scholars argued that "pragmatism," rather than idealism, had become India's "new" approach to the world.[94] These scholars defined pragmatism not in terms unique to India, but rather in terms of power politics. According to this line of argument, which has been dubbed "substantial pragmatism," India had suddenly woken up in the post–Cold War era and had begun to emphasize its own national interests, the utility of alliances, and the futility of ideology—in other words, it had jettisoned all previous ideas, and was now attuned to the realities of power politics.[95] This argument was implausible for many reasons, including the implicit assumption that India had been oblivious for decades to its own security interests.[96] In fact, as many have argued, established ideas are "sticky" and difficult to oust, so new ideas were introduced only incrementally into Indian foreign policy.[97] Consequently, if we examine Indian foreign policy ideas in the 1990s, drawing on known experts, senior officials, and Indian party manifestos, we find both a lingering of the old ideas of non-alignment, anti-imperialism, and suspicion of great power intervention alongside a new grappling with the changed geopolitical situation and India's domestic capacity to face it. The push and pull of these ideas advocated reaction rather than action, and a focus on nation-building rather than great-power-building. Moreover, this combination, along with India's traditional emphasis on the value of its moral leadership, promoted the conviction that India would continue to be an exemplary force in world politics, as it always had been.

We can observe the entrenchment of old foreign policy ideas through, for example, manifestos of major parties in India released prior to general elections. Unsurprisingly, the Indian National Congress, the party of Nehru and Indira Gandhi, continued to emphasize non-alignment and its accompanying mores. The Congress's election manifesto from 1991 stated: "This is a critical juncture in world history and for the nonaligned movement. The dramatic transformation taking place in relations between the superpowers is not merely a major opportunity but also [a] major challenge. It is for us to ensure that the ending of the Cold War does not mean domination by any one power center. It is for us to ensure that the emergence of new economic powers . . . works for the betterment of the poor and not only for the enrichment of the rich."[98] The manifesto from 1998 included the line: "It is a great tribute to the foresight and wisdom of Jawaharlal Nehru that the foreign policy framework crafted by him remains intact in its basics and fundamentals."[99] But even in the manifestos of the Bharatiya Janata Party (BJP) between 1991 and 2004—a party vastly dissimilar from the Congress and said to be pragmatic—we find a consistent emphasis on India as "an autonomous power center in the world,"[100] a declaration of the need for "sovereign equality among nations and a rejection of political hegemonism,"[101] and a commitment to "making India the voice of the developing world."[102] Curiously, the BJP manifestos claimed these old ideas even while declaring non-alignment to have "lost relevance."[103]

India had always seen itself as a great civilization that could lead by cultural example. During the Cold War period, India also prided itself on its moral leadership, and considered itself to be setting a moral example to the world.[104] Morality in international relations was intertwined with Indian conceptions of liberal internationalism. India stood for the developing countries and the weak countries against the machinations of superpower politics. India stood against injustices like racism, imperialism, and colonialism. It opposed any great power interference in the sovereignty of countries. Its insistence on autonomy and non-alignment was a belief in a moral right to "freedom in decision making."[105] Thus,

India's opposition to the nuclear weapons states was not simply about power; it was also about protesting the injustice of a world where only a very few "haves" were allowed to possess nuclear weapons while the "have-nots" were not just excluded, but dictated to by norms imposed by those few. In a famous article for *Foreign Affairs*, published in 1998, Minister of Defense Jaswant Singh wrote that in testing the nuclear bomb that year, India had stood up "against nuclear apartheid."[106]

The idea of India as exemplary continued in the post–Cold War era. As former ambassador and Foreign Secretary Shyam Saran pointed out in a conversation with this author, "We have a sense of ourselves as a civilizational entity. We want to play the role of an independent actor in a complex environment. Present ourselves as a bridge. Neither East nor West."[107] Party manifestos, across party lines, often held up this idea of India as exemplar. An example is the BJP Manifesto in 1998: "The idea of *vasudhaiva kutumbakam*—world as family—is integral to the concept of *sanatana dharma* [eternal path/duty] . . . [and is] synonymous with Indian nationalism. . . . This gigantic idea is an exclusively Indian contribution to world peace . . . thousands of years before any League of Nations or United Nations was thought of to avoid global strife."[108] Moreover, India was acutely conscious that it was *not China*: that is, it had a robust democracy and the rest of the world held a perception of India that was mostly benign.[109] Thus, as Saran noted, "We don't have [the China] problem. What you want to ensure is that as your footprint increases, you don't tarnish that [existing] image."[110]

At the same time, along with India's changing capabilities, there was a recognition that India needed to focus on economic nation-building. While the necessity of nation-building might seem paradoxical for a country so many decades after independence, India's diversity meant that this continued to be a crucial civic concept for India.[111] For India, nation-building meant not only the ongoing project of political unification across the country's complex diversity of religious, linguistic, ethnic, and caste groups; it also meant that alongside the economic reforms implemented by the government in the 1990s, there was a crucial and newly urgent sense of the need for unification through economic development. Economic development was seen as necessary for political nation-building and for India's national security. In 2012, I conducted interviews across the Ministry of External Affairs with very senior Indian Foreign Service officials, both serving and retired. It was striking how almost every single officer, when talking about India's foreign policy, national security, and national interests, consistently emphasized the connection with economics. At the same time, they were remarkably candid about their discomfort with new ideas about India's role in the world, particularly about India attaining great power. In other words, considerations of economic development had primacy over considerations of great power. One very influential former ambassador to a major Western country remarked,

> When [we] talk about our breakthroughs abroad, [we] think of how much difference [we] can make to an average Indian. . . . [We think] one cow is sick, and the person has two cows, well, that's half her livelihood. . . . [We] think how do you make a difference so economic diplomacy is at the center. . . . We can't operate like China or the United States. We should have a national security policy. We don't have one because the economy is critical. . . . [We cannot] delink from domestic economic issues. [The] imperative for growth is [for us] not just in terms of projection of power but to maintain social cohesion.[112]

Similarly, another very senior official in the Ministry of External Affairs stated,

> [Our] primary focus is national development. This has many implications—economic content, access to resources, trade, a peaceful periphery. From the late 1990s, there was a hysterical sense encouraged by the West of [India's] rise. Every time a foreign leader came to India and wanted to get banner headlines, [he] would talk of India as the next superpower. [The] obsession with great power status was among the upper classes. Seductive labels [of rising or great power] can lead to foolish choices. In external affairs, Indians tend to be very restrained. In the Ministry of External Affairs I don't think anybody has ever acted on the premise that we are a big power.[113]

A third senior official said, "[The] Indian way of thinking [is that we are] not an aggressive power. [We have] no territorial ambitions. Most of our priorities are driven by domestic goals because we are a poor country."[114] Another pointed out, "National interest means India needs peace and security [internally through economic development]."[115] The focus on economic development can be seen in party manifestos, too, which often tied together foreign policy interests with economic development. For example, the Congress Party manifesto of 1999 created a detailed work plan of development while also explicitly vowing to pursue membership in the Asia-Pacific Economic Forum (APEC).[116] Similarly, BJP manifestos delivered detailed domestic economic plans. For instance, the manifesto from 1998 promised to make India a "software superpower" and a "global economic power." At the same time, it promised to reject abroad "all forms of economic hegemonism . . . and actively [resist] such efforts."[117]

The combination of strongly entrenched older ideas and inward-focused ideas of nation-building resulted in notions that were reactive rather than creative. That is, India often responded to situations, rather than building upon or creating opportunities for active leadership. This thread can be seen in the transcripts from a national security seminar organized in 2000 by the United Services Institution, a Delhi-based security and defense think tank (first set up in 1870 to support the British Indian military and intelligence through analyses and reports). The seminar was a series of discussions and individual sessions by leading officers in the military and foreign service, both retired and active. They underlined, on the one hand, the need for economic development, and on the other, the absence both of a national security structure and of strategic thinking about international order, and great power. For example, Lt. General Chandra Shekhar emphasized that the most important factor for developing India's power was economic power and that India needed to consolidate its economy—that was the step that was crucial to achieving comprehensive national strength and growth as a global power. But, he also asserted that India had not demonstrated capability to think through long-term issues and had been mostly reactive, managing short-term national security interests.[118] This point was further taken up by Commander C. Uday Bhaskar, who reiterated that India had consistently been "reticent" and "reactive" and had not adequately comprehended the "relevance of macro-military power in the realization of larger national objectives."[119] Ambassador Arundhati Ghosh argued that India needed to be clear on its national objectives;[120] she pointed out that the focus on economic prosperity was important, but that there was no country in the world that had been able to build economic prosperity without developing its thinking on security.[121] Ambassador J. N. Dixit reiterated that India had an "insular acquisitiveness about power and status."[122] In short, India had little to say about the norms of great power or the path it might take to attain such power.

Conclusion: A Reticent Rise

The seesawing Indo-US relationship and the halting progression of India's LEP during this period can be understood in the context of these narratives—the pull of the old foreign policy ideas and the push of the need for domestic economic development, combined with the absence of narratives about great power norms. Thus, despite India's clearly increasing military strength and astonishing economic growth—between 1980 and 2018 India's growth averaged 4.6%, with no decadal average falling below 3%, a feat only nine countries in the world have achieved[123]—its behavior stayed reticent.

In early 1998, C. V. Gopalakrishnan, the then deputy editor of *The Hindu*, pointed out in a book commissioned by the Foreign Service Institute in New Delhi that "one has to be incredibly optimistic to refuse to accept that the US and India have been drifting apart, and there is no likelihood of the global perceptions becoming closer."[124] To understand this strong conviction, held even *before* the blow of the US sanctions on India after its nuclear tests, one must understand the continuity of old ideas combined with the focus on domestic development.

Traditionally, India, despite the perception that the United States often pushed its own interests at the expense of India's, never attributed "malevolence" to US intentions.[125] But while the United States was never India's enemy, neither had it ever been perceived as an empathetic friend who would understand India's security imperatives. Despite non-alignment, one of the reasons India had eventually leaned toward the Soviet Union was because the Russians, unlike the Americans, grasped the crucial importance that India assigned to its independence, and to equality in bilateral foreign relations. As a result of this more perceptive treatment of Indian ideas, the Soviets were held by India to be the lesser of the two evils of a bipolar world. Indian officials were convinced that equality in bilateral dealings and complete autonomy of action were conditions that America would never provide.[126] India's threat perceptions also remained consistent into the post–Cold War era. Pakistan had always been the enemy, and China the adversary.[127]

American overtures toward India beginning in the late 1980s, and India's economic reforms, made the United States hopeful of a reframed Indo-US relationship. But India's suspicions of the United States and its overreach, its mistrust of the US-Pakistani relationship, and its continued desire for autonomy meant that it did not embrace America's vision—that India would provide a counterbalance to China. Forging a partnership with the United States in the 1990s was seen as a dichotomous choice between Pax Americana or an independent (Nehruvian) foreign policy.[128] This choice played out, for example, during the 1991 Gulf War. While some pointed that there were "now unprecedented opportunities" for India to effect strategic change in Asia by offering support to the United States and moving it away from Pakistan as its primary South Asian partner, many remained strongly doubtful of American intentions. When India allowed an American war plane to refuel on Indian soil, critics condemned the alleged "tilt" toward the United States as an encroachment on India's autonomy.[129] India continued to believe through the 1990s that "an uncritical alliance with the United States could significantly affect [its] credibility as an independent power."[130] Thus, even with improved Indo-US defense cooperation in the early 2000s, with the Indo-US nuclear deal and continued US overtures to India (President Bush's National Security Strategy explicitly named India as a potential great power alongside China), India remained "cautious and tempered by past legacies."[131]

The push and pull of old ideas, combined with India's inward focus rather than on current great power norms, also affected its "Look East" policy. During the early years after independence, India had often claimed solidarity with other Asian countries, citing their common values and opposition to Western imperialism. For a long time, these ideas took a backseat to non-alignment, but they emerged again with the LEP, as Indian politicians recalled India's "cultural affinity" with Asia, implicitly claimed anti-West solidarity, and extolled the value of the Asian path to modernization.[132,133] As political scientist Christopher Jaffrelot has shown, the conception of Asia propagated by Indians, and most especially by the Hindu nationalist movement that was the backbone of the BJP, was strongly tied to India's civilizational greatness as exemplar. That is, India didn't believed it needed to create a new path or forge new links in Asia. Rather, India would Asianize itself by regenerating its *own* culture and "reestablishing links with its own timeless traditions."[134] Thus, in 1996 the electoral manifesto of the BJP announced the "promotion of Asian solidarity" even while declaring it would not accept "any outside interference in this region" or "any interference in our country's internal affairs, and would "reject the very thought of patronage by anybody."[135] And the Hindu nationalist weekly, the *Organiser*, while touting the importance of the Indian diaspora in Southeast Asia, explained that "on account of the large number of temples in the country, Malaysia looks like another Hindustan."[136] Again, despite India sharing ASEAN's concerns about China, Indian ideas of autonomy meant that it continued to be reluctant to play the role of the balancer. The persistence of old ideas, the strongly Indo-centric framing of Asia, and reluctance to commit to any path that could infringe upon its independence precluded a path for India to strongly develop relations with Southeast Asian nations. India was simply not an active rising power; instead, it continued to be more comfortable in its old pattern of emphasizing bilateral relationships. The absence of narratives of great power and continuity of entrenched foreign policy ideas meant that it was unable to position itself as centrally important to Southeast Asia.

Thoughts on Power Transitions, Past and Future

The world has always worried about the rise of new powers. Society sees rising powers as challengers to the international system. They are considered countries that will upend the status quo, remake the international order, and cause war and chaos in the process. As a result, countries are constantly looking over their shoulders to see which other countries are emerging as challengers and whom, consequently, they should fear. But, as it turns out, we are not very good at identifying which countries are rising, whether they truly are challengers, and whether conflict is inevitable. Beyond that, we have a hard time gauging why we should or should not fear them.

When I set out to research this project I wanted primarily to understand which countries can be considered rising powers and whether both China and India fit the definition. In many ways, China seemed to be embracing its rise while India did not. I also wanted to understand what we should expect, if anything at all, of rising powers in general, and of China and India in particular. After finding that there was little consensus on rising powers, I decided to look to the past. I thought (as it turned out, with some naïveté) that I could do this by identifying one other country that had once been a rising power and comparing China and India to that country. I began, thus, with simply one case—the United States in the late 19th century, when it was acknowledged by many historians to be a rising power.

It was my first time exploring and researching American history from that time period. I found myself fascinated by the narratives and raucous deliberations that existed during that period. I found historian Robert Beisner's *Twelve against Empire*, an old classic about the elite intellectual revolt after the Spanish-American War of 1898, a particularly gripping read. Through the exploration of the beliefs of twelve influential American men, Beisner recounted how the antipathy to America becoming a colonizing great power united individuals with

Why Nations Rise. Manjari Chatterjee Miller, Oxford University Press (2021). © Oxford University Press.
DOI: 10.1093/oso/9780190639938.003.0007

many different, even opposing, stances, and from many walks of life. Yet, in the end, despite spirited debates, they failed to keep the United States from acquiring a colony. Reading the many rich accounts of this period, I began to realize that although the United States would eventually remake the international system, as a rising power it was often startlingly accommodational in its behavior. And as Beisner's work, among many others, detailed, the narratives that accompanied this accommodational behavior were not only about becoming a great power but about recognizing what great power was: *great power was acquiring colonies.* The question was whether America should follow that path, and for a while, it did. The United States was an active rising power. The accompanying narratives tried to reconcile becoming a colonial great power with previous and continuing ideas of exceptionalism and liberty—in essence, promoting accommodation of late 19th-century norms of great power. It was only after this period of active and accommodational behavior that the United States would become activist, remake the international order, and reject colonialism as an essential part of great power.

I questioned, however, whether the existence of such narratives was perhaps a late 19th-century Western and democratic phenomenon. American elites had these narratives about great power because they had the luxury to do so in a vibrant democracy, one that was founded on Western liberal ideas. Perhaps it was only Western countries that even considered colonialism and colonies a symbol of great power, and perhaps it was only democracies that had such a marketplace of narratives. I turned, therefore, to an Asian monarchy, Meiji Japan. All I really knew of Meiji Japan was from my school days in Asia and Africa—that Japan's victory over Russia in 1905 was considered a triumph for non-Western nations. I had always been taught to think of Japan as revisionist, its victory heralding as it did the arrival of an Asian, not a Western, country as a great power-to-be. But as I researched Meiji Japan, I was astonished to find that Japan too was not only active in its behavior as a rising power but accommodational of the great power norms of the time. Meiji elites were acutely aware of what great power was and what it was not, and they were very clear that Japan should be a colonizing great power like those of the West. And unlike the United States, Japan was not conflicted about becoming a colonizer—rather, its narratives debated how to colonize most effectively.

Now I wondered whether there was any country at that time in the late 19th century that did not engage in active behavior despite having material wealth. A chance conversation with a friend who had just read an article on *gidsland*, or the Dutch idea of being a good country, a *moral* country, pointed me toward the Netherlands, a small and extremely rich country that did not capitalize on opportunities and remained reticent even when compared to countries of its size. Finding very few sources in English on this period, I visited the country to talk to historians, hired a Dutch-speaking research assistant, and began my research. To my surprise and some amusement, I was often met with puzzlement that I was interested in a period when the Netherlands gave up colonies, rather than the period of the Golden Age when it was at the height of its power. One academic even claimed with a laugh that many of the research grants currently provided by the Dutch government were for further research to add to the already copious amount on the Golden Age rather than on the late 19th century—even though that era has been called a second Golden Age. The Netherlands was a fascinating case—here was a rich country with colonies, acknowledged to be the second greatest colonial power after Great Britain, and yet it remained highly reticent. This reticence was accompanied not by narratives of becoming a great power or even by acknowledgment of the Netherlands' wealth and existing colonies, but narratives of it being a small ethical non-imperial state, very different from the colonial powers of the time. And this case made me think again of Japan but at a different time—the Cold War era. Cold War–era Japan was heralded in its rise by countless international books and newspapers. It had massive economic wealth but engaged in highly reticent behavior, with its narratives strikingly different from those of the elites of Meiji Japan.

The cases I selected for the book to understand China and India varied across culture, time, and regime type. They had one element in common—they each had some increasing amount of material capability, as well as the opportunity to be considered a country whose power was increasing relative to the status quo. In some cases, this was internationally recognized—late 19th-century America, and post–Cold War Japan were both considered rising powers. Meiji Japan took a while for recognition—it cemented its role as a rising power after its victory over Russia. And the Netherlands in the late 19th century was somewhat overlooked, despite its increasing material power and acknowledged mastery of colonies. Before turning to China and India, I studied these earlier cases to lay out the patterns I found—I examined the United States and the Netherlands in detail, and Meiji and post–Cold War Japan as mini-cases. In cases where these countries engaged in active behavior (the United States, Meiji Japan), they were also accommodational. Their accommodational behavior was accompanied by narratives that recognized the prevalent norms of great power and debated how to become a great power in accordance with those norms. In cases where these countries engaged in reticent behavior (the Netherlands, Cold War Japan), their behavior was indifferent to or even rejecting of typical great power behavior. Their narratives did not advocate becoming a great power, even though they recognized what the current norms of great power were.

I realized that we treat rising powers as countries that will become great powers and fear them accordingly, but this is because we primarily use material power to categorize them, and their quest for material power to mark their behavior. This tautological truism does not allow us to understand that all rising powers are not the same, and that when they are different it is not necessarily attributable to a divergence in capabilities. Active rising powers recognize the prevalent norms of great power and are accommodational of them. Reticent rising powers are either indifferent to them or reject them. The difference between them can be captured not just through their dissimilarities in behavior, but also through the narratives that accompany that behavior. Now turning to examine the early post–Cold War period—a period in which China and India were increasingly referred to as rising powers and when their capabilities were comparable (something that would change by the middle of the first decade of the 2000s)—I found that the ways these two countries were rising were indeed different from each other. China and India were different in their behavior, and also in their narratives about great power. China became an active rising power in the 1990s, and its behavior was accommodational of the great power norms of the day; and this behavior was accompanied by narratives about *becoming* a great power in the style of prevalent great power norms. India was a reticent power, indifferent and sometimes even hostile to the great power norms of the day, and its narratives continued to primarily draw on older institutionalized ideas. Thus, this book has four important conclusions.

The first conclusion is that countries that are active rising powers are on the path to great power because they have three elements: economic power, military power, *and* narratives about becoming a great power, which I also call *idea advocacy*. Those that simply have increasing economic power and/or military power but no idea advocacy are reticent powers, and are not on the path to great power. The United States and Meiji Japan had all three elements and behaved like active rising powers—in addition to increasing their military and economic might, they globalized their interests and took on authority and responsibility in the international system; they displayed internal recognition of their changing status and explained their policies for a domestic and international audience. The Netherlands and Cold War Japan behaved in some of the ways we typically expect of rising powers—the Dutch substantially increased their economic clout, and attempted to shore up their defensive military clout; Japan attempted to become a trading state. But they lacked idea advocacy and remained reticent powers. China and India, despite being labeled rising powers and having comparable capabilities, behaved very differently: China had all three elements and behaved as other active rising powers have done in the past. India had increasing military and economic power but failed to develop narratives of becoming a great power, and stayed reticent.

The second conclusion of this book is that active rising powers recognize and play by the prevalent norms and institutions that mark great power behavior, and *rise to become great powers by accommodating, not revising, those norms.* In other words, rising powers do not rise by challenging the current international order but rather by accepting it. Some international relations experts who have examined other historical cases of rising powers acknowledge this—Stacie Goddard shows, for example, how Prussia used established norms and rhetoric to justify its expansion, and as a result it rose virtually unopposed,[1] while Iver Neumann shows how Russia constantly attempted to adopt European behaviors in order to be recognized as a great power.[2] This book expands on this foundational work to show that rising powers globalize because they recognize what the great power norms are in the current international order, and that what we think of as the symbol of great power is dependent on the era in which we live. It would be unacceptable today, for example, for China to attempt to be a great power by acquiring or acting as if it owns colonial territories—China is, in fact, incredibly sensitive to the fact that its push into Africa has sometimes been dubbed imperialistic. The flip side of this is that reticent powers sometimes do *not* accept important elements of the international order. The Netherlands in the 19th century rejected the idea of itself as an imperialist country, even though it held colonies and was considered a model of colonialism by other countries of the time; rather, it thought of itself as non-imperialist and morally above the other colonizing countries. Cold War Japan thought that by focusing on being a trading state, and eschewing military might, great power would eventually follow at some point. India in the 1990s, and even today in many aspects, rejects the idea of great power responsibility through institutional leadership, seeing it as a thinly veiled intrusion on its sovereignty.

The third conclusion is that idea advocacy—or the lack of it—is not a constant; just as there are many factors that spur countries to begin increasing their economic and military power, narratives about becoming a great power arise for many reasons too. And countries that do not have idea advocacy can, in the future, develop these narratives. It has been argued by many that new ideas about identity, culture, or policy—or the replacement of older ideas—can occur when there is some sort of an exogenous shock to the system.[3] Particularly, this has been shown to be the case with economic ideas which, spurred by a shock, can provide a map for new institutions to be created, and reduce societal and political uncertainty by offering solutions to a "moment of crisis."[4] These shocks therefore result in ideas that can be transformative for the country as a whole.[5]

Others have argued that the emergence of new ideas can be related to the type of government that is in place; that is, in some countries the structure of the government is such that ideas do not "diffuse" or "transfer" very easily. If elites have very strong control over policies, then the speed with which ideas diffuse can be affected—the stronger the control, the slower the pace of diffusion.[6] New or recombined ideas can also arise due to embedded cultural, religious, and historical institutions in the country.[7] In each case in this book we find these and other reasons for why idea advocacy occurred. In the United States, the Spanish-American War was indeed an exogenous shock, but ideas about expansion and American greatness were not completely new, and were also rooted in identity and ideas of the past. America had always talked about national greatness, but now it also talked about international greatness. Japan, too, one could argue, suffered a shock to its system because of the forcible opening up of the country in the mid-19th century. But it would be a mistake to attribute its idea advocacy entirely to this one major event. The Meiji Restoration that followed was also a formative experience, as were the deliberate policy steps Japanese elites took, such as sending many of its finest abroad to learn from Western countries. And while many of the ideas about regaining great power were indeed new, in that Japan, a hitherto isolated nation, now embraced Western laws and notions of co-lonial great power, there were also links to uniquely Japanese codes of honor and self-esteem that merged with its rising nationalism.[8] The case of Cold War Japan is interesting to think of in this context because there were some signs that idea advocacy *could* have re-emerged. Not only was there resistance among some Japanese elites to their country's reticent foreign policy—in 1970, the novelist Mishima Yukio committed suicide at Self-Defense Forces headquarters to pro-test Japan's loss of its samurai spirit; a decade later, Matsuoka Hideo, a prominent foreign affairs commentator, declared Japan's reticence to be the "diplomacy of cowardice"[9]—but when Prime Minister Nakasone came to power, he appointed a private brain trust, the Maekawa Commission, to discuss the topic of interna-tionalization and to propagate a new, more active vision for Japan. Ultimately, as we saw in Chapter 4, Nakasone's agenda remained unrealized, and by the 1990s, the economic crisis had overtaken the country.

In some ways, one could argue post–Cold War China made a deliberate in-stitutionalized effort to generate narratives about how to become a great power. A Chinese academic with whom I was once chatting in Beijing put forward a related, interesting, if slightly implausible, argument; when we were discussing my project he mused out loud that perhaps China had such narratives and India did not because there was a long Confucian tradition in China of intellectuals as-piring to offer their thoughts about strategy and the country's place in the world to the government. This is because, he said, Confucius himself had once been a mandarin (*guan*) or bureaucrat-scholar (although one who had failed at the job). While this academic's take was striking to contemplate, it did not explain for me the difference between modern China and India, particularly because the latter also has a tradition of scholar-bureaucrats (Kautilya, the author of the *Arthashastra*, a 2nd-century BC treatise on how to rule an empire, comes to mind).

But it was clear that the Chinese government in many respects was trying to replicate the American model of vibrant foreign policy discussions between the government and an elite brain trust in the form of think tanks, but with a twist—acknowledgment of the authoritarian state, which meant that, publicly at least, ideas could not deviate from the official party line. Yet while early post–Cold War China was not a democracy, neither was it a country with a monolithic narrative. In addition to supporting the Chinese government's top-down ideas—"peaceful rise" (*heping jueqi*) and "peaceful development" (*heping fazhan*)—experts at think tanks were often deliberately drafted into the process of producing ideas. Think tanks in China are not independent in the Western sense—they cannot determine the mission and timing of research to be undertaken. However, they are "stable and autonomous" and conduct research and provide advice on policy issues.[10] Some of the most influential think tanks in China today on foreign security policy include the Chinese Institutes of Contemporary International Relations, or CICIR (*Zhongguo xiandai guoji guanxi yanjiuyuan*), China Institute of International Studies (*Zhongguo guoji wenti yanjiuyuan*), Shanghai Institute of International Studies (*Shanghai guoji wenti yanjiuyuan*), Centre for International and Strategic Studies, Peking University (*Beijing daxue guoji zhanlue yanjiusuo*), and the Institute of International Studies, Tsinghua University (*Qinghua daxue guoji guanxi yanjiuyuan*). These bodies regularly provide reports and research, and they convene meetings on specific issues, many times at the request of the Chinese government, that are attended by government personnel. Key academics and analysts from these think tanks are often also invited to high-level meetings in government.

The nexus between these think tanks and the Chinese government was not limited to the discussion of specific policy issues. In addition, government officials regularly asked them to brainstorm and interpret ideas. For example, before one of Xi Jinping's early visits to the United States as Chairman, officials from the Ministry of Foreign Affairs (*waijiao bu*) asked a major think tank to convene a conference on one of the concepts Xi had begun espousing—*xinxing daguo guanxi*, or "new type of great power relations." Multiple interviewees in Beijing and Shanghai told me that *waijiao bu* officials attended the conference, took copious notes that would be sent up through the appropriate channels, but did not say a word during the proceedings. Other interviewees claimed that the concept itself had first been espoused by an expert at CICIR in an internal seminar, and then had eventually wended its way up to Xi, who endorsed it by publicly including it in a speech.[11]

While Indian think tanks still do not have the reach and influence of Chinese think tanks, and the Indian government does not utilize them in a similar fashion, there are some indications of efforts to move in this direction. The Observer Research Foundation (ORF), for example, is making a conscious effort to produce a body of work on Indian foreign policy and power. The organization is stymied somewhat, however, in that its reputation is still more as an organizer of networking conferences (particularly the Raisina Dialogue, which it organizes annually in partnership with the Indian Ministry of External Affairs) rather than as a trust of substantive consultative expertise.

As a corollary, let me say that I'm not making a value judgment about countries that do or don't develop idea advocacy. Whether a country is an active rising power and rises to become a great power or stays a reticent power is not a matter of superiority versus inferiority, either of culture or of government. In some ways, one could argue that reticence can sometimes serve a country well. India's reticence has indeed earned it frustration on the part of its partners but, on the other hand, despite this and despite its increasing capabilities, its reputation is one that China has reason to envy. Even when India does not play by the norms of the international order—witness its bid to enter the Nuclear Security Group (NSG) despite its continuing refusal to sign the Nuclear Nonproliferation Treaty (NPT), a prerequisite for NSG members—it is not seen or feared as a revisionist power.[12]

The final, and perhaps most important, conclusion is that when trying to understand China and India today, we need to understand that idea advocacy or the lack of it can explain much of why they behave differently—understanding and even mapping these domestic narratives early on are crucial to understanding their behavior as well as the content of their nationalism. And such an understanding is crucial in terms of managing our relationships with these countries.

Active rising powers that are initially accommodational may in fact eventually become activist; that is, they will attempt to revise the international order. Convinced of the need to *act* like a great power, China has slowly, since the 1990s, been transitioning its reputation from an opposer of norms to a shaper of norms.[13] China is also today searching for a *Chinese* as opposed to a Western path to great power. A multilateral initiative like the Belt and Road Initiative (BRI)—a centerpiece of Chinese foreign policy which promises to connect China to nearly seventy countries through infrastructure development and investments—is an expression of the search for a Chinese path to great power, even as China uses the norms of the liberal international order to anchor the initiative. In 2020, Fareed Zakaria pronounced that "the new consensus on China's economic behavior holds that China forced multinational companies to transfer their technology, has subsidized its 'national champions,' and has placed formal and informal barriers in the path of foreign firms seeking to enter its market. Beijing has, in short, used the open international economy to bolster its own statist and mercantilist system."[14] While the thrust of Zakaria's piece was that one should not exaggerate the threat from China, he pointed to the BRI as exemplifying the fact that China's foreign policy has under Xi become much more "ambitious and assertive." But what Zakaria and others need to understand is that BRI is not a sudden new outcome—it is the result of a longer process of China's rise that first encompassed active behavior before Beijing attempted any activism. In other words, China today displaying intentions to create new rules in international politics and undertake reform to prominent international institutions so that they would better serve Chinese interests[15] is part of a process that began in the 1990s. Thus, any management of a rising power needs to be strategized when it displays active behavior not simply as a belated reaction to activist behavior.

It is also important to remember that activism, even China's activism, is not a given. BRI is very subnational at its core—that is, local Chinese governments play a large role in BRI,[16] leading to fragmented rather than consolidated implementation.[17] This means that BRI is not driven by a single monolithic idea, but rather that narratives will continue to play a role in shaping BRI as it evolves. Its very "hazy[ness]"[18] means that there may be room to impact the narratives, and the fact that BRI is primarily about China's desire to articulate an alternate "Chinese" path and reshape global governance[19] (the official government language about the policy suggests that BRI is supposed to "understand the world, change the world, and profoundly shape the destiny of humanity"[20]) means that attempting to shape the narratives is important. Moreover, since idea advocacy is a marketplace of narratives, by definition there are narratives that do not win out. It may be significant for the United States and others to look at these losing narratives, and the elites who espouse them, and understand why they lost out.

In India's case, the United States needs to tamp down its expectations. American frustration with India continued in the twenty-first century as India pursued interests that seemed inimical to cooperation. For example, India enacted the Civil Liability for Nuclear Damage Act in 2010, casting a "pall" over any optimism on America's part; India bought the French Rafale fighter jet over an American jet; and, outraged by the arrest of an Indian diplomat in the United States by US Attorney for the Southern District of New York, Preet Bharara, the Indian government ordered that the security barriers around the American Embassy in New Delhi be pulled away, leaving the embassy vulnerable to attack, particularly by vehicles approaching at high speeds.[21] Even as recently as 2018, a former US ambassador to India, Richard Verma, acknowledged at a conference in New Delhi that the Indo-US relationship never seemed to "quite get there."[22]

This could explain, in turn, India's lack of deep engagement in constructing a multilateral initiative like the Indo Pacific Quad.[23] Even though India is deeply worried about the Indo-Pacific region and, particularly, about China's BRI activities in the region (and even though its ruling party, the BJP, has advocated that India give up its "strategic reticence"[24]), it continues to frustrate its partners with its unwillingness to commit to or build any new initiative to counterbalance China or even draw in Southeast Asian countries.[25] The Look East policy, first begun in 1991, was tacitly acknowledged to have failed when Prime Minister

Modi decided to reboot the policy shortly after coming to power in 2014 and to rebrand it as "Act East." But as one expert acknowledged in 2016, India still remained "peripheral" to Southeast Asia as a "minor player" with "limited influence."[26] Another stated that while it was clearly in India's interests to support ASEAN vis-à-vis China, and there was "little doubt about New Delhi's desires," ASEAN valued "actual deliveries rather than promises."[27]

Today India's GDP is the third largest in the world after China and the United States in purchasing power parity terms,[28] and India is the world's third largest military spender.[29] But many of the narratives of its elites continue to be inward rather than outward looking—in international and domestic speeches, Prime Minister Modi (unlike Xi, for example) rarely, if ever, actively talks of Indian leadership in the world, and he espouses no *Indian* way to emulate.[30] Rather, he makes clear that his goals are to develop the Indian economy and attract investment. This was recently confirmed to me by a very high-ranking Indian official who said s/he believed that Modi's goal was to make India a rich country, not a powerful one, which explained why Indian diplomats in major partner countries, like the United Sates for example, were consistently instructed to meet with businessmen, and virtually ignore their counterparts in the US State Department.

Why Nations Rise also raises a number of questions that provide fertile ground for further research. Can we find patterns for why some countries develop narratives about becoming a great power, and others do not? In the cases that I chose, I found a number of different reasons for each country's narratives. But in no case did I find that the presence or absence of these narratives was predetermined. The case of Japan in two time periods demonstrates that very clearly. If we could pinpoint critical junctures at which some countries become more likely than others to propagate these narratives, we could begin to understand even more about the causes and consequences of a country's rise.

We saw in this book that material capabilities which we consistently rely on to identify rising powers are certainly necessary but not sufficient for a country to behave as a rising power. But what if there were a country that had narratives about becoming a great power but not the capability to do so? What could be the outcome of such narratives? A potential, and somewhat chilling, case that came to my mind after discussions with historian colleagues is that of Weimar Germany between the two World Wars.[31]

The Enabling Act of March 1933 that brought Hitler unrestricted power to rule Germany was a seminal event that resulted in the military resurgence of Germany. When interwar Germany is discussed as a rising power by international relations experts, the period under scrutiny is invariably post-1933 when Hitler ascended to power and set in motion Germany's overt rearmament. Between 1933 and 1939, the rise of Germany, the failure to contain it, and the outbreak of World War II led to much hand-wringing about the policy of appease-ment, where it came from, who propagated it, and who was to blame. Weimar Germany, by contrast, had emerged from national defeat, and was militarily and economically weak. However, interestingly, while Weimar Germany indeed had neither the military nor the economic power that would lead us to consider it to be a rising power, it had narratives about regaining great power: German elites strongly believed that Germany was destined to again become a great power, even if that led to another war.[32]

Historians accept that Nazi ideology had historical roots. Many elements such as "territorial unity and independence of all racial Germans," the need for "living space" (*Lebensraum*) to match the territory with the economic needs of a people, and the idea of an enlarged state engaging in worldwide imperial poli-tics derived from pre-1914 German beliefs about the nation's role in the world.[33] There was no significant break between the ideas of pre-1914 and subsequent Nazi ideology, and a consistent emphasis on the need for Germany to reassert itself as a great power. These beliefs were enhanced by various factors, such as the humiliating "war guilt" clause in the Treaty of Versailles, the psycholog-ical burden of reparations, the unfair imposition of the borders in the eastern frontiers, counter-revolutionary strands that drew on Pan-German ideas, and imperialist dreams of world power and colonial grandeur. And even though Germany at this time did not have the capabilities, elite ideas about regaining great power strongly promoted rearmament. The "stab in the back" legend (when Germany's defeat became clear, its military leaders quickly installed a civil government that would be held responsible by the German public for their nation's loss) helped sustain the idea that the German empire had been de-feated because the army had been "betrayed."[34] Army manuals made it clear that Germany was "a major military power" with a modern army, helping the officers avoid the bleak reality of the present and think instead of a bright military fu-ture.[35] Moreover, the German military (Reichswehr) and the German Foreign Office began demanding that Germany's armed forces be allowed to gain parity with other countries.[36] The Reichswehr under General Schleicher also began to move away from reorganizing existing units to long-term plans for rearmament and "became more active politically" as it sought to align these plans "with the revisionist foreign policy of the government."[37] "The persistence of the mystique of nationalist integration and the desire to reassert Germany's position as a great power also helped inspire the revanchist shift in foreign policy that began in 1929–1930."[38] In short, Weimar Germany could represent a somewhat worrying case of a country with narratives of (re)gaining great power; these narratives played no small role in its rearmament, that is, in Germany's regaining both eco-nomic and military might.

Charting the emergence and decline of narratives is also interesting to consider. Some narratives win out. Others do not. Why? Does it have to do with the fortunes of the elites who hold them, or is there some other reason? Are there certain kinds of elites who are more likely to hold some narratives over others? Can a status quo power be successful in promoting some narratives over others within a rising power in order to better manage the relationship?

As I finish this book in the middle of a global pandemic, I wonder how an unprecedented geopolitical crisis can affect narratives. Will India feel compelled to develop narratives of great power in self-preservation if the United States and the international liberal order decline? India currently has a Hindu nationalist government in power under Prime Minister Modi which has been even more aggressively vocal about the rising threat of China than previous Indian governments—will Hindu nationalist narratives eventually turn to India's changing status in the world and advocate active behavior? Will China tamp down narratives of becoming a great power if it sees itself either as compelled to cooperate with the United States to tackle the crisis[39] (in effect taking on collective responsibility on a larger scale and faster than it has done thus far) or if a second wave of the pandemic hits? There are divisions among Chinese elites today about tackling the global health crisis, from those who believe that China should focus on de-escalating the rivalry with the United States, to those who advocate for China to take on the responsibility of helping countries to recover, to those who think China should seize the moment and take on leadership in public health institutions.

Finally, this book is not intended to be a crystal ball and definitively predict that if countries do not develop narratives about becoming a great power they will certainly not become great powers, and that if they do, they will. Rather, what it does is show that, all else being equal, we can look to history to learn fascinating patterns of behavior in countries that have increased their economic and military power, and/or had opportunities to rise, and use these patterns to understand China and India today. *Why Nations Rise* is intended to give us a different way to think about China, India, and other rising powers, and open the path for future scholars to ask more questions about power transitions in the world.

NOTES

Chapter 1

1. Private conversation with author, July 2018.
2. Max Fisher, "India Says It Wants to Be a Great Power. It Didn't Act like One This Week," *Washington Post*, December 18, 2013. https://www.washingtonpost.com/news/worldviews/wp/2013/12/18/india-says-it-wants-to-be-a-great-power-it-didnt-act-like-one-this-week/.
3. Stephen P. Cohen and Sumit Ganguly, "The Case Studies: India," in *The Pivotal States: A New Framework for US Policy in the Developing World*, eds. Robert Chase, Emily Hill, and Paul Kennedy (New York: W. W. Norton, 1999), 41.
4. Alyssa Ayres, "Will India Start Acting like a Global Power?," *Foreign Affairs* 96 no. 6 (November–December 2017).
5. As part of the acronym BRICS.
6. Tarik Oguzlu, "Making Sense of Turkey's Rising Power Status: What Does Turkey's Approach within NATO Tell Us?," *Turkish Studies* 14, no. 4 (2013), 774–796.
7. "Brazil's Unrest: A Rising Power Is Wracked by Social Turmoil," *Pittsburgh Post-Gazette*, June 22, 2013. https://www.post-gazette.com/opinion/editorials/2013/06/22/Brazil-s-unrest-A-rising-power-is-wracked-by-social-turmoil/stories/201306220144
8. "The Rise and Rise of Iran: How Tehran has Become Pivotal to the Future of the Middle East," *The Conversation*, September 1, 2017. https://theconversation.com/the-rise-and-rise-of-iran-how-tehran-has-become-pivotal-to-the-future-of-the-middle-east-83160.
9. Jonathan Adelman, "The Surprising Resurgence of Russia as a Great Power," *Huffington Post*, September 8, 2015. https://www.huffpost.com/entry/the-surprising-resurgence_b_8104486?guccounter=1&guce_referrer=aHR0cHM6Ly93d3cuZ29vZ2xlLmNvbS8&guce_referrer_sig=AQAAAFxJzlX4FQyl-IUb0yIYyXvcT1eIL8sJP8ixeZLQ3eodzI1WcQp_vqbe04gdx8ozU1V3uze_6Q2dXfWQBwHTICex0ftE90GUqy6W5gelJi-VdcQu3yrRf5-ZiFezkgOaflQKAbVds8s-maYjsIA7-9W7kyM1oDmlVb3mTgEzmxMQ
10. Douglas Lemke and Ronald Tammen, "Power Transition Theory and the Rise of China," *International Interactions* 29, no. 4 (2003): 269.
11. Robert Gilpin, *War and Change in World Politics* (Cambridge, UK: Cambridge University Press, 1981), 13.
12. A. F. K. Organski, *World Politics* (New York: Alfred A. Knopf, 1958), 361.
13. Organski, *World Politics*; A. F. K. Organski and Jacek Kugler, *The War Ledger* (Chicago: Chicago University Press, 1980); Jacek Kugler and Douglas Lemke, eds., *Parity and War: Evaluations and Extensions of the War Ledger* (Ann Arbor: University of Michigan Press, 1996); Raimo Vayrynen, "Economic Cycles, Power Transitions, Political Management and Wars between Major Powers," *International Studies Quarterly* 27, no. 4 (December 1983): 389–418; David Sobek and Jeremy Wells, "Dangerous Liaisons: Dyadic Power Transitions and the Risk of Militarized Disputes," *Canadian Journal of Political Science* 46, no. 1 (June 2013): 69–92;

Brian Efird, Jacek Kugler, and Gaspare Genna, "From War to Integration: Generalizing Power Transition Theory," *International Interactions* 29, no. 4 (October 2003): 293–313.

14. Some examples of power transition theorists applying their findings to specific cases like China are Jacek Kugler and Ronald Tammen, "Regional Challenge: China's Rise to Power," in *The Asia-Pacific: A Region in Transition*, ed. Jim Rolfe (Honolulu: Asia-Pacific Center for Security Studies, 2004), 33–53; David Rapkin and William Thompson, "Power Transition, Challenge and the (Re-) Emergence of China," *International Interactions* 29, no. 4 (2003): 315–342.

15. See, for example, Jack S. Levy, "Misperception and the Causes of War: Theoretical Linkages and Analytical Problems," *World Politics* 36, no. 1 (October 1983): 76–99; Christopher Layne, "The Unipolar Illusion: Why New Great Powers Will Rise," *International Security* 17, no. 4 (Spring 1993): 5–51; Stacie Goddard, *When Right Makes Might: Rising Powers and World Order* (Ithaca, NY: Cornell University Press, 2018); David. M. Edelstein, *Over the Horizon: Time, Uncertainty and the Rise of Great Powers* (Ithaca, NY: Cornell University Press, 2017).

16. There is a large body of excellent work by country experts on China and India that provides insight into their domestic politics and foreign policy and how they affect their rise. A variation on this also focuses on the implications of each one's rise for the United States and the international system. Examples of the latter are Alastair Iain Johnston, "Is China a Status Quo Power," *International Security* 27, no. 3 (Spring 2003): 5–56; John Mearsheimer, "China's Un-peaceful Rise," *Current History* 105, no. 690 (April 2006): 160–162; G. John Ikenberry, "The Rise of China and the Future of the West: Can the Liberal System Survive?," *Foreign Affairs* 87, no. 1 (January–February 2008): 23–37; Barry Buzan, "China in International Society: Is 'Peaceful Rise' Possible?" *Chinese Journal of International Politics* 3, no. 1 (2010): 5–36; Andrew F. Hart and Bruce D. Jones, "How Do Rising Powers Rise?" *Survival* 52, no. 6 (2010): 63–88; Graham Allison, *Destined for War: Can America and China Escape Thucydides' Trap?* (Boston and New York: Houghton Mifflin Harcourt, 2017).

17. This is the smallest body of work. Examples include Robyn Meredith, *The Elephant and the Dragon: The Rise of India and China and What It Means for All of Us* (New York: W.W. Norton, 2008); Pranab Bardhan, *Awakening Giants, Feet of Clay: Assessing the Economic Rise of India and China* (Princeton, NJ: Princeton University Press, 2010); George Gilboy and Eric Heginbotham, *Chinese and Indian Strategic Behavior: Growing Power and Alarm* (New York: Cambridge University Press, 2012); T. V. Paul, ed., *The China-India Rivalry in the Globalization Era* (Washington, DC: Georgetown University Press, 2018).

18. More specifically, "capabilities are an aggregation of world population, urban population, military expenditures, military personnel, iron and steel production, and coal and oil consumption" (Kugler and Tammen, "Regional Challenge," 38). At its broadest, it implies a combination of hard and soft power.

19. Joseph S. Nye, "Soft Power and American Foreign Policy," *Political Science Quarterly* 119, no. 2 (Summer 2004): 256.

20. Hart and Jones, "How Do Rising Powers Rise?," 65.

21. Sheena Chestnut and Alastair Iain Johnston, "Is China Rising?," in *Global Giant: Is China Changing the Rules of the Game*, eds. Eva Paus et al. (New York: Palgrave MacMillan, 2009), 239–240.

22. Jehangir Pocha and Ha Jin, "The Rising 'Soft Power' of India and China," *New Perspectives Quarterly* 20, no. 1 (Winter 2003): 6–13; Yanzhong Huang and Sheng Ding, "Dragon's Underbelly: An Analysis of China's Soft Power," *East Asia* 23, no. 4 (December 2006): 22–44; Li Mingjiang, "China Debates Soft Power," *The Chinese Journal of International Politics* 2, no. 2 (October 2008): 287–308; Jacques Hymans, "India's Soft Power and Vulnerability," *India Review* 8, no. 3 (2009): 234–265.

23. Organski, *World Politics*, 366–367; Jacek Kugler and A. F. K. Organski, "The Power Transition: A Retrospective and Prospective Evaluation," *Handbook of War Studies* 1 (1989): 173.

24. Cornel Ban and Mark Blyth, "The BRICs and the Washington Consensus: An introduction," *Review of International Political Economy* 20, no. 2 (2013): 242; Marion Fourcade, "The Material and Symbolic Construction of the BRICs: Reflections Inspired by the RIPE Special Issue," *Review of International Political Economy* 20, no. 2 (2013): 262.

25. Fourcade, "The Material and Symbolic Construction," 261.

26. Chelsea Geach, "Four Reasons for SA's Low Life Expectancy," *Western Cape,* December 22, 2014. https://www.iol.co.za/news/south-africa/western-cape/four-reasons-for-sas-low-life-expectancy-1798106

27. Chestnut and Johnston, "Is China Rising?," 244.

28. Eric Heginbotham et al., *The US-China Military Scorecard: Forces, Geography, and the Evolving Balance of Power, 1996–2017* (Santa Monica, CA: RAND, 2015).

29. John Mearsheimer, *The Tragedy of Great Power Politics* (New York: W. W. Norton, 2001)

30. Defined as "an activist foreign policy that ranges from attention to international events to increases in diplomatic legations to participation in great-power diplomacy." Fareed Zakaria, *From Wealth to Power: The Unusual Origins of America's World Role* (Princeton, NJ: Princeton University Press, 1998), 4–5

31. That is, when rising powers engage in expansionist behavior, we should apparently expect them to do so because either they can (they have the relative material power to do so) or they must (they have the material power to do so and they perceive a threat). See Sean Lynn Jones, "Realism and America's Rise: A Review Essay," *International Security* 23, no. 2 (Fall 1998): 170.

32. Michael Mazarr, Timothy Heath, and Astrid Cevallos, "China and the International Order," *RAND Report* (Santa Monica, CA: RAND, 2018); Alastair Iain Johnston, "China and International Order: Which Order?" (working paper, Gov. James Albert Noe and Linda Noe Laine Professor of China in World Affairs, Harvard University, Cambridge, MA, 2018).

33. Manjari Chatterjee Miller, "India's Authoritarian Streak: What Modi Risks with His Divisive Populism," *Foreign Affairs* (May 2018). https://www.foreignaffairs.com/articles/india/2018-05-30/indias-authoritarian-streak

34. Josh Shifrinson, *Rising Titans, Falling Giants: How Great Powers Exploit Power Shifts* (Ithaca, NY: Cornell University Press, 2018), 17–20.

35. Property is given meaning only because actors share belief it has meaning [Marina Duque, "Recognizing International Status: A Relational Approach" (unpublished paper, 2016)].

36. "Yearbook: Armaments, Disarmament and International Security," Stockholm International Peace Research Institute (SIPRI), 2018, http://data.worldbank.org/indicator/MS.MIL.XPND.GD.ZS.

37. "2020 Military Strength Ranking," Global Firepower List, http://www.globalfirepower.com/countries-listing.asp.

38. Miles Kahler, "Rising Powers and Global Governance: Negotiating Change in a Resilient Status Quo," *International Affairs* 89, no. 3 (May 2013): 721.

39. Mingjiang Li, ed., *Soft Power: China's Emerging Strategy in International Politics* (Lanham, MD: Lexington Books, 2009).

40. Hart and Jones, "How Do Rising Powers Rise?," 65; Chestnut and Johnston, "Is China Rising?," 237.

41. Levy, *War and the Modern Great Power System,* 8.

42. Manjari Chatterjee Miller, "The Role of Beliefs in Identifying Rising Powers," *The Chinese Journal of International Politics* 9, no. 2 (April 2016): 221.

43. George Modelski, *World Power Concentrations: Typology, Data, Explanatory Framework* (Morristown, NJ: General Learning Press, 1974).

44. Daniel S. Geller and J. David Singer, *Nations at War: A Scientific Study of International Conflict* (Cambridge: Cambridge University Press, 1998), 58.

45. Melvin Small and Joel David Singer, *Resort to Arms: International and Civil Wars, 1816–1980* (Beverly Hills, CA: Sage Publications, 1982).

46. An example of this is Turkey and the United States in 1845, both of which ranked higher than Prussia using the COW scale, but only the latter is identified as a great power (Levy, *War and the Modern Great Power System,* 16).

47. Levy, *War and the Modern Great Power System,* 16; R. Corbetta et al., "Major Powers, Major Power Status and Status Inconsistency in International Politics" (unpublished paper, 2008), 3; Joel David Singer, "Reconstructing the Correlates of War Data Set on Material Capabilities of States, 1816–1985," *International Interactions* 14, no. 2 (1988): 119.

48. Singer, "Reconstructing the Correlates of War Data Set," 119–120; Levy, *War and the Modern Great Power System*, 17–18.

49. Oystein Tunsjo, *The Return of Bipolarity in World Politics: China, the United States and Geostructural Realism* (New York: Columbia University Press, 2018), 7–16.

50. Tunsjo, *The Return of Bipolarity*, 90.

51. Iver B. Neumann, "Russia as a Great Power: 1815–2007," *Journal of International Relations and Development* 11, no. 2 (June 2008): 144.

52. Neumann, "Russia As a Great Power," 145.

53. This sometimes has been the case even when great powers have expanded. Stacie Goddard shows how Prussia used established norms and rhetoric to justify expansion, and essentially rose unopposed. Stacie Goddard, "When Right Makes Might: How Prussia Overturned the European Balance of Power," *International Security* 33, no. 3 (Winter 2009): 110–142.

54. We already know that countries in general attach importance to social reputation as an end in itself. The purpose is to achieve and manage "social standing, legitimacy and influence in international and national politics." Jennifer Erickson, *Dangerous Trade: Arms Exports, Human Rights and International Reputation* (New York: Columbia University Press, 2015), 32. We also know that rising powers need to be recognized by established great powers in order to feel that their quest for great power is legitimate. Michelle Murray, *The Struggle for Recognition in International Relations: Status, Revisionism and Rising Powers* (Oxford: Oxford University Press, 2018).

55. Quoted in Neumann, "Russia as a Great Power," 130.

56. Louise Emmerji, Richard Jolly, and Thomas G. Weiss, "Economic and Social Thinking in the UN in Historical Perspective," *Development and Change* 36, no. 2 (2005): 211–235.

57. Also called norms. Martha Finnemore and Kathryn Sikkink, "International Norm Dynamics and Political Change," *International Organization* 52, no. 4 (1998): 891.

58. Judith Goldstein and Robert O. Keohane, eds., *Ideas and Foreign Policy: Beliefs, Institutions and Political Change* (Ithaca, NY, and London: Cornell University Press, 1993); Kathleen Knight, "Transformations of the Concept of Ideology in the Twentieth Century," *American Political Science Review* 100, no. 4 (2006): 619–626.

59. Goldstein and Keohane, *Ideas and Foreign Policy*; Jeffrey Checkel, *Ideas and International Political Change: Soviet/Russian Behavior and the End of the Cold War* (New Haven, CT: Yale University Press, 1997); Matthew Evangelista, *Unarmed Forces: The Transnational Movement to End the Cold War* (Ithaca, NY, and London: Cornell University Press, 1999); Daniel Béland and Robert Henry Cox, eds., *Ideas and Politics in Social Science Research* (New York: Oxford University Press, 2010).

60. Vivien Schmidt, "Reconciling Ideas and Interests Through Discursive Institutionalism," in *Ideas and Politics in Social Science Research*, eds. Daniel Béland and Robert Henry Cox (New York: Oxford University Press, 2010), 58.

61. Daniel Béland and Robert Henry Cox, "Introduction," in *Ideas and Politics in Social Science Research*, eds. Daniel Béland and Robert Henry Cox (New York: Oxford University Press, 2010), 5.

62. Schmidt, "Reconciling Ideas and Interests," 54.

63. William B. Gartner, "What Are We Talking about When We Talk about Entrepreneurship?," *Journal of Business Venturing* 5, no. 1 (1990): 15–28.

64. There are some exceptions. See, for example, Stacie Goddard, "Brokering Change: Networks and Entrepreneurs in International Politics," *International Theory* 1, no. 2 (2009): 249–281.

65. Peter Hall, "Policy Paradigms, Social Learning, and the State: The Case of Economic Policymaking in Britain," *Comparative Politics* (1993): 275–296; Martin B. Carstensen, "Ideas Are Not as Stable as Political Scientists Want Them to Be: A Theory of Incremental Ideational Change," *Political Studies* 59, no. 3 (2011): 596–615.

66. Adam D. Sheingate, "Political Entrepreneurship, Institutional Change, and American Political Development," *Studies in American Political Development* 17, no. 2 (2003): 188.

67. Sheingate, "Political Entrepreneurship," 188. Note that idea entrepreneurship may also include elite norm entrepreneurs who pressure the state to enact policy as part of a transnational advocacy network because it is appropriate great power behavior. See, for example, R. Charli Carpenter, "Setting the Advocacy Agenda: Theorizing Issue Emergence and Nonemergence

in Transnational Advocacy Networks," *International Studies Quarterly* 51, no. 1 (2007): 99–120; Thorsten Benner, "Brazil as a Norm Entrepreneur: The 'Responsibility while Protecting' Initiative" (working paper, Global Public Policy Institute, Berlin, March 2013).

68. Peter Haas, "Epistemic Communities and International Policy Coordination," *International Organization* 46, no. 1 (1992): 1–35; John L. Campbell and Ove K. Pederson, "Knowledge Regimes and Comparative Political Economy," in *Ideas and Politics in Social Science Research*, eds. Daniel Béland and Robert Henry Cox (New York: Oxford University Press, 2010): 172–190; Daniel L. Byman and Kenneth M. Pollack, "Let Us Now Praise Great Men: Bringing the Statesman Back In," *International Security* 25, no. 4 (Spring 2001): 107–146.

69. Schmidt, "Reconciling Ideas and Interests," 57.

70. Campbell and Pederson, "Knowledge Regimes," 174.

71. Schmidt, "Reconciling Ideas and Interests," 47, 56.

72. Robert Jervis, *Perception and Misperception in International Politics* (Princeton, NJ: Princeton University Press, 1976); Sheri Berman, *The Social Democratic Moment: Ideas and Politics in the Making of Interwar Europe* (Cambridge, MA: Harvard University Press, 1998); Craig Parsons, *A Certain Idea of Europe* (Ithaca, NY: Cornell University Press, 2003).

73. Hal Brands, *What Good Is Grand Strategy?: Power and Purpose in American Statecraft from Harry S. Truman to George W. Bush* (Ithaca, NY: Cornell University Press, 2014), 24.

74. Stacie Goddard, *When Right Makes Might: Rising Powers and World Order* (Ithaca, NY: Cornell University Press, 2018), 12.

75. David. M. Edelstein, *Over the Horizon: Time, Uncertainty and the Rise of Great Powers* (Ithaca, NY: Cornell University Press, 2017), 77.

76. Any state that is actively increasing its material capabilities also usually has a grand strategy. Grand strategy is a difficult concept to define, encapsulating as it does "grand plans" (deliberate planning by elites), "grand principles" (principles held by elites to guide their behavior), and "grand behavior" (repeating patterns of behavior); Nina Silove, "Beyond the Buzzword: The Three Meanings of 'Grand Strategy,'" *Security Studies* 27, no. 1 (2017): 3. However, its essence is the ability of political leaders, using all resources at the disposal of a country, to integrate both military and non-military policies in order to preserve and advance the country's long-term interests during war and peace; Paul M. Kennedy, ed., *Grand Strategies in War and Peace* (New Haven, CT: Yale University Press, 1991), 4–5. Silove points out that the commonalities between the differing conceptions of grand strategy are the focus on ends and means, its holistic nature and the advancing of the most important interests; "Beyond the Buzzword," 19–20.

77. Avery Goldstein, *Rising to the Challenge: China's Grand Strategy and International Security* (Stanford, CA: Stanford University Press, 2005); Silove, "Beyond the Buzzword," 25.

78. Wang Jisi, "China's Search for a Grand Strategy," *Foreign Affairs* (March–April 2011): 68–79.

79. This has been claimed explicitly with respect to rising powers by both classical power transition theorists like Robert Gilpin and more recent scholars: T. V. Paul, Deborah Welch Larson, and William Wohlforth, *Status in World Politics* (Cambridge: Cambridge University Press, 2014); Steven Ward, *Status and the Challenge of Rising Powers* (Cambridge: Cambridge University Press, 2017); Xiaoyu Pu, *Rebranding China: Contested Status Signaling in the Changing Global Order* (Stanford, CA: Stanford University Press, 2019); as well as by scholars who argue that all seek status within their own status community, see Jonathan Renshon, *Fighting for Status: Hierarchy and Conflict in World Politics* (Princeton, NJ: Princeton University Press, 2017).

80. Basil Liddell Hart, *Strategy* (New York: Praeger, 1954); John M. Collins, *Grand Strategy: Principles and Practices* (Annapolis, MD: Naval Institute Press, 1973); Hal Brands, *What Good Is Grand Strategy?*

81. Kennedy, *Grand Strategies in War and Peace*; Richard Rosecrance and Arthur Stein, eds., *The Domestic Bases of Grand Strategy* (Ithaca, NY: Cornell University Press, 1993).

82. John Mueller, "The Impact of Ideas on Grand Strategy," in *The Domestic Bases of Grand Strategy*, eds. Richard Rosecrance and Arthur Stein, *The Domestic Bases of Grand Strategy* (Ithaca, NY: Cornell University Press, 1993): 48–62.

83. Paul M. Kennedy, ed., *Grand Strategies in War and Peace*, 4–5. Silove points out that the commonalities between the differing conceptions of grand strategy are the focus on ends

and means, its holistic nature, and the advancing of the most important interests ("Beyond the Buzzword," 19–20).

84. Goldstein and Keohane, *Ideas and Foreign Policy*; Checkel, *Ideas and International Political Change*; Evangelista, *Unarmed Forces*; Béland and Cox, *Ideas and Politics*.

85. Elites in great powers have been shown to engage in narratives that lead to overexpansion (Jack Snyder, *Myths of Empire*).

86. Gilpin encouraged scholars to "think of any international system as temporary . . . to look for underlying causes of change which accumulate slowly but are realized in rare, concentrated bursts . . . to be on the lookout for gaps between the capabilities of states and the demands placed upon them by their international roles." William Wohlforth, "Gilpinian Realism and International Relations," *International Relations* 25, no. 4 (2011): 504.

87. Paul M. Kennedy, *The Rise and Fall of the Great Powers: Economic Change and Military Conflict from 1500–2000* (New York: Penguin Random House, 1987), 143.

88. Kennedy, *Rise and Fall*, 150.

89. Frank Ninkovich, *The United States and Imperialism* (Oxford: Blackwell, 2001), 10.

90. Kennedy, *Rise and Fall*, 151.

91. Adam Taylor, "Map: The Rise and Fall of the British Empire," *Washington Post*, September 8, 2015. https://www.washingtonpost.com/news/worldviews/wp/2015/09/08/map-the-rise-and-fall-of-the-british-empire/

92. Ninkovich, *United States and Imperialism*.

93. Quoted in Kennedy, *Rise and Fall*, 195.

94. There were undoubtedly some differences in the "real strength" of these countries when they became great powers, consequently varying their "great power effectiveness" (Kennedy, *Rise and Fall*, 202).

95. Kennedy, *Rise and Fall*, 203.

96. Zakaria, *From Wealth to Power*, 4–5

97. Zakaria, *From Wealth to Power*, 4–5

98. Sean Lynn-Jones, "Realism and America's Rise," 170.

99. Michael H. Hunt, *Ideology and U.S. Foreign Policy* (New Haven, CT: Yale University Press, 1997), 19.

100. Hunt, *Ideology and U.S. Foreign Policy*, 18.

101. Hunt, *Ideology and U.S. Foreign Policy*, 30, 32, 37.

102. Jeffrey W. Meiser, *Power and Restraint: The Rise of the United States, 1898–1941* (Washington, DC: Georgetown University Press, 2015), xvii.

103. Kenneth B. Pyle, *Japan Rising: The Resurgence of Japanese Power and Purpose* (New York: PublicAffairs, 2007), 98.

104. Pyle, *Japan Rising*, 98.

105. Pyle, *Japan Rising*, 99.

106. W. G. Beasley, *Japanese Imperialism 1894–1945* (Oxford: Oxford University Press, 1987), 27.

107. Beasley, *Japanese Imperialism*, 30.

108. Pyle, *Japan Rising*, 110.

109. Pyle, *Japan Rising*, 32.

110. Beasley, *Japanese Imperialism*; Pyle, *Japan Rising*.

111. Fabian Hilfrich, *Debating American Exceptionalism: Empire and Democracy in the Wake of the Spanish-American War* (New York: Palgrave MacMillan, 2012).

112. Paulo E. Coletta, "McKinley, the Peace Negotiations," *The Pacific Historical Review* 30, no. 4 (1961): 341–350.

113. Robert Jackson, *Quasi-States: Sovereignty, International Relations and the Third World* (Cambridge: Cambridge University Press, 1990).

114. Paul K. MacDonald, "Those Who Forget History Are Doomed to Republish It: Empire, Imperialism and Contemporary Debates about American Power," *Review of International Studies* 35, no. 1 (2009): 49–50. See also Ian Tyrrell and Jay Sexton, eds., *Empire's Twin: US Anti-Imperialism from the Founding Era to the Age of Terrorism* (Ithaca, NY: Cornell University Press, 2015), which argues that the United States has always had imperialist traditions and ends; others say the idea of the United States as an empire is "false"; see, for example, Elizabeth Cobbs Hoffman, *American Umpire* (Cambridge University Press, 2013), 5.

115. Robert Keohane, "Multilateralism: An Agenda for Research," *International Journal* 45, no. 4 (1990): 731.

116. Jonathan R. Macey and Jeffrey P. Miller, "The End of History and the New World Order: The Triumph of Capitalism and the Competition between Liberalism and Democracy," *Cornell International Law Journal* 25, no. 2 (1992): 283.

117. Anne-Marie Slaughter, "America's Edge: Power in the Networked Century," *Foreign Affairs* 88 (January–February 2009): 95.

118. A more controversial term.

119. Charles Maier, *Among Empires: American Ascendancy and Its Predecessors* (Cambridge, MA: Harvard University Press, 2006), 32.

120. Pyle, *Japan Rising*, 4.

121. Pyle, *Japan Rising*, 2.

122. Cited in Pyle, *Japan Rising*, 4.

123. Charles P. Kindleberger, "Dominance and Leadership in the International Economy: Exploitation, Public Goods, and Free Rides," *International Studies Quarterly* 25, no. 2 (June 1981): 242–254.

124. Andrew Nathan, "Domestic Factors in the Making of Chinese Foreign Policy," *China Report* 52, no. 3 (June 2016): 185.

125. See, for example, Ward's work on the struggles between hardline and moderate elites in rising powers, which can push these countries to radical revisionism (Ward, *Status and the Challenge*).

Chapter 2

1. Niall Ferguson, "America: An Empire in Denial," *The Chronicle of Higher Education* 28, March 2003, 317.

2. Eric Heginbotham et al., *The US-China Military Scorecard: Forces, Geography and the Evolving Balance of Power 1996–2017* (Santa Monica, CA: RAND, 2015).

3. Ernest May, *Imperial Democracy: The Emergence of America as a Great Power* (New York: Harcourt, Brace and World, 1961), 5.

4. May, *Imperial Democracy*, 3, 7.

5. Quoted in Robert W. Johannsen, "The Meaning of Manifest Destiny," in *Manifest Destiny and Empire: American Antebellum Expansionism*, eds. Sam W. Haynes and Christopher Morris (College Station: Texas A&M University Press, 1997), 15.

6. Dexter Perkins, *A History of the Monroe Doctrine* (Boston and Toronto: Little, Brown, 1955), 58.

7. Paul Kennedy, "The Rise of the United States to Great Power Status," in *Imperial Surge: The United States Abroad, the 1890s–early 1900s*, eds. Thomas G. Paterson and Stephen G. Rabe (Lexington: D. C. Heath, 1992), 5.

8. Walter LaFeber, *The New Empire: An Interpretation of American Expansion 1860–1898* (Ithaca, NY, and London: Cornell University Press, 1998), 9.

9. John Steele Gordon, *An Empire of Wealth: The Epic History of American Economic Power* (New York: HarperCollins, 2004), 259.

10. Gordon, *An Empire of Wealth*, 259.

11. Gordon, *An Empire of Wealth*, 254.

12. Robert J. Gordon, *The Rise and Fall of American Growth: The US Standard of Living since the Civil War* (Princeton, NJ: Princeton University Press, 2016), 27.

13. Value added is the difference between the value of a good and the cost of materials used in producing that good.

14. LaFeber, *New Empire*, 67.

15. LaFeber, *New Empire*, 18.

16. Figures and statistics quoted in Peter Trubowitz, *Defining the National Interest: Conflict and Change in American Foreign Policy* (Chicago: University of Chicago Press, 1998), 32–33.

17. Gordon, *An Empire of Wealth*, 260.

18. Frank Ninkovich, *The United States and Imperialism* (Hoboken, NJ: Wiley, 2001), 17–18.

19. Gordon, *An Empire of Wealth*, 277.

20. Paul Kennedy, *The Rise and Fall of the Great Powers: Economic Change and Military Conflict from 1500 to 2000* (New York: Penguin Random House, 1987), 154, 179.

21. Samuel Huntington, *The Soldier and the State: The Theory and Politics of Civil Military Relations* (Cambridge, MA: Harvard University press, 1957), 228.

22. Zakaria, *From Wealth to Power*, 122.

23. Quoted in Donald Chisholm, *Waiting for Dead Men's Shoes: Origins and Development of the US Navy's Office Personnel System 1793–1941* (Stanford, CA: Stanford University Press, 2001), 167.

24. Robert Kagan, *Dangerous Nation: America's Foreign Policy from Its Earliest Days to the Dawn of the Twentieth Century* (New York: Alfred A. Knopf, 2006), 341, 342.

25. Kagan, *Dangerous Nation*, 342.

26. "Personnel of the Navy: Nearly Half of the Enlisted Men Are Foreigners," *New York Times*, December 28, 1891.

27. Zakaria, *From Wealth to Power*, 123–124.

28. Zakaria, *From Wealth to Power*, 125.

29. Zakaria, *From Wealth to Power*, 125.

30. Secretary of War, Annual Report, A. 72597, pt. 1 (1874), 10, https://hdl.handle.net/2027/coo.31924095656017.

31. Secretary of War, Annual Report, A. 46298, pt. 1 (1891), 13–14, https://hdl.handle.net/2027/coo.31924095656348.

32. Secretary of the Navy, Annual Report, vol. 1 (1889), 4, https://catalog.hathitrust.org/Record/012202882

33. Zakaria, *From Wealth to Power*, 130.

34. Trubowitz, *Defining the National Interest*, 38.

35. Zakaria, *From Wealth to Power*, 48.

36. Jay Sexton, *The Monroe Doctrine: Empire and Nation in Nineteenth Century America* (New York: Farrar, Straus, and Giroux, 2011), 163.

37. David M. Edelstein, *Over the Horizon: Time, Uncertainty, and the Rise of Great Powers* (Ithaca, NY: Cornell University Press, 2017), 78.

38. Sexton, *The Monroe Doctrine*, 168.

39. Bailey, "America's Emergence," 1.

40. He argued that in fact the United States was a world power the day it was born, July 2, 1776 (Bailey, "America's Emergence").

41. Ephraim K. Smith, "William McKinley's Enduring Legacy: The Historiographical Debate on the Taking of the Philippine Islands," in *Crucible of Empire: The Spanish-American War and Its Aftermath*, ed. James C. Bradford (Annapolis: Naval Institute Press, 1993), 210.

42. Robert Beisner, *Twelve against Empire: The Anti-Imperialists 1898–1900* (New York: McGraw-Hill, 1968), xv.

43. There were certainly other earlier periods of time when the United States sought recognition from the great powers; see Eliga H. Gould, *Among the Powers of the Earth: The American Revolution and the Making of a New World Empire* (Cambridge, MA: Harvard University Press, 2012). But now the United States displayed behavior that was in accordance with accepted and recognized great power norms.

44. Selected articles on the Monroe Doctrine (New York: H. W. Wilson, 1915), 48, https://hdl.handle.net/2027/uc2.ark:/13960/t1fj2c48k.

45. Ninkovich, *The United States and Imperialism*, 14.

46. Perkins, *A History of the Monroe Doctrine*, 185.

47. Edelstein, *Over the Horizon*, 78.

48. Sexton, *The Monroe Doctrine*, 209.

49. Quoted in Sexton, *The Monroe Doctrine*, 208.

50. Historians such as William Appleman Williams and Walter LaFeber argued in the 1950s and 1960s that business interests played a role in America's expansion. But other than overemphasizing the hold that American business exerted on foreign policy, they concentrated their explanations on the late 1890s, and did not explain non-expansion. See Zakaria, *From Wealth to Power*, 51; Ninkovich, *United States and Imperialism*.

51. Ninkovich, *United States and Imperialism*, 15.

52. Ninkovich, *United States*, 16.

53. Ninkovich, *United States*, 16.

54. Zakaria, *From Wealth to Power*.

55. H. W. Brands, *Bound to Empire: The United States and the Philippines* (Oxford: Oxford University Press, 1992), 21.

56. Paulo E. Coletta, "McKinley, the Peace Negotiations, and the Acquisition of the Philippines," *Pacific Historical Review* 30, no. 4 (November 1961): 341–350.

57. Quoted in Edward P. Crapol, "Coming to Terms with Empire: The Historiography of Late 19th Century American Foreign Relations," *Diplomatic History* 16, no. 4 (October 1992): 578.

58. Luis A. Perez Jr., *The War of 1898: The United States and Cuba in History and Historiography* (Chapel Hill: University of North Carolina Press, 1998); Philip S. Foner, *The Spanish-Cuban-American War and the Birth of American Imperialism, 1895 to 1902* (New York: Monthly Review Press, 1972).

59. See Crapol, "Coming to Terms," 573–598, for an overview of the historical debate. For a more contemporary take, see Ian Tyrrell and Jay Sexton, eds., *Empire's Twin: US Anti-imperialism from the Founding Era to the Age of Terrorism* (Ithaca, NY: Cornell University Press, 2015), 172–174.

60. Thomas A. Bailey, "America's Emergence as a World Power: The Myth and the Verity," *Pacific Historical Review* 30, no. 1 (February 1961): 1–16.

61. Quoted in Samuel Flagg Bemis, *John Quincy Adams and the Foundations of American Foreign Policy* (New York: A. A. Knopf, 1949), 180.

62. Rohan Mukherjee, *Ascending Order: Rising Powers and the Institutional Politics of Status* (book manuscript).

63. Michael Hunt, *Ideology and U.S. Foreign Policy* (New Haven, CT: Yale University Press, 1987), 41.

64. Sean Lynn-Jones, "Realism and America's Rise," *International Security* 23, no. 2 (Fall 1998): 168.

65. James C. Bradford, ed., "Introduction," in *Crucible of Empire: The Spanish-American War and Its Aftermath* (Annapolis, MD: Naval Institute Press, 1993), xiv.

66. Beisner, *Twelve against Empire*, xiv.

67. James Monroe, "Monroe Doctrine" (speech, Washington, DC, December 2, 1823), ourdocuments.gov, https://www.ourdocuments.gov/doc.php?flash=false&doc=23.

68. 1853 is one of the earliest instances of any mention of a doctrine (Perkins, *A History of the Monroe Doctrine*, 99).

69. Perkins, *A History of the Monroe Doctrine*, 31, 57.

70. Perkins, *A History of the Monroe Doctrine*, 30.

71. Sexton, *The Monroe Doctrine*, 60.

72. John Louis O'Sullivan, "Annexation," *Democratic Review* 17 (1845): 5.

73. Robert W. Johannsen, "The Meaning of Manifest Destiny," in *Manifest Destiny and Empire: American Antebellum Expansionism*, eds. Sam W Haynes and Christopher Morris (Arlington: University of Texas at Arlington, 1997), 9.

74. Thomas R. Hietala, "'This Splendid Juggernaut': Westward a Nation and Its People," in *Manifest Destiny and Empire: American Antebellum Expansionism*, eds. Sam W. Haynes and Christopher Morris (Arlington: University of Texas at Arlington, 1997), 51.

75. Sexton, *The Monroe Doctrine*, 160.

76. Sexton, *The Monroe Doctrine*, 162.

77. Sexton, *The Monroe Doctrine*, 163.

78. Quoted in Sexton, *The Monroe Doctrine*, 181.

79. Sexton, *The Monroe Doctrine*, 206, 210.

80. Ninkovich, *United States and Imperialism*, 12.

81. Ninkovich, *United States and Imperialism*, 29.

82. Fabian Hilfrich, *Debating American Exceptionalism: Empire and Democracy in the Wake of the Spanish-American War* (New York: Springer, 2012).

83. Ninkovich, *United States and Imperialism*, 19–21.

84. Coletta, "McKinley, the Peace Negotiations," 342.

85. Ninkovich, *United States*, 21.

86. Kagan, *Dangerous*, 409–410.
87. Crapol, "Coming to Terms," 573–598.
88. Michael Patrick Cullinane, *Liberty and American Anti-Imperialism 1898–1909* (New York: Springer, 2012), 17.
89. Beisner, *Twelve against Empire*, xii.
90. Frank Friedel, "Dissent in the Spanish-American War and the Philippine Insurrection," *Proceedings of the Massachusetts Historical Society* 81 (1969): 175.
91. Cullinane, *Liberty and American Anti-Imperialism*, 31.
92. Letter from the Hon. George F. Hoar, March 29, 1899, Library of Congress, http://lcweb2. loc.gov/service/gdc/scd0001/2007/20071206001le/20071206001le.pdf.
93. Fred H. Harrington, "The Anti-Imperialist Movement in the United States 1898–1900," *The Mississippi Valley Historical Review* 22, no. 2 (September 1935): 214.
94. Paolo E. Coletta, "Bryan, McKinley and the Treaty of Paris," *Pacific Historical Review* 26, no. 2 (May 1957): 132, 134.
95. David Mayers, *Dissenting Voices in America's Rise to Power* (Cambridge: Cambridge University Press, 2007), 199.
96. Harrington, "Anti-Imperialist Movement," 218.
97. Hilfrich, *Debating American Exceptionalism*, 42.
98. Stuart Creighton Miller, *Benevolent Assimilation: The American Conquest of the Philippines 1899–1903* (New Haven, CT: Yale University Press, 1984), 26.
99. Mayers, *Dissenting Voices*, 199.
100. Mayers, *Dissenting Voices*, 199, 200.
101. James A. Field Jr., "American Imperialism: The Worst Chapter in Almost Any Book," *The American Historical Review* 83, no. 3 (June 1978): 651.
102. Beisner, *Twelve against Empire*, 174, 178.
103. Beisner, *Twelve against Empire*, 61.
104. Michael H. Hunt, "American Ideology: Visions of National Greatness and Racism," in *Imperial Surge: The United States Abroad, the 1890s–early 1900s*, eds. Thomas G. Paterson and Stephen G. Rabe (Lexington: D. C. Heath, 1992), 16.
105. Walter LaFeber, "The Business Community's Push for War," in *Imperial Surge: The United States Abroad, the 1890s–early 1900s*, eds. Thomas G. Paterson and Stephen G. Rabe (Lexington: D. C. Heath, 1992); LaFeber, *New Empire*.
106. Hunt, "American Ideology," 17.
107. Henry Cabot Lodge, "The Retention of the Philippine Islands" (speech, Washington, DC, March 7, 1900), Harvard College Library, 15, https://ia600301.us.archive.org/13/items/ retentionphilip00lodggoog/retentionphilip00lodggoog.pdf.
108. Hunt, *Ideology and U.S. Foreign Policy*, 43.
109. Theodore Roosevelt, "Expansion and Peace," *Independent* 51, December 21, 1899.
110. David H. Burton, "Theodore Roosevelt: Confident Imperialist," *The Review of Politics* 23, no. 3 (July 1961): 358.
111. Jeffrey A. Engel, "The Democratic Language of American Imperialism: Race, Order and Theodore Roosevelt's Personifications of Foreign Policy Evil," *Diplomacy and Statecraft* 19 (December 2008): 679, 680.
112. Quoted in Engel, "The Democratic Language of American Imperialism," 679.
113. Quoted in Engel, "The Democratic Language of American Imperialism," 680.
114. Albert J. Beveridge, "The Development of a Colonial Policy for the United States," *The Annals of the American Academy of Political and Social Science* 30 (July 1907): 3–4.
115. LaFeber, *New Empire*, 91.
116. Smith, "McKinley's Enduring Legacy."
117. Louis J. Gould, "President McKinley's Strong Leadership and the Road to War," in *Imperial Surge: The United States Abroad, the 1890s–early 1900s*, eds. Thomas G. Paterson and Stephen G. Rabe (Lexington: D. C. Heath, 1992), 41; Smith, "McKinley's Enduring Legacy," 207.
118. Gould, "McKinley's Strong Leadership," 41.
119. LaFeber, *New Empire*, 95–98.
120. Burton, "Theodore Roosevelt," 358.
121. Burton, "Theodore Roosevelt."

122. For a summary of some ongoing debates, see Charles S. Maier, "Review: Empire without End: Imperial Achievements and Ideologies," *Foreign Affairs* 89, no. 4 (2010): 153–159.

123. Daniel Immerwahr, *How to Hide an Empire: A Short History of the Greater United States* (New York: Farrar, Strauss and Giroux, 2019); Tyrrell and Sexton, eds., *Empire's Twin*; Adam Burns, *American Imperialism: The Territorial Expansion of the United States 1783–2013* (Edinburgh: Edinburgh University Press, 2017).

124. Elizabeth Cobbs Hoffman, *American Umpire* (Cambridge, MA: Harvard University Press, 2013), 13.

125. Hoffman, *American Umpire*, 12–13.

126. The work of historians such as Paul Kramer details US imperialism in the Philippines and how it played out; see Kramer, *The Blood of Government: Race, the United States and the Philippines* (Chapel Hill: University of North Carolina Press, 2006).

127. Some date the United States' giving up of colonialism to post–World War II; see Immerwahr, *How to Hide an Empire*.

128. Hoffman, *American Umpire*, 13.

Chapter 3

1. The Dutch Golden Age lasted from approximately 1568 to 1648. Until the Twelve Years' Truce in 1609, the height of the Golden Age, the Netherlands' physical territory was approximate to the post-1840 (when the partition from Belgium occurred) territory. See maps comparison: *The Dutch Revolt*, 1566–1609, The Map Archive, https://www.themaparchive.com/the–dutch–revolt–15661609.html; Alvin Jewett Johnson, cartographer, *Map of Holland, Belgium, and Switzerland*, 1867, 15.5 x 22.5 in., Geographicus Rare Antique Maps, https://www.geographicus.com/P/AntiqueMap/HollandSwitzerland–johnson–1870.

2. I am indebted to Corné Smit, Leiden University, for his research assistance and translation of Dutch articles, books, and primary texts.

3. Quoted in Bernard Hubertus and Maria Vlekke, *Evolution of the Dutch Nation* (New York: Roy, 1945), 326–327.

4. Paul Kennedy, *The Rise and Fall of the Great Powers: Economic Change and Military Conflict from 1500 to 2000* (New York: Random House, 1987), 100.

5. Wim Klinkert, *Het vaderland verdedigd. Plannen en opvattingen over de verdediging van Nederland 1874–1914* [The Fatherland defended: plans and views on the defense of the Netherlands 1874–1914] ('s-Gravenhage: Sectie Militaire Geschiedenis, 1992), 4.

6. Maarten Kuitenbrouwer, "Review of *The Netherlands and the Rise of Modern Imperialism: Colonies and Foreign Policy, 1870–1902*, by D. K. Fieldhouse," *The International History Review* 15, no. 3 (August 1993): 584.

7. In Japan, the Dutch controlled the port of Deshima (known today as Dejima). Dutch India consisted of Dutch Ceylon, Dutch Coromandel, Dutch Bengal, and Dutch Surat. The portion of the East Coast controlled by the Dutch consisted of parts of New York, New Jersey, Delaware, Connecticut, Pennsylvania, and Rhode Island and was known as the New Netherlands. The area of Dutch Brazil was called New Holland.

8. Henk L. Wesseling, "The Giant That Was a Dwarf, or the Strange Case of Dutch Imperialism," in *Imperialism and Colonialism: Essays on the History of European Expansion*, ed. Henk L. Wesseling (Westport, CT: Greenwood Press, 1997), 78.

9. Henk L. Wesseling, "The Netherlands as a Colonial Model," in *Imperialism and Colonialism: Essays on the History of European Expansion*, ed. Henk L. Wesseling (Westport, CT: Greenwood Press, 1997), 49.

10. Wesseling, "The Netherlands as a Colonial Model," 44.

11. Wesseling, "The Netherlands as a Colonial Model," 42.

12. Frances Gouda, *Dutch Culture Overseas: Colonial Practice in the Netherlands Indies, 1900–1942* (Amsterdam: Amsterdam University Press, 1995), 41, 42.

13. Maarten Kuitenbrouwer, *The Netherlands and the Rise of Modern Imperialism: Colonies and Foreign Policy, 1817–1902*, trans. Hugh Beyer (Oxford: Berg, 1992), 33.

14. Although the Netherlands industrialized later than some of the European great powers, it has been argued that this did not mean it was "a backward country." Rather, the process

of economic growth had, first, not been driven by the expansion of industry, and second, had been gradual rather than "spectacular." See Richard T. Griffiths, "Backward, Late or Different? Aspects of the Economic Development of the Netherlands in the 19th Century," in *The Economic Development of the Netherlands since 1870*, ed. Jan Luiten van Zanden (Cheltenham, UK: Elgar, 1996), 2, 5, 6.

15. Jan Luiten van Zanden and Arthur van Riel, *Nederland 1780–1914: Staat, instituties en economische ontwikkeling* (Amsterdam: Balans, 2000), 344.

16. Friso Wielenga, *A History of the Netherlands: From the Sixteenth Century to the Present Day*, trans. Lynne Richards (London: Bloomsbury, 2015), 181.

17. Luiten van Zanden and van Riel, *Nederland 1780–1914*, 285.

18. Paul F. State, *A Brief History of the Netherlands* (New York: Facts on File, 2008), 146–147.

19. Luiten van Zanden and van Riel, *Nederland 1780–1914*, 377.

20. Luiten van Zanden and van Riel, *Nederland 1780–1914*, 289.

21. Joost Jonker, "The Alternative Road to Modernity: Banking and Currency, 1814–1914," in *A Financial History of the Netherlands*, eds. Marjolein 't Hart, Joost Jonker, and Jan Luiten van Zanden (Cambridge: Cambridge University Press, 1997), 114.

22. Wielenga, *A History of the Netherlands*, 182.

23. Jacco Pekelder, "Nederland en de Duitse kwestie [The Netherlands and the German question]," in *De wereld volgens Nederland: Nederlandse buitenlandse politiek in historisch perspectief*, eds. J. Pekelder, Remco Raben, and Mathieu Segers, *De wereld volgens Nederland: Nederlandse buitenlandse politiek in historisch perspectief* [The world according to the Netherlands: Dutch foreign policy in historical perspective] (Amsterdam: Boom, 2015), 68.

24. Thomas Lindblad, "De handel tussen Nederland en Nederlands–Indië, 1874–1939 [The trade between the Netherlands and the Dutch Indies, 1874–1939]," *Economisch: en sociaal-historisch jaarboek* 51 (1988), 246.

25. Marjolein 't Hart, Joost Jonker, and Jan Luiten van Zanden, "Introduction," in *A Financial History of the Netherlands*, eds. Marjolein 't Hart, Joost Jonker, and Jan Luiten van Zanden (Cambridge: Cambridge University Press, 1997), 8.

26. Calculated in 1990 dollars. Kennedy, *Rise and Fall*, 234.

27. Luiten van Zanden and van Riel, *Nederland 1780–1914*, 359.

28. Willem Bevaart, *De Nederlandse defensie (1839–1874)* [The Dutch defense] ('s–Gravenhage: Sectie Militaire Geschiedenis, 1993), 278.

29. Bevaart, *De Nederlandse defensie*, 125.

30. Bevaart, *De Nederlandse defensie*, 279.

31. Bevaart, *De Nederlandse defensie*, 466.

32. The complex Dutch plan was to make invasion so costly for an attacking power that others would feel safe enough not to attack the Dutch first. That is, they assumed that none of the great powers would allow another power to capture the Netherlands, and that since all of them had an interest in keeping the Dutch neutral, they would only attack them if another power threatened to do so.

33. Klinkert, *Het Vaderland Verdedigd*, 6.

34. Bevaart, *De Nederlandse defensie*, 561.

35. Ben Schoenmaker and Floribert Baudet, *Officieren aan het woord: De geschiedenis van de Militaire Spectator 1832–2007* [Officers speaking: The history of the Military Spectator 1832–2007] (Amsterdam: Boom, 2007), 58, 68.

36. Wim Klinkert, "The Salutary Yoke of Discipline: Military Opinion on the Social Benefit of Conscription," in *Images of the Nation: Different Meanings of Dutchness 1870–1940*, eds. Annemieke Galema, Barbara Henkes, and Henk te Velde (Amsterdam: Rodopi, 1993), 22.

37. Klinkert, "The Salutary Yoke," 24.

38. In the civil militia it was once a month or so, depending on the size of the village or municipality.

39. E.W.R. Van Roon, "De dienstplicht op de markt gebracht: Het fenomeen dienstvervanging in de negentiende eeuw [Conscription brought to the market place: The phenomenon of service replacement in the nineteenth century]," *BMGN: Low Countries Historical Review* 109, no. 4 (1994): 613.

40. Klinkert, "The Salutary Yoke," 24.

41. Klinkert, "The Salutary Yoke," 20.
42. Schoenmaker and Baudet, *Officieren aan het woord*, 68.
43. Klinkert, *Het Vaderland Verdedigd*, 391–392.
44. Klinkert, *Het Vaderland Verdedigd*, 335.
45. Kennedy, *Rise and Fall*, 203.
46. Klinkert, *Het Vaderland Verdedigd*, 37.
47. Klinkert, *Het Vaderland Verdedigd*, 50, 55, 294–295.
48. In European armies, typically, it was only after a declaration of war that a commander of a field army was appointed. Only after that appointment would the staff be formed and given the task of drawing up and executing plans. The Dutch modernized and improved their military readiness by appointing a field army commander in peace time who could prepare for war in advance and quickly. That the Dutch took this unique step demonstrates the importance of the field army in Dutch defense plans after 1907. See Klinkert, *Het Vaderland Verdedigd*, 315.
49. Klinkert, *Het Vaderland Verdedigd*, 479–481.
50. C. Antunes and J. Gommans, *Exploring the Dutch Empire: Agents, Networks and Institutions, 1600–2000* (London: Bloomsbury), 49.
51. Friso Wielenga, *Geschiedenis van Nederland: Van de Opstand tot heden* (Amsterdam: Boom 2012), 259.
52. State, *A Brief History*, 168.
53. Henk L. Wesseling, *Indië verloren, rampspoed geboren en andere opstellen over de geschiedenis van de Europese expansie* [Indies lost means adversity born and other essays concerning the history of European expansion] (Amsterdam: B. Bakker, 1988), 193.
54. Elsbeth Locher-Scholten, "Dutch Expansion in the Indonesian Archipelago around 1900 and Imperialism Debate," *Journal of South East Asian Studies* 25, no. 1 (March 1994): 95.
55. Henk L. Wesseling, "The Netherlands and the Partition of Africa," in *Imperialism and Colonialism: Essays on the History of European Expansion*, ed. Henk L. Wesseling (Westport, CT: Greenwood Press, 1997), 105.
56. Kuitenbrouwer, *The Netherlands and the Rise of Modern Imperialism*, 61.
57. Quoted in Kuitenbrouwer, *The Netherlands and the Rise of Modern Imperialism*, 64–65.
58. Quoted in Kuitenbrouwer, *The Netherlands and the Rise of Modern Imperialism*, 143.
59. Kuitenbrouwer, *The Netherlands and the Rise of Modern Imperialism*, 125.
60. Kuitenbrouwer, *The Netherlands and the Rise of Modern Imperialism*, 138, 140, 142.
61. Organized by Otto van Bismarck to discuss regulating European trade in Africa, which eventually led to a massive increase in colonial activity in the continent.
62. Immanuel Wallerstein, "Implicit Ideology in Africa: A Review of Books by Kwame Nkrumah," *The Journal of Conflict Resolution* 11, no. 4 (December 1967): 521.
63. Wesseling, "The Berlin Conference of 1884–1885," in *Imperialism and Colonialism: Essays on the History of European Expansion*, ed. Henk L. Wesseling (Westport, CT: Greenwood Press, 1997), 89, 91.
64. Wesseling, "The Netherlands and the Partition of Africa," 111.
65. Kuitenbrouwer, *The Netherlands and the Rise of Modern Imperialism*, 25–26.
66. Wesseling, "The Giant That Was a Dwarf," 75.
67. Term used by Cees Fasseur to denote the initiative for colonialism coming from the peripheral territories rather than the center. Quoted in J. Thomas Lindblad, "Economic Aspects of the Dutch Expansion in Indonesia, 1870–1914," *Modern Asian Studies* 23, no. 1 (1989): 3.
68. Kuitenbrouwer, *The Netherlands and the Rise of Modern Imperialism*.
69. Gerlof D. Homan, "Review of *The Netherlands and the Rise of Modern Imperialism: Colonies and Foreign Policy, 1870–1902*, by Maarten Kuitenbrouwer," *The American Historical Review* 98, no. 1 (February 1993): 190.
70. Lindblad, "Economic Aspects of the Dutch Expansion," 4–5, 6.
71. Locher-Scholten, "Dutch Expansion in the Indonesian Archipelago," 93, 96.
72. Locher-Scholten, "Dutch Expansion in the Indonesian Archipelago," 93.
73. Lindblad, "Economic Aspects of the Dutch Expansion," 14.
74. Lindblad, "Economic Aspects of the Dutch Expansion," 2.
75. Gouda, *Dutch Culture Overseas*, 47.
76. Hubertus and Vlekke, *Evolution of the Dutch Nation*, 318.

77. Kennedy, *Rise and Fall*, 245.
78. Wesseling, "The Netherlands and the Partition of Africa," 111.
79. J. Ellis Barker, *The Rise and Decline of the Netherlands: A Political and Economic History and a Study in Practical Statesmanship* (London: Smith, Elder, 1906), 441.
80. Wesseling, "The Giant That Was a Dwarf," 60.
81. Mentioned by a Dutch historian, conversation with the author, October 9, 2017.
82. Prof. James Kennedy, conversation with the author, February 9, 2017.
83. For comparison, that is less than twice the size of New Jersey. See "Europe: Netherlands," The World Factbook, Central Intelligence Agency, last modified February 7, 2020, https://www.cia.gov/library/publications/the–world–factbook/geos/nl.html.
84. Kennedy, *Rise and Fall*, 2.
85. P. D. M. Blaas, "The Touchiness of a Small Nation with a Great Past: The Approach of Fruin and Blok to the Writing of the History of the Netherlands," in *Clio's Mirror: Historiography in Britain and the Netherlands*, eds. A. C. Duke and C. A. Tamse (Zatphen: Walburg, 1985), 133–161.
86. Abraham Kuyper, *Ons Program, 1879* (Amsterdam: J. H. Kruyt, 1879), 330. The document which formed the basis of Kuyper's Anti-Revolutionary party founded the same year contains some ideas on colonial politics.
87. Nicholas C. F. van Sas, "Varieties of Dutchness," in *Images of the Nation: Different Meanings of Dutchness 1870–1940*, eds. Annemieke Galema, Barbara Henkes, and Henk te Velde (Amsterdam: Rodopi, 1993), 11–12.
88. Quoted in Kuitenbrouwer, *The Netherlands and the Rise of Modern Imperialism*, 61–62.
89. Quoted in Kuitenbrouwer, *The Netherlands and the Rise of Modern Imperialism*, 61–62.
90. Kuitenbrouwer, *The Netherlands and the Rise of Modern Imperialism*, 62.
91. Quoted in Kuitenbrouwer, *The Netherlands and the Rise of Modern Imperialism*, 64.
92. Quoted in Kuitenbrouwer, *The Netherlands and the Rise of Modern Imperialism*,133–134.
93. Quoted in Wesseling, "The Netherlands and the Partition of Africa," 110.
94. Quoted in Kuitenbrouwer, *The Netherlands and the Rise of Modern Imperialism*,137.
95. Quoted in Thomas R. Rochon, *The Netherlands: Negotiating Sovereignty in an Interdependent World* (Boulder, CO: Westview Press, 1999), 232.
96. Quoted in Thomas R. Rochon, *The Netherlands*, 232.
97. Henk te Velde, "How High Did the Dutch Fly? Remarks on Stereotypes of Burger Mentality," in *Images of the Nation: Different Meanings of Dutchness 1870–1940*, eds. Annemieke Galema, Barbara Henkes, and Henk te Velde (Amsterdam: Rodopi, 1993), 61.
98. Cited in te Velde, "How High Did the Dutch Fly?," 63–64.
99. te Velde, "How High Did the Dutch Fly?," 61.
100. Thanks to Prof. Maartje Janse for bringing this to my attention.
101. The highest-ranking Dutch official in a colonial district.
102. Cees Fasseur, "Purse or Principle: Dutch Colonial Policy in the 1860s and the Decline of the Cultivation System," *Modern Asian Studies* 25, no. 1 (February 1991): 44.
103. Quoted in Wesseling, "The Giant That Was a Dwarf,"60.
104. Maartje Janse, "Representing Distant Victims: The Emergence of an Ethical Movement in Dutch Colonial Politics," *BMGN: Low Countries Historical Review* 128, no. 1 (2013): 60–61.
105. C. Th. van Deventer, "Een Eereschuld [A debt of honor]," *De Gids* (1899), 210, 217, 228.
106. P. Brooshooft, *De ethische koers in de koloniale politiek* [The ethical direction in colonial policy] (Amsterdam: J. H. De Bussy, 1901), 14.
107. Brooshooft, *De ethische koers*, 30–31.
108. Brooshooft, *De ethische koers*, 77.
109. Kuyper, *Ons Program*, 332, 337.
110. Queen Wilhelmina, "Troonrede," 1901. http://www.troonredes.nl/troonrede-van-17-september-1901/
111. Fasseur, "Purse or Principle," 34.
112. Janse, "Representing Distant Victims," 74–75.
113. The word "empire" lacks a direct translation in the Dutch language. Prof. Vincent Kuitenbrouwer, conversation with author.

114. Kuitenbrouwer, *The Netherlands and the Rise of Modern Imperialism*, 18.
115. René Koekkoek, Anne–Isabelle Richard, and Arthur Weststeijn, "Visions of Dutch Empire: Towards a Long-Term Global Perspective," *BMGN: Low Countries Historical Review* 132, no. 2 (2017): 93.
116. Peter Lawler, "The Good State: in Praise of Classical Internationalism," *Review of International Studies* 31 (July 2005): 443.
117. B. W. Schaper, "Nieuwe opvattingen over het nieuwe imperialisme [New views on new imperialism]," *BMGN: Low Countries Historical Review* 1 (1971): 8.
118. Quoted in Hubertus and Vlekke, *Evolution of the Dutch Nation*, 326–327.
119. Wesseling, "The Netherlands and the Partition of Africa," 110.
120. Lindblad, "Economic Aspects of the Dutch Expansion," 13.
121. Lindblad, "Economic Aspects of the Dutch Expansion," 18.
122. Lindblad, "Economic Aspects of the Dutch Expansion," 7.
123. Locher-Scholten, "Dutch Expansion in the Indonesian Archipelago," 93.
124. Gouda, *Dutch Culture Overseas*.
125. "The Asian Century Is Set to Begin," *Financial Times*, March 25, 2019. https://www.ft.com/content/520cb6f6-2958-11e9-a5ab-ff8ef2b976c7

Chapter 4

1. The United States Immigration Act of 1924 banned Japanese immigrants to the country, in effect putting Japan in its place as an Asian country on par with China rather than the West (Rohan Mukherjee, *Ascending Order: Rising Powers and the Institutional Politics of Status*, book manuscript).
2. Peter Duus, *Modern Japan*, 2nd ed. (Boston: Houghton Mifflin, 1998), 39.
3. Duus, *Modern Japan*, 75.
4. Duus, *Modern Japan*, 80–81.
5. Duus, *Modern Japan*, 85.
6. Tokugawa society had four classes: the samurai, farmers, craftsmen, and merchants. The samurai as a social class had been declining since the 1840s but the Meiji Restoration and its reforms struck it a death blow (Hidehiro Sonoda, "The Decline of the Japanese Warrior Class 1840–1880," *Japan Review* no. 1 (1990): 73–111.
7. Marius B. Jansen, "The Meiji Restoration," in *The Emergence of Meiji Japan*, ed. Marius B. Jansen (Cambridge: Cambridge University Press, 1995), 144.
8. Duus, *Modern Japan*, 85–87.
9. Akira Iriye, "Japan's Drive to Great Power Status," in *The Emergence of Meiji Japan*, ed. Marius B. Jansen (Cambridge: Cambridge University Press, 1995), 278.
10. Quoted in Kenneth B. Pyle, *Japan Rising: The Resurgence of Japanese Power and Purpose* (New York: Public Affairs, 2007), 9.
11. William Lockwood, *Economic Development of Japan: Growth and Structural Change 1868–1938* (Princeton, NJ: Princeton University Press, 1954).
12. Lockwood, *Economic Development of Japan*, 12.
13. Lockwood, *Economic Development of Japan*, 14.
14. Lockwood, *Economic Development of Japan*, 12.
15. Lockwood, *Economic Development of Japan*, 16.
16. Lockwood, *Economic Development of Japan*, 20.
17. Lockwood, *Economic Development of Japan*, 14.
18. Lockwood, *Economic Development of Japan*, 22.
19. Emily Goldman, "Cultural Foundations of Military Diffusion," *Review of International Studies* 32, no. 1 (January 2006): 83.
20. Jansen, "The Meiji Restoration," 185.
21. Hyman Kublin, "The 'Modern' Army of Early Meiji Japan," *The Far Eastern Quarterly* 9, no. 1 (November 1949): 31.
22. Goldman, "Cultural Foundations," 84.
23. Goldman, "Cultural Foundations," 84.
24. Kublin, "The 'Modern' Army," 23.

25. Richard Samuels, "Reinventing Security: Japan since Meiji," *Daedalus* 120, no. 4 (Fall 1991): 49.

26. Peter Duus, *The Abacus and the Sword: The Japanese Penetration of Korea, 1895–1910* (Berkeley and Los Angeles: University of California Press, 1995), 19.

27. Even during periods when these countries did not pay tribute to the Chinese emperor, they did not fall outside of the system—they stayed within the system even when they perceived their interests to lie outside of it. Manjari Chatterjee Miller, "China, India and Their Differing Conceptions of International Order," in *The China-India Rivalry in the Globalization Era*, ed. T. V. Paul (Washington DC: Georgetown University Press, 2018), 79.

28. Duus, *The Abacus and the Sword*, 31.

29. Marlene J. Mayo, "The Korean Crisis of 1873 and Early Meiji Foreign Policy," *The Journal of Asian Studies* 31, no. 4 (August 1972), 798.

30. Duus, *The Abacus and the Sword*, 48.

31. Duus, *The Abacus and the Sword*, 48.

32. James L. Huffman, *Japan and Imperialism, 1853–1945* (Ann Arbor, MI: Association for Asian Studies, 2010), 19–20.

33. Huffman, *Japan and Imperialism*, 19–20.

34. Huffman, *Japan and Imperialism*, 21.

35. Ramon H. Myers and Mark R. Peattie, "Introduction," in *The Japanese Colonial Empire, 1895–1945*, eds. Ramon H. Myers and Mark R. Peattie (Princeton, NJ: Princeton University Press, 1984), 16.

36. Alexis Dudden, Jaishree Odin, and Peter T. Manicas, *Japan's Colonization of Korea: Discourse and Power* (Honolulu: University of Hawaii Press, 2004), 63.

37. Duus, *Modern Japan*, 87–89.

38. Iriye, "Japan's Drive," 282–283.

39. Rotem Kowner, "Becoming an Honorary Civilized Nation: Remaking Japan's Military Image during the Russo-Japanese War, 1904–1905," *The Historian* 64, no. 1 (2001): 27–28.

40. Kowner, "Becoming an Honorary Civilized Nation," 27.

41. Duus, *The Abacus*, 48.

42. Mark Peattie, "Japanese Attitudes Towards Colonialism, 1895–1945," in *The Japanese Colonial Empire, 1895–1945*, eds. Raymond H. Myers and Mark R. Peattie (Princeton, NJ: Princeton University Press, 1984), 84.

43. Peter Duus, "Economic Dimensions of Meiji Imperialism: The Case of Korea, 1895–1910," in *The Japanese Colonial Empire, 1895–1945*, eds. Raymond H. Myers and Mark R. Peattie (Princeton, NJ: Princeton University Press, 1984), 137–138.

44. Dudden et al., *Japan's Colonization of Korea*, 110–112.

45. Dudden et al., *Japan's Colonization of Korea*, 113, 115.

46. Dudden et al., *Japan's Colonization of Korea*, 116; Daniel V. Botsman, *Punishment and Power in the Making of Modern Japan* (Princeton, NJ: Princeton University Press, 2005), 12.

47. T. V. Paul, *Asymmetric Conflicts: War Initiation by Weaker Powers* (Cambridge: Cambridge University Press, 1994), 42.

48. Duus, *The Abacus and the Sword*, 24.

49. Iriye, "Japan's Drive," 323–324.

50. Barton Hacker, "The Weapons of the West: Military Technology and Modernization in 19th-century China and Japan," *Technology and Culture* 18, no. 1 (January 1977): 55.

51. Iriye, "Japan's Drive," 294.

52. Iriye, "Japan's Drive," 323–324.

53. Akira Iriye, *Across the Pacific: An Inner History of American-East Asian Relations* (New York: Harcourt, Brace & World, 1967), 65.

54. Hacker, "The Weapons of the West," 52.

55. Hacker, "The Weapons of the West," 53.

56. Goldman, "Cultural Foundations," 88.

57. Goldman, "Cultural Foundations," 88.

58. Kublin, "The 'Modern' Army," 28–29.

59. Quoted in Samuels, "Reinventing Security," 47.

60. Michio Kitahara, "The Rise of Four Mottos in Japan: Before and after the Meiji Restoration," *Journal of Asian History* 20, no.1 (1986): 55.
61. Kitahara, "The Rise of Four Mottos in Japan," 60–61.
62. Kitahara, "The Rise of Four Mottos in Japan," 61–62.
63. Quoted in John H. Miller, "The Reluctant Asianist: Japan and Asia," *Asian Affairs: An American Review* 31, no. 2 (Summer 2004): 75.
64. Quoted in Urs Mathias Zachman, *China and Japan in the late Meiji Period: China Policy and the Japanese Discourse on National Identity, 1852–1904* (Abingdon and New York: Routledge, 2009), 19.
65. Quoted in Sandra Wilson, "The Discourse of National Greatness in Japan 1890–1919," *Japanese Studies* 25, no. 1 (2005): 46.
66. Kitahara, "The Rise of Four Mottos," 62.
67. Miller, "The Reluctant Asianist," 76.
68. Andrew Gordon, *A Modern History of Japan: From Tokugawa Times to the Present*, 2nd ed. (New York: Oxford University Press, 2009), 110.
69. Kitahara, "The Rise of Four Mottos," 57.
70. Dudden et al., *Japan's Colonization of Korea*, 43.
71. Iriye, "Japan's Drive," 282.
72. Dudden et al., *Japan's Colonization of Korea*, 28.
73. Iriye, "Japan's Drive," 294, 297.
74. Gordon, *A Modern History of Japan*, 115.
75. Wilson, "The Discourse of National Greatness," 37.
76. Quoted in Mark R. Peattie, "Japanese Attitudes Towards Colonialism, 1895–1945," in *The Japanese Colonial Empire, 1895–1945*, eds. Ramon H. Myers and Mark R. Peattie (Princeton, NJ: Princeton University Press, 1984), 83.
77. Quoted in Huffman, "Japan and Imperialism," 20.
78. Cited in Peattie, "Japanese Attitudes Towards Colonialism," 73.
79. Iriye, "Japan's Drive," 309.
80. Quoted in Iriye, "Japan's Drive," 309.
81. Dudden et al., *Japan's Colonization of Korea*, 47.
82. Quoted in Dudden et al., *Japan's Colonization of Korea*, 48.
83. Peattie, "Japanese Attitudes Towards Colonialism," 84.
84. Cited in Peattie, "Japanese Attitudes Towards Colonialism," 95.
85. Duus, *The Abacus and the Sword*, 15.
86. Quoted in Peattie, "Japanese Attitudes Towards Colonialism," 95.
87. Peattie, "Japanese Attitudes Towards Colonialism," 92–93.
88. Peattie, "Japanese Attitudes Towards Colonialism," 86–87.
89. Duus, *The Abacus and the Sword*, 51–52.
90. Quoted in Pyle, *Japan Rising*, 2.
91. Paul Kennedy, *The Rise and Fall of the Great Powers: Economic Change and Military Conflict from 1500–2000* (New York: Random House, 1987).
92. Quoted in Pyle, *Japan Rising*, 4.
93. John W. Dower, *Embracing Defeat: Japan in the Wake of World War II* (London: W. W. Norton, 2000), 73.
94. Pyle, *Japan Rising*, 219–220.
95. While earlier work on the American occupation of Japan portrayed it as beneficial, later scholars derided it as "barely legitimate." However, many Japanese experts, even recently, have talked of the positive effects of the democratic institutions imposed on Japan by the occupation (Laura Hein, "Revisiting America's Occupation of Japan," *Cold War History* 11, no. 4 (November 2011): 581.
96. Dower, *Embracing Defeat*, 75.
97. Dower, *Embracing Defeat*, 75.
98. Chalmers Johnson, *MITI and the Japanese Miracle: The Growth of Industrial Policy, 1925–1975* (Redwood City, CA: Stanford University Press, 1982), 20.
99. Chalmers Johnson, *MITI and the Japanese Miracle*, 23–24.

100. Richard Samuels, *Machiavelli's Children: Leaders and Their Legacies in Italy and Japan* (Ithaca, NY: Cornell University Press, 2003), 191.
101. Chalmers Johnson, *MITI and the Japanese Miracle*, 25–26.
102. Pyle, *Japan Rising*, 246.
103. Aaron Forsberg, *America and the Japanese Miracle: The Cold War Context of Japan's Postwar Economic Revival, 1950–1960* (Chapel Hill: University of North Carolina Press, 2000), 69.
104. Michael Beckley, Yusaku Horiuchi, and Jennifer M. Miller, "America's Role in the Making of Japan's Economic Miracle," *Journal of East Asian Studies* 18, no. 1 (March 2018): 5.
105. Forsberg, *America and the Japanese Miracle*, 46.
106. Beckley et al., "America's Role," 1.
107. Yukio Noguchi, "The 'Bubble' and Economic Policies in the 1980s," *The Journal of Japanese Studies* 20, no. 2 (Summer 1994): 292.
108. Quoted in Gordon, *A Modern History of Japan*, 244.
109. Beckley et al., "America's Role," 1.
110. Edward J. Lincoln, "Japanese Trade and Investment Issues," in *Japan's Emerging Global Role*, eds. Danny Unger and Paul Blackburn (Boulder, CO: Lynn Reiner, 1993), 135.
111. Dennis Yasutomo, "Why Aid? Japan as an 'Aid Great Power,'" *Pacific Affairs* 62, no. 4 (Winter 1989–1990): 490–491.
112. Yasutomo, "Why Aid?," 492–493.
113. Theodore H. White, "The Danger from Japan," *New York Times*, July 28, 1985. https://www.nytimes.com/1985/07/28/magazine/the-danger-from-japan.html
114. Robert B. Reich, "Is Japan Out to Get Us?," *New York Times*, February 9, 1992. https://www.nytimes.com/1992/03/15/books/l-is-japan-out-to-get-us-537892.html
115. Pyle, *Japan Rising*, 4.
116. Forsberg, *America and the Japanese Miracle*, 69.
117. Pyle, *Japan Rising*, 220.
118. Thomas R. Havens, *Fire across the Sea: The Vietnam War and Japan 1965–1975* (Princeton, NJ: Princeton University Press, 1987), 8.
119. Jennifer Lind, "Pacifism or Passing the Buck? Testing Theories of Japanese Security Policy," *International Security* 29, no. 1 (Summer 2004): 95.
120. Akitoshi Miyashita, "Where Do Norms Come From? Foundations of Japan's Postwar Pacifism," *International Relations of the Asia-Pacific* 7 (2007): 100.
121. Paul Midford, "The Logic of Reassurance and Japan's Grand Strategy," *Security Studies* 11, no. 3 (Spring 2002): 10.
122. Midford, "The Logic of Reassurance," 11.
123. Midford, "The Logic of Reassurance," 11.
124. Miyashita, "Where Do Norms Come From?," 104.
125. Pyle, *Japan Rising*, 229.
126. Pyle, *Japan Rising*, 228.
127. Pyle, *Japan Rising*, 229.
128. Havens, *Fire across the Sea*, 22.
129. Michael Schaller, *Altered States: The United States and Japan since the Occupation* (New York: Oxford University Press, 1997), 186.
130. Schaller, *Altered States*, 190.
131. Schaller, *Altered States*, 188.
132. Quoted in Schaller, *Altered States*, 202.
133. Amy Catalinac, "Identity Theory and Foreign Policy: Explaining Japan's Responses to the 1991 Gulf War and the 2003 US War in Iraq," *Politics and Policy* 35, no. 1 (February 2007): 61.
134. Yoichi Funabashi, "Japan and the New World Order," *Foreign Affairs* 70 (Winter 1991/1992): 58.
135. Catalinac, "Identity Theory and Foreign Policy," 62.
136. Catalinac, "Identity Theory and Foreign Policy," 62.
137. Funabashi, "Japan and the New World Order," 58.
138. Lawrence Freedman and Efraim Karsh, *The Gulf Conflict: 1990–1991: Diplomacy and War in the New World Order* (Princeton, NJ: Princeton University Press, 1993), 121.

139. Catalinac, "Identity Theory and Foreign Policy," 63.
140. Akio Watanabe, "Foreign Policymaking, Japanese-Style," *International Affairs* 54, no. 1 (January 1978): 87.
141. Alan Rix, "Japan's Foreign Aid Policy: A Capacity for Leadership?," *Pacific Affairs* 62, no. 4 (Winter 1989/1990): 3.
142. Kent Calder, "Japanese Foreign Economic Policy: Explaining the Reactive State," *World Politics* 40, no. 4 (July 1988): 520, 523.
143. Calder, "Japanese Foreign Economic Policy," 524.
144. W. W. Rostow, "Is There a Need for Economic Leadership?: Japanese or US?" *American Economic Review* 75, no. 2 (May 1985): 285–291.
145. Charles P. Kindleberger, "Dominance and Leadership in the International Economy," *International Studies Quarterly* 25 no. 2 (June 1981): 242–254.
146. Calder, "Japanese Foreign Economic Policy," 527.
147. Yoshihide Soeya, "Japan: Normative Constraints versus Structural Imperatives," in *Asian Security Practice: Material and Ideational Influences*, ed. Muthiah Alagappa (Redwood City, CA: Stanford University Press 1998), 226.
148. Peter Katzenstein, *Cultural Norms and National Security: Police and Military in Postwar Japan* (Ithaca, NY: Cornell University Press 1996), 194–195.
149. Lind, "Pacifism or Passing the Buck."
150. Eric Heginbotham and Richard Samuels, "Mercantile Realism and Japanese Foreign Policy," *International Security* 22, no. 4 (Spring 1998): 171–203.
151. Midford, "The Logic of Reassurance," 16.
152. Heginbotham and Samuels, "Mercantile Realism," 178.
153. Heginbotham and Samuels, "Mercantile Realism," 176.
154. Pyle, *Japan Rising*, 225–226.
155. Thomas Berger, "From Sword to Chrysanthemum: Japan's Culture of Anti-Militarism," *International Security* 17, no. 4 (Spring 1993): 133.
156. Pyle, *Japan Rising*, 227.
157. Pyle, *Japan Rising*, 227–228.
158. Pyle, *Japan Rising*, 229.
159. Pyle, *Japan Rising*, 230.
160. Pyle, *Japan Rising*, 229.
161. Berger, "From Sword to Chrysanthemum," 137–138.
162. Pyle, *Japan Rising*, 231–232.
163. Quoted in Pyle, *Japan Rising*, 232–233.
164. Quoted in Pyle, *Japan Rising*, 236.
165. Havens, *Fire across the Sea*, 19.
166. Havens, *Fire across the Sea*, 25.
167. Schaller, *Altered States*, 187.
168. Schaller, *Altered States*, 192.
169. Quoted in Pyle, *Japan Rising*, 265.
170. Quoted in Pyle, *Japan Rising*, 267.
171. Richard J. Samuels, *Securing Japan: Tokyo's Grand Strategy and the Future of East Asia* (Ithaca, NY: Cornell University Press, 2007), 36.
172. Berger, "From Sword to Chrysanthemum," 143.
173. Pyle, *Japan Rising*, 272–276.
174. Berger, "From Sword to Chrysanthemum," 145.
175. Funabashi, "Japan and the New World Order," 60.
176. Yoshihide Soeya, "A 'Normal' Middle Power: Interpreting Changes in Japanese Security Policy in the 1990s and After," in *Japan as a "Normal" Country?: A Nation in Search of Its Place in the World*, eds. Yoshihide Soeya, Mayasuki Tadokoro, and David A. Welch (Toronto: University of Toronto Press, 2011), 91.
177. Michael J Green, *Japan's Reluctant Realism: Foreign Policy Challenges in an Era of Uncertain Power* (New York: Council on Foreign Relations, 2001), 17.
178. Quoted in Samuels, *Securing Japan*, 36.
179. Green, *Japan's Reluctant Realism*, 17.

Chapter 5

1. Barber B. Conable, Jr., and David M. Lampton, "China: The Coming Power," *Foreign Affairs* 71, no. 5 (Winter 1992): 133–149.
2. Nicholas Kristof, "The Rise of China," *Foreign Affairs* 72, no. 5 (November–December 1993): 59.
3. Gungwu Wang, "The Fourth Rise of China: Cultural Implications," *China: An International Journal* 2, no. 2 (September 2004): 318.
4. Jim Impoco, "Life after the Bubble: How Japan Lost a Decade," *New York Times*, October 18, 2008. https://www.nytimes.com/2008/10/19/weekinreview/19impoco.html
5. Samuel Kim, "China's Pacific Policy: Reconciling the Irreconcilable," *International Journal* 50, no. 3 (Summer 1995): 462.
6. William Callahan, "Forum: The Rise of China, 'How to Understand China: The Dangers and Opportunities of Being a Rising Power,'" *Review of International Studies* 31 (October 2005): 702.
7. Charles Krauthammer, "Why We Must Contain China," *Time*, July 31, 1995. http://content.time.com/time/magazine/article/0,9171,983245,00.html
8. Robert Ross, "China II: Beijing as a Conservative Power," *Foreign Affairs* 76 (March–April 1997): 33–44.
9. Bill Gertz, *The China Threat: How the People's Republic Targets America* (Washington, DC: Regnery, 2000).
10. David M. Lampton, *Following the Leader: Ruling China from Deng Xiaoping to Xi Jinping* (Oakland: University of California Press, 2014), 14.
11. Daniel Griswold, "Trade and the Transformation of China," (speech, Latrobe, November 6, 2002), Cato Institute, https://www.cato.org/publications/speeches/trade-transformation-china.
12. Eswar Prasad, ed., "China's Growth and Integration into the World Economy: Prospects and Challenges," Occasional Paper 232, International Monetary Fund (2004): 1.
13. Prasad, ed., "China's Growth and Integration," 1.
14. Griswold, "Trade and the Transformation of China," n.p.
15. William C. Triplett II, "Inside China's Scary New Military-Industrial Complex," *Washington Post*, May 8, 1994. https://www.washingtonpost.com/archive/1994/05/08/inside-chinas-scary-new-military-industrial-complex/24d132d0-a7aa-453f-bd11-cd87c938ced3/
16. Triplett II, "Inside China's Scary New Military-Industrial Complex." https://www.washingtonpost.com/archive/1994/05/08/inside-chinas-scary-new-military-industrial-complex/24d132d0-a7aa-453f-bd11-cd87c938ced3/
17. Denny Roy, "The 'China Threat' Issue: Major Arguments," *Asian Survey* 36, no. 8 (1996): 759.
18. David Shambaugh, "China's Military: Real or Paper Tiger?," *The Washington Quarterly* 19, no. 2 (Spring 1996): 23.
19. Roy, "The 'China Threat' Issue," 759.
20. Shambaugh, "China's Military," 28.
21. "Military Expenditure by Country as Percentage of Gross Domestic Product, 1988–2002," Stockholm International Peace Research Institute (SIPRI) Military Expenditure Database, https://www.sipri.org/sites/default/files/3_Data%20for%20all%20countries%20from%20 1988%E2%80%932017%20as%20a%20share%20of%20GDP.pdf.
22. Ross, "China II," 2.
23. Shambaugh, "China's Military," 23.
24. David Shambaugh, "Growing Strong: China's Challenge to Asian Security," *Survival* 36, no. 2 (1994): 44.
25. Triplett II, "Inside China's Scary New Military-Industrial Complex."
26. Triplett II, "Inside China's Scary New Military-Industrial Complex." https://www.washingtonpost.com/archive/1994/05/08/inside-chinas-scary-new-military-industrial-complex/24d132d0-a7aa-453f-bd11-cd87c938ced3/
27. Allen S. Whiting, "ASEAN Eyes China: The Security Dimension," *Asian Survey* 37, no. 4 (April 1997): 311.
28. Quoted in Roy, "The 'China Threat' Issue," 760.

29. Evan S. Medeiros and M. Taylor Fravel, "China's New Diplomacy," *Foreign Affairs* 82, no. 6 (November–December 2003): 24.
30. David Shambaugh, *China Goes Global: The Partial Power* (New York: Oxford University Press, 2013).
31. Medeiros and Fravel, "China's New Diplomacy," 22.
32. Medeiros and Fravel, "China's New Diplomacy," 24.
33. Medeiros and Fravel, "China's New Diplomacy."
34. Yong Deng, *China's Struggle for Status: The Realignment of International Relations* (Cambridge: Cambridge University Press, 2008), 131.
35. Deng, *China's Struggle for Status*, 134.
36. Deng, *China's Struggle for Status*, 137.
37. Deng, *China's Struggle for Status*, 137.
38. Lowell Dittmer, "China's New Internationalism," in *China Turns to Multilateralism: Foreign Policy and Regional Security*, eds. Guoguang Wu and Helen Lansdowne (London and New York: Routledge, 2008), 21.
39. Dittmer, "China's New Internationalism," 28.
40. Dittmer, "China's New Internationalism," 28.
41. Bates Gill and Yangzhong Huang, "Sources and Limits of Chinese 'Soft Power,'" *Survival* 48, no. 2 (May 2006): 22.
42. Jean A. Garrison, "China's Prudent Cultivation of 'Soft' Power and Implications for U.S. Policy in East Asia," *Asian Affairs: An American Review* 32, no. 1 (2005): 26.
43. Garrison, "China's Prudent Cultivation of Soft Power," 27.
44. Dittmer, "China's New Internationalism," 31.
45. Jing-dong Yuan, "The New Player in the Game: China, Arms Control and Multilateralism," in *China Turns to Multilateralism: Foreign Policy and Regional Security*, eds. Guoguang Wu and Helen Lansdowne (London and New York: Routledge 2008), 58–59.
46. Yuan, "The New Player in the Game," 58.
47. Yuan, "The New Player in the Game," 62.
48. Wenran Jiang, "China Makes 'Great Leaps Outward' in Regional Diplomacy," *International Journal* 61, no. 2 (June 2006): 331.
49. Kuniko Ashizawa, "Tokyo's Quandary, Beijing's Moment in the Six-Party Talks: A Regional Multilateral Approach to Resolve the DPRK's Nuclear Problem," *Pacific Affairs* 79, no. 3 (September 2006): 424.
50. Ashizawa, "Tokyo's Quandary," 425.
51. Courtney Fung, "What Explains China's Deployment to UN Peacekeeping Operations?," *International Relations of the Asia-Pacific* 16, no. 3 (September 2016): 6.
52. Courtney Fung, "What Explains China's Deployment," 7.
53. Andrew Nathan, "China's Rise and International Regimes: Does China Seek to Overthrow Global Norms?," in *China in the Era of Xi Jinping: Domestic and Foreign Policy Challenges*, eds. Robert S. Ross and Jo Inge Bekkevold (Washington, DC: Georgetown University Press, 2016), 171.
54. Nathan, "China's Rise and International Regimes," 173.
55. Nathan, "China's Rise and International Regimes," 176.
56. Nathan, "China's Rise and International Regimes," 173.
57. M. Taylor Fravel, *Strong Borders, Secure Nation: Cooperation and Conflict in China's Territorial Disputes* (Princeton, NJ: Princeton University Press, 2008), xv.
58. Medeiros and Fravel, "China's New Diplomacy."
59. Nathan, "China's Rise and International Regimes," 172.
60. Medeiros and Fravel, "China's New Diplomacy."
61. Medeiros and Fravel, "China's New Diplomacy," 27.
62. Nicola Leveringhaus and Kate Sullivan de Estrada, "Between Conformity and Innovation: China's and India's Quest for Status and Responsible Nuclear Powers," *Review of International Studies* 44, no. 3 (March 2018): 489.
63. Leveringhaus and Sullivan de Estrada, "Between Conformity and Innovation," 490.
64. Alistair Iain Johnston, "International Structures and Chinese Foreign Policy," in *China and the World: Chinese Foreign Policy Faces the New Millennium*, ed. Samuel Kim (Boulder, CO: Westview Press, 1998), 75.

65. Julie Klinger, "China, India and Outer Space: Cooperation and Competition in the Global Commons, in *Routledge Handbook of China-India Relations*, eds. Kanti Bajpai, Selina Ho, and Manjari Chatterjee Miller (Abingdon: Routledge, 2020), 526.

66. Ashizawa, "Tokyo's Quandary," 417.

67. David Shambaugh, "China Engages Asia: Reshaping the Regional Order," *International Security* 29, no. 3 (Winter 2004–2005): 68.

68. Ashizawa, "Tokyo's Quandary," 423–424.

69. Liu Jinghua, "Ershi yi shiji 20–30 niandai zhongguo jueqi ji waijiao zhanlue xuanze [China's rise and foreign policy strategic options in the 21st century]," *Zhanlue yu guanli [Strategy and Management]* 3 (1994): 119–120.

70. Ye Zicheng, " 'Daguo fei daguo' yu zhongguo de guoji diwei [A Great Power that is not really a great power and China's international status]," *Guoji zhengzhi yanjiu [International Politics Research]* 4 (1994): 1–5.

71. Robert Sutter, *Chinese Foreign Relations: Power and Policy Since the Cold War*, 2nd ed. (Lanham, MD: Rowman & Littlefield, 2010), 10.

72. Thomas W. Robinson, "Interdependence in China's Foreign Relations," in *China and the World: Chinese Foreign Relations in the Post-Cold War Era*, 3rd ed., ed. Samuel Kim (Boulder, CO: Westview Press, 1994): 193.

73. Michael Oksenberg, "The China Problem," *Foreign Affairs* 70, no. 3 (Summer 1991): 11.

74. Mianlinzhe xuduo gongtong de wenti he tiaozhan. Ren Xiao, "Dangdai shijie yu zhengzhi xue: ji guoji zhengzhi xuehui di 15 jie shijie dahui [Contemporary world and politics meeting: remembering the 15th session of the international political conference]," *Fudan xuebao [Fudan Journal]* (January 31, 1992): 11.

75. Yao biyao yong mingtian de yanguang lai kandai xin de quanqiuxing xianghu yicun; Shijie zhong de yige zhenzheng de huoban. Han Suyin and Wu Ming, "Xin de quanqiuxing huxiang yicun [The new global interdependence]," *Liaowang zhoukan [Weekly Outlook]* (March 2, 1991): 17.

76. Wang Yizhou, *Dangdai guoji zhengzhi xilun* [Analysis of contemporary international politics] (Shanghai: Shanghai *renmin chubanshe*, 1995), 43.

77. Zhonguo de fazhan libukai shijie. Liu Jingbo, "Lun xianghu yicun tiaojian xia de guoji guanxi xin tedian [Theorizing the new characteristics of international relations under the conditions of interdependence]," *Shijie jingji yu zhengzhi [World Economics and Politics]* (April 14, 1995): 51.

78. Jisi Wang, "Pragmatic Nationalism: China Seeks a New Role in World Affairs," *Oxford International Review* 6, no. 1 (1994): 30, 51.

79. "The Sino-Russian Partnership Agreement," quoted in Michael Yahuda, "China's Search for a Global Role," *Current History* 98 (1999): 269.

80. Huang Renguo, "Xin shiji zhongguo de mulin waijiao zhengce shuping [Commentary on China's good neighbor and foreign relations policy at the beginning of the new century]," *Chenzhou shifan gaodeng zhuanke xuexiao [Journal of Chenzhou Teacher's College]* 6 (2002): 1.

81. "Full text of Jiang Zemin's Report at the 14th Party Congress," Government Documents, Bejing Review.com, last modified March 29, 1991, http://www.bjreview.com.cn/document/txt/2011–03/29/content_363504_10.htm.

82. Shambaugh, "China Goes Global," 21–22.

83. Wang, "Pragmatic Nationalism," 30.

84. Manjari Chatterjee Miller, *Wronged by Empire: Post-Imperial Ideology and Foreign Policy in India and China* (Stanford, CA: Stanford University Press, 2013).

85. He Hongze, "Zai meiguo waijiao zhengce xiehui shang Qian Qichen waizhang tan zhongmei guanxi zhichu: shuangfang yingben zhe huxiang zunzhong, pingdeng xiangdai, xinshou nuoyan, zunshou xieyi de jingshen chuli liangguo guanxi ["Foreign minister Qian Qichen discusses Sino-American relations at the US foreign policy association meeting: Both sides should adopt the spirit of mutual respect, mutual equality, keeping promises, and respecting agreements to handle bilateral relations]," *Renmin ribao [People's Daily]*, September 24, 1992.

86. A crisis that is traced to 1992 when the US government, in violation of the 1982 US-China arms communiqué, sold Taiwan 150 F-16 warplanes; the crisis erupted in 1995 when the United States, in a first for any Taiwanese president, granted President Lee Teng-hui a visa

to enter the country. In retaliation, China conducted military exercises and missile tests near Taiwan, shocking US officials with the confrontation.

87. Suisheng Zhao, "China's Periphery Policy and Its Asian Neighbors," *Security Dialogue* 30, no. 3 (1999): 336.

88. Zhu Tinghchang, "Lun zhongguo mulin zhengce de lilun yu shijian [The theory and practice of the good neighbor policy]," *Guoji guancha: Guoji zhengzhi yanjiu* [*International Survey: Research on International Politics*] 2 (2001): 3.

89. Huang Renguo, "Xin shiji zhongguo de mulin waijiao zhengce shuping [Commentary on China's good neighbor and foreign relations policy at the beginning of the new century]," *Chenzhou shifan gaodeng zhuanke xuexiao* [*Journal of Chenzhou Teacher's College*] 6 (2002).

90. Zhang Yiping, "Lengzhanhou shijie de xin anquan guan [The new security relations of the post-Cold War world]," *Xiandai guoji guanxi* [*Contemporary International Relations*], February 20, 1997.

91. When, in fact, such threats were the result of whether or not a country sought hegemony (*chengba*), attempted to expand (*kuozhang*), invaded (*qinlue*) or intervened in the affairs of other countries (*ganshe taguoshi*). See Yan Xuetong, "Zhongguo de xin anquan guan yu anquan hezuo gouxiang [China's new security relations and the concept of security cooperation]," *Xiandai guoji guanxi* [*Contemporary International Relations*], November 20, 1997, 28.

92. Yan, "Zhongguo de xin anquan guan [China's new security relations]," 32.

93. Wang Yong, "Lun zhongguo de xin anquan guan [On China's new security relations]," *Shijie jingji yu zhengzhi* [*World Economics and Politics*], (January 14, 1999), 43.

94. Richard Baum, "The Fifteenth National Party Congress: Jiang Takes Command?," *The China Quarterly* 153 (March 1998): 148.

95. Rosemary Foot, "Chinese Strategies in a US-Led Hegemonic Global Order: Accommodating and Hedging," *International Affairs* 82, no. 1 (January 2006), 79.

96. Kaishi fazhan duobian junshi lianxi jiaqiang quyuxing anquan hezuo. Zhang Wu, "Dongmeng guojia quyuxing anquan hezuo de quxiang [The trend of regional security cooperation in ASEAN countries]," *Guoji zhanwang* [*Global Survey*], April 13, 1991, 1.

97. Susan Shirk, "Chinese Views on Asia-Pacific Regional Security Cooperation," *National Bureau of Asian Research* 5, no. 5 (1994): 8.

98. Quoted in Banning Garrett and Bonnie Glaser, "Multilateral Security in the Asia-Pacific Region and Its Impact on Chinese Interests: Views from Beijing," *Contemporary Southeast Asia* 16, no. 1 (June 1994): 15.

99. Garrett and Glaser, "Multilateral Security in the Asia-Pacific Region," 19–21.

100. Even as recently as 2018, the author was present at a conference where a former extremely high-level US government official credited Zoellick with calling on and thereby inspiring the Chinese to think of themselves in those terms.

101. He, "Zai meiguo waijiao zhengce xiehui shang."

102. Hoo Tiang Boon, *China's Global Identity: Considering the Responsibilities of Great Power* (Washington, DC: Georgetown University Press, 2018), 40.

103. Xiao Huanrong, "Zhongguo de daguo zeren yu diquzhuyi zhanlue [China's responsibility as a great power and its regionalism strategy]," *Shijie jingji yu zhengzhi* [*World Economics and Politics*] (January 2003), 49.

104. Ta yaoqiu daguo renting duoyuan gongchu he xianghu yicun wei dangjin guojia shehui de jiben tezheng. Qu Congwen, "Fuzenren de daguo guan [The concept of a responsible great power]," *Shijie jingji yu zhengzhi* [*World Economics and Politics*] (October 2002), 77.

105. Canjia duobian hezuo. Zhu Kaibing, "Guoji shehui duili chongtu de daguo zeren [The great power responsibility of opposing conflict in international society]," *Nanjing zhengzhi xueyuan xuebao* [*Journal of Nanjing Institute of Politics*] (January 2002), 44.

106. We can particularly see these narratives percolate in various think tanks around China which play host to a marketplace of ideas through meetings, conferences, and publications. Think tanks in China are not independent in the Western sense—they cannot determine the mission and timing of research to be undertaken. However, they are "stable and autonomous" and conduct research and provide advice on policy issues. See Xufeng Zhu and Lan Xue, "Think Tanks in Transitional China," *Public Administration and Development* 27, no. 5 (2007), 453. Some of the most influential think tanks in China today on foreign

security policy include the Chinese Institutes of Contemporary International Relations, or CICIR [*Zhongguo xiandai guoji guanxi yanjiuyuan*], China Institute of International Studies [*Zhongguo guoji wenti yanjiuyuan*], Shanghai Institute of International Studies [*Shanghai guoji wenti yanjiuyuan*], Centre for International and Strategic Studies, Peking University [*Beijing daxue guoji zhanlue yanjiusuo*], and the Institute of International Studies, Tsinghua University [*Qinghua daxue guoji guanxi yanjiuyuan*]. They regularly provide reports and research that may even be actively solicited by the government; they convene meetings, again often on request from the government, on specific issues that are attended by government personnel; and key academics and analysts from these think tanks are often invited to high-level meetings.

107. Contemporary International Relations [xiandai guoji guanxi].
108. See Manjari Chatterjee Miller, "The Role of Beliefs in Identifying Rising Powers," *The Chinese Journal of International Politics* 9, no. 2 (April 2016): 211–238 for a more detailed discussion.
109. Bonnie S. Glaser and Evan S. Medeiros, "The Changing Ecology of Foreign Policy-Making in China: The Ascension and Demise of the Theory of 'Peaceful Rise,'" *China* Quarterly 190 (2007): 300.
110. Miller, "The Role of Beliefs in Identifying Rising Powers."
111. Chen Longshan, "Dongbeiya duobian anquan hezuo jizhi jianyi [A discussion on multilateral security cooperation mechanisms in Northeast Asia]," *Dongdai yatai* [*Journal of Contemporary Asia Pacific*] (April 25, 1997); Zhu Feng and Zhu Zaiyou, "Duobian jizhi yu dongya anquan [Multilateral mechanisms and East Asian security]," *Dongdai yatai* [*Journal of Contemporary Asia Pacific*] (October 25, 1997).
112. Ningken yunyong duobian jizhi erbushi caiqu danbian xingdong. Wang Yizhou, "Sikao 'duojihua' [Thinking about multipolarity]," *Guoji jingji pinglun* [*International Economic Review*] (October 15, 1998), 26.
113. Shambaugh, "China Engages Asia," 68.
114. Wang Fei-ling quoted in Sutter, "Chinese Foreign Relations," 12.
115. Jisi Wang, "The Role of the United States as a Global and Pacific Power: A View from China," *The Pacific Review* 10, no. 1 (1997): 13.
116. Jianwei Wang and Zhimin Li, "Chinese Perceptions in the Post–Cold War Era: Three Images of the United States," *Asian Survey* 32, no. 10 (October 1992): 906.
117. Wang and Li, "Chinese Perceptions in the Post–Cold War Era," 908.
118. Andrew J. Nathan and Andrew Scobell, "How China Sees America: The Sum of Beijing's Fears," *Foreign Affairs* (September–October 2012), 33.
119. Xiao, "Zhongguo de daguo zeren," 49.

Chapter 6

1. Richard K. Betts, "Wealth, Power and Instability: East Asia and the United States after the Cold War," *International Security* 18, no. 3 (1993/94), 34.
2. "India Releases Pictures of Nuclear Tests," *CNN*, May 17, 1998, http://www.cnn.com/WORLD/asiapcf/9805/17/india.nuke.tests/.
3. Salil Tripathi, "Escaping the 'Hindu Rate of Growth,'" *The Guardian*, June 13, 2006, https://www.theguardian.com/commentisfree/2006/jun/13/escapingthehindurateofgro.
4. Gary S. Fields, *Poverty, Inequality, and Development* (Cambridge: Cambridge University Press, 1980), 204.
5. Ramesh Thakur, "India in the World: Neither Rich, Powerful, nor Principled," *Foreign Affairs* 76, no. 4 (July–August 1997), 18.
6. Arvind Panagariya, *India: The Emerging Giant* (New York: Oxford University Press, 2008), 93.
7. "India's Economy: One More Push," *The Economist*, July 21, 2011, https://www.economist.com/leaders/2011/07/21/one-more-push.
8. Panagariya, *India*, 21.
9. "India's Economy: One More Push."
10. Panagariya, *India*, xviii.

11. There is some debate over whether India's economic transformation should be traced to the 1980s, when "attitudinal shifts" among the Indian elite pushed for economic change; see Dani Rodrik and Arvind Subramanian, "From 'Hindu Growth' to Productivity Surge: The Mystery of the Indian Growth Transition," NBER Working Paper no. 10376 (March 2004). Panagariya points out that while a change in the attitudes of Indian officials may indeed have occurred, it is only through the subsequent changes in policies and implementation that they could be conveyed to entrepreneurs; see Arvind Panagariya, "India in the 1980s and 1990s: A Triumph of Reforms," IMF Working Paper, International Monetary Fund (March 2004).

12. Panagariya, *India*, 22.

13. Swaminathan S. Anklesaria Aiyar, "Twenty-Five Years of Indian Economic Reform," *Cato Institute*, Policy Analysis no. 803 (October 26, 2016).

14. Manjari Chatterjee Miller, *Wronged by Empire: Post-Imperial Ideology in India and China* (Stanford, CA: Stanford University Press, 2013), 63.

15. Stephen P. Cohen, *India: Emerging Power* (Washington, DC: Brookings Institution Press, 2001), 133, 145.

16. Pravin Joshi, "India's Defense Expenditure: Historical Perspective," in *Emerging India: Security and Foreign Policy Perspectives*, eds. N. S. Sisodia and C. Uday Bhaskar (New Delhi: Institute for Defense Studies and Analyses, 2005): 138–139.

17. Jaswant Singh, *Defending India* (London: MacMillan Press, 1999), 225.

18. Joshi, "India's Defense Expenditure," 138–139.

19. There was a slight dip toward the end of the 1980s, but this picked up again by 1992–1993.

20. Sandy Gordon, *India's Rise to Power in the Twentieth Century and Beyond* (London: Macmillan, 1995), 66.

21. Gordon, *India's Rise to Power*, 68.

22. Deba R. Mohanty, "Future of Indian Defence Industry," in *Emerging India: Security and Foreign Policy Perspectives*, eds. N. S. Sisodia and C. Uday Bhaskar (New Delhi: Institute for Defence Studies and Analyses, 2005), 123–124, 127.

23. "Armed Forces Personnel Data," World Bank, https://data.worldbank.org/indicator/MS.MIL.TOTL.P1?end=2000&locations=IN&start=1990.

24. William W. Bain, "Sino-Indian Military Modernization: The Potential for Destabilization," *Asian Affairs: An American Review* 21, no. 3 (1994): 139.

25. Raju Thomas, "South Asian Security in the 1990s," *The Adelphi Papers* 33, no. 278 (1993): 66.

26. Cited in John F. Burns, "India Sets 3 Nuclear Blasts, Defying a Worldwide Ban; Tests Bring a Sharp Outcry," *New York Times*, May 12, 1998, https://www.nytimes.com/1998/05/12/world/india-sets-3-nuclear-blasts-defying-a-worldwide-ban-tests-bring-a-sharp-outcry.html.

27. Manjari Chatterjee Miller, "India's Authoritarian Streak: What Modi Risks with His Divisive Populism," *Foreign Affairs* (May 2018). https://www.foreignaffairs.com/articles/india/2018-05-30/indias-authoritarian-streak

28. "Sri Lankan Puts Hid Trust in Gandhi," *New York Times*, August 8, 1987. https://www.nytimes.com/1987/08/08/world/sri-lankan-puts-hid-trust-in-gandhi.html

29. "Regional Powers Cast Shadow over Australia," *Sydney Morning Herald*, May 9, 1989.

30. Perry L. Wood, "India's Uncertain Future," *Christian Science Monitor*, July 22, 1991, https://www.csmonitor.com/1991/0722/22191.html.

31. Teresita C. Shaffer, "Building a New Partnership with India," *The Washington Quarterly* 25, no. 2 (Spring 2002): 31.

32. Lloyd Macauley Richardson, "Now Play the India Card," *Policy Review* (October–November 2002): 21.

33. Manjari Chatterjee Miller, "India's Authoritarian Streak," *Foreign Affairs*, May 2018. https://www.foreignaffairs.com/articles/india/2018-05-30/indias-authoritarian-streak

34. ASEAN member states are Brunei, Cambodia, Indonesia, Laos, Malaysia, Myanmar, Philippines, Singapore, Thailand, and Vietnam.

35. Dennis Kux, *India and the United States: Estranged Democracies, 1941–1991* (Darby: Diane, 1992).

36. S. D. Muni, "India and the Post-Cold War World: Opportunities and Challenges," *Asian Survey* 31, no. 9 (September 1991): 866.

37. Robert W. Cox, "Multilateralism and World Order," *Review of International* Studies 18, no. 2 (1992): 164.
38. J. Mohan Malik, "India's Response to the Gulf Crisis: Implications for Indian Foreign Policy," *Asian Survey* 31, no. 9 (September 1991): 848.
39. Malik, "India's Response to the Gulf Crisis," 850.
40. Malik, "India's Response to the Gulf Crisis," 852.
41. Gordon, *India's Rise to Power*, 252.
42. Allen Carlson, "Helping to Keep the Peace (Albeit Reluctantly): China's Recent Stance on Sovereignty and Multilateral Intervention," *Pacific* Affairs 77, no. 1 (2004): 15.
43. Robert Benjamin, "Beijing Neutral but Many Chinese Applauded Gulf War," *Baltimore Sun*, February 12, 1991, https://www.baltimoresun.com/news/bs-xpm-1991-02-12-1991043071-story.html.
44. Gordon, *India's Rise to Power*, 253.
45. Taylor Branch, *The Clinton Tapes: Conversations with a President 1993–2001* (New York: Simon & Schuster, 2009), 247.
46. Quoted in Rudra Chaudhuri, *Forged in Crisis: India and the United States since 1947* (New York: Oxford University Press, 2014), 180.
47. Strobe Talbott, *Engaging India: Diplomacy, Democracy and the Bomb* (Washington, DC: Brookings Institution Press, 2004), 58.
48. Talbott, *Engaging India*.
49. Chaudhuri, *Forged in Crisis*, 185.
50. Chaudhuri, *Forged in Crisis*, 184–185.
51. Chaudhuri, *Forged in Crisis*, 186.
52. Ashley Tellis, "Review of *Forged in Crisis: India and the United States since 1947*, by Rudra Chaudhuri," *International Affairs* 91, no. 2 (March 2015): 441.
53. Chintamani Mahapatra, "Indo-US Relations into the 21st Century," in *Indian Foreign Policy: Agenda for the 21st Century*, vol. 2, eds. Lalit Mansingh et al. (New Delhi: Foreign Service Institute, 1997), 322.
54. Howard B. Schaffer, *Limits of Influence: America's Role in Kashmir* (Washington, DC: Brookings Institution Press, 2009), 171.
55. Chaudhuri, *Forged in Crisis*, 189.
56. James Chiriyankandath, "Realigning India: Indian Foreign Policy after the Cold War," *The Roundtable: The Commonwealth Journal of International Affairs* 93, no. 374 (2004): 209.
57. Quoted in Seema Sirohi, "I Do, I Don't," *Outlook Magazine*, November 17, 2003. https://magazine.outlookindia.com/story/i-do-i-dont/222087
58. Sirohi, "I Do, I Don't."
59. UN Security Council, Resolution 1483, On Lifting the Economic Sanctions on Iraq Imposed by Resolution 661, S/RES/1483 (May 22, 2003), https://digitallibrary.un.org/record/495555?ln=en.
60. Quoted in Chaudhuri, *Forged in Crisis*, 199.
61. Jyothi Malhotra, "India Wants to be a Lackey," *The Indian Express*, June 3, 2003.
62. Ashley Tellis, "India as a New Global Power: An Action Agenda for the United States," *Carnegie Endowment for International Peace* (July 2005): 6.
63. Chaudhuri, *Forged in Crisis*, 221–222.
64. C. Raja Mohan, *Impossible Allies: Nuclear India, United States and the Global Order* (New Delhi: India Research Press, 2006), 4.
65. "India's Look East Policy: A Critical Assessment," *Institute of Peace and Conflict Studies* (October 2009): 1–10.
66. Tridib Chakraborti, "India's Conviviality with Southeast Asia: Traversing the Saga of 'Look East' Achievements-Hindrances Dichotomy," in *Rising India in the Changing Asia-Pacific: Strategies and Challenges*, eds. Ganganath Jha and Vibhanshu Shekhar (New Delhi: Pentagon Press, 2012), 119.
67. Christopher Jaffrelot, "India's Look East Policy: An Asianist Strategy in Perspective," *India Review* 2, no. 2 (April 2003): 45.
68. Sumit Ganguly, "India's Foreign Policy Grows Up," *World Policy Journal* 20, no. 4 (Winter 2003–2004): 44.

69. Chakraborti, "India's Conviviality with Southeast Asia," 121.
70. Chakraborti, "India's Conviviality with Southeast Asia," 129.
71. Shankari Sundaraman, "Politics and Security in South-East Asia: Prospects for India-ASEAN Cooperation," *International Studies* 41, no. 4 (2004): 384.
72. Chakraborti, "India's Conviviality with Southeast Asia," 121.
73. Sundaraman, "Politics and Security in South-East Asia," 384–385.
74. G. V. C. Naidu, "Future of Institutionalism in the Asia-Pacific: The ARF and its Implications for India," *Strategic Analysis* 23, no. 11 (2000): 1967.
75. Jagannath P. Panda, "From Look East to Act East: India as a Security Actor and Security Provider" (working paper, East Asia Institute, Institute for Defense Studies and Analyses, Seoul), 15.
76. Vibhanshu Shekhar, "Two Decades of India's Look East Policy," in *Rising India in the Changing Asia-Pacific: Strategies and Challenges,* eds. Ganganath Jha and Vibhanshu Shekhar (New Delhi: Pentagon Press 2012), 13.
77. Rajeswari Pillai Rajagopalan, "Minding the Gaps in India's Act East Policy," *The Diplomat,* September 17, 2018, https://thediplomat.com/2018/09/minding-the-gaps-in-indias-act-east-policy/.
78. Shekhar, "Two Decades of India's Look East Policy," 15.
79. Antony L. Smith, "ASEAN's Ninth Summit: What Did It Achieve?," *India Quarterly: A Journal of International Affairs* 60, no. 3 (July 2004), 20.
80. Faizal Yahya, "India and Southeast Asia: Revisited," *Contemporary Southeast Asia: A Journal of International and Strategic Affairs* 25, no. 1 (April 2003): 86.
81. Panda, "From Look East to Act East," 6–7.
82. Panda, "From Look East to Act East," 19.
83. Chakraborti, "India's Conviviality with Southeast Asia," 137.
84. "India's Look East–Act East Policy: A Bridge to the Asian Neighborhood" (Conference Proceedings, Symbiosis Institute of International Studies, Symbiosis International University, and the Ministry of External Affairs, Government of India, 2014), 32.
85. Jaffrelot, "India's Look East Policy," 48, 54–55.
86. "India's Look East–Act East Policy," 15.
87. Panda, "From Look East to Act East," 6–7.
88. Panda, "From Look East to Act East," 1.
89. Panda, "From Look East to Act East," 6–7.
90. Panda, "From Look East to Act East," 3.
91. Chakraborti, "India's Conviviality with Southeast Asia," 139.
92. A. Lakshmana Chetty, "India and East Asia Summit: A New Opportunity in Engaging East Asia," in *Rising India in the Changing Asia-Pacific: Strategies and Challenges,* eds. Ganganath Jha and Vibhanshu Shekhar (New Delhi: Pentagon Press, 2012), 94.
93. Stephen P. Cohen, *India: Emerging Power* (Washington, DC: Brookings Institution Press, 2001), 38; Chiriyankandath, "Realigning India," 200; Ganguly, "India's Foreign Policy," 42.
94. C. Raja Mohan, *Crossing the Rubicon: The Shaping of India's New Foreign Policy* (New Delhi: Viking Adult, 2003); Ganguly, "India's Foreign Policy"; Deepa Ollapally and Rajesh Rajagopalan, "The Pragmatic Challenge to Indian Foreign Policy," *Washington Quarterly* 34, no. 2 (Spring 2011): 145–162; Deepa M. Ollapally and Rajesh Rajagopalan, "India: Foreign Policy Perspectives of an Ambiguous Power," in *Worldviews of Aspiring Powers: Domestic Foreign Policy Debates in China, India, Iran, Japan, and Russia,* eds. Henry R. Nau and Deepa M. Ollapally (New York: Oxford University Press, 2012), 73–113.
95. Manjari Chatterjee Miller and Kate Sullivan de Estrada, "Pragmatism in Indian Foreign Policy: How Ideas Constrain Modi," *International Affairs* 93, no. 1 (January 2017): 27–49.
96. Miller and Sullivan de Estrada, "Pragmatism in Indian Foreign Policy," 30–31.
97. Rajesh Basrur, "Paradigm Shift: India during and after the Cold War," in *The Engagement of India: Strategies and Responses,* ed. Ian Hall (Washington, DC: Georgetown University Press, 2014), 169–183; Miller and Sullivan de Estrada, "Pragmatism in Indian Foreign Policy," 34–35.
98. 1991 Indian National Congress Manifesto, 72.

99. 1998 Indian National Congress Manifesto.

100. 1991 Bharatiya Janata Party Manifesto, 352.

101. 1996 Bharatiya Janata Party Manifesto, 271.

102. 1999 National Democratic Alliance, 133.

103. 1991 Bharatiya Janata Party Manifesto, 350.

104. William J. Barnds, "India and America at Odds," *International Affairs* 49, no. 3 (July 1973): 374.

105. Author interview, Ministry of External Affairs, New Delhi, India, June 21, 2012.

106. Jaswant Singh, "Against Nuclear Apartheid," *Foreign Affairs* 77 (September–October 1998): 41–52.

107. Shyam Saran, Conversation with author, June 18, 2012.

108. 1998 Bharatiya Janata Party Manifesto, 141.

109. Miller, "India's Authoritarian Streak."

110. Shyam Saran, Conversation with author, June 18, 2012.

111. Mohammed Ayoob, "Nuclear India and Indian-American Relations," *Orbis* 43, no. 1 (Winter 1999): 60.

112. Author interview, New Delhi, India, July 5, 2012.

113. Author interview, Ministry of External Affairs, New Delhi, India, July 3, 2012.

114. Author interview, Ministry of External Affairs, New Delhi, India, June 29, 2012.

115. Author interview, Ministry of External Affairs, June 19, 2012.

116. 1999 Indian National Congress Manifesto.

117. 1998 Bharatiya Janata Party Manifesto, 156, 193, 227.

118. Lt. General Chandra Shekhar, "Perception of the Role India Needs to Play in the Subcontinent, the Region and at the Global Level in the Short Term, Medium Term and the Long Term," 2nd session, in United Services Institution of India, USI National Security Series 2000 (New Delhi, India, 2001), 81, 95.

119. Commander C. Uday Bhaskar, "Observations by Discussants," 2nd session, in United Services Institution of India, USI National Security Series 2000 (New Delhi, India, 2001), 141.

120. Ambassador Arundhati Ghosh, "Open Discussion," 1st session, in United Services Institution of India, USI National Security Series 2000 (New Delhi, India, 2001), 75.

121. Ghosh, "Open Discussion," 1st session, 145.

122. J. N. Dixit, "Evolution of the Existing National Security Apparatus," 1st session, in United Services Institution of India, USI National Security Series 2000 (New Delhi, India, 2001), 51.

123. Rohit Lamba and Arvind Subramanian, "Dynamism with Incommensurate Development: The Distinctive Indian Model," *Journal of Economic Perspectives* 34, no. 1 (Winter 2020): 6.

124. C. V. Gopalakrishnan, "India and the US: The Widening Rift," in *Indian Foreign Policy: Agenda for the 21st Century*, vol. 2, eds. Lalit Mansingh et al. (New Delhi: Foreign Service Institute, 1997), 299.

125. Ayoob, "Nuclear India and Indian-American Relations," 63.

126. Author interview, March 2017.

127. Manjari Chatterjee Miller, "Foreign Policy à la Modi: India's Next Worldview," *Foreign Affairs* (April 2014).

128. Muni, "India and the Post-Cold War World," 865.

129. Malik, "India's Response to the Gulf Crisis," 854–855.

130. S. D. Muni and C. Raja Mohan, "Emerging Asia: India's Options," *International Studies* 41, no. 3 (August 2004): 318.

131. Chiriyankandath, "Realigning India," 208, 209.

132. Jaffrelot, "India's Look East Policy," 36, 46.

133. Jaffrelot, India's Look East Policy," 36.

134. Jaffrelot, India's Look East Policy," 56.

135. 1996 Bharatiya Janata Party Manifesto, 271.

136. Quoted in Jaffrelot, "India's Look East Policy," 61.

Chapter 7

1. Stacie Goddard, "When Right Makes Might: How Prussia Overturned the European Balance of Power," *International Security* 33, no. 3 (Winter 2009): 110–142.

2. Iver B. Neumann, "Russia as a Great Power: 1815–2007," *Journal of International Relations and Development* 11, no. 2 (2008): 128–151.

3. Peter Hall, "Policy Paradigms, Social Learning, and the State: The Case of Economic Policymaking in Britain," *Comparative Politics* 25, no. 3 (1993): 275–296; Martin B. Carstensen, "Ideas Are Not as Stable as Political Scientists Want Them to Be: A Theory of Incremental Ideational Change," *Political Studies* 59, no. 3 (2011): 596–615.

4. Mark Blyth, *Great Transformations: Economic Ideas and Institutional Change in the Twentieth Century* (Cambridge: Cambridge University Press, 2002), 11, 35.

5. Blyth, *Great Transformations*.

6. Jeffrey Checkel, *Ideas and International Political Change: Soviet/Russian Behavior and the End of the Cold War* (New Haven, CT: Yale University Press, 1997), 4; "Norms, Institutions and National Identity in Contemporary Europe," *International Studies Quarterly* 43, no. 1 (1999): 85.

7. Yinan He, *The Search for Reconciliation: Sino-Japanese and Polish-German Relations since World War II* (Cambridge: Cambridge University Press, 2009); Samuel Huntington, *The Clash of Civilizations and the Remaking of World Order* (New York: Touchstone, 2011); Charles A. Kupchan, *How Enemies Become Friends: The Sources of Stable Peace* (Princeton, NJ: Princeton University Press, 2010).

8. Kenneth B. Pyle, *Japan Rising: The Resurgence of Japanese Power and Purpose* (New York: Public Affairs, 2007), 132.

9. Pyle, *Japan Rising*, 266–268.

10. Xufeng Zhu and Lan Xue, "Think Tanks in Transitional China," *Public Administration and Development* 27, no. 5 (2007): 453.

11. Interviews in Beijing and Shanghai, June 2013.

12. Manjari Chatterjee Miller, "India's Authoritarian Streak," *Foreign Affairs* (May 2018). https://www.foreignaffairs.com/articles/india/2018-05-30/indias-authoritarian-streak

13. Courtney Fung, "Rhetorical Adaptation, Normative Resistance, and International Order-Making: China's Advancement of the Responsibility to Protect," *Cooperation and Conflict* (2019), 3.

14. Fareed Zakaria, "The New China Scare: Why America Shouldn't Panic about Its Latest Challenger," *Foreign Affairs* 99, no. 1 (January–February 2020): 57.

15. Angela Poh and Mingjiang Li, "A China in Transition: The Rhetoric and Substance of Chinese Foreign Policy under Xi Jinping," *Asian Security* 13, no. 2 (2017): 84.

16. Li, "China's Economic Power in Asia," 278.

17. Min Ye, *The Belt Road and Beyond: State-Mobilized Globalization in China: 1998–2018* (Cambridge: Cambridge University Press, 2020).

18. Yuen Yuen Ang, "Demystifying Belt and Road: The Struggle to Define 'China's Project of the Century,'" *Foreign Affairs* (May 2019). https://www.foreignaffairs.com/articles/china/2019-05-22/demystifying-belt-and-road

19. Weifeng Zhou and Mario Esteban, "Beyond Balancing: China's Approach Towards the Belt and Road Initiative," *Journal of Contemporary China* 27, no. 112 (2018): 487–501.

20. Quoted in Ang, "Demystifying Belt and Road." https://www.foreignaffairs.com/articles/china/2019-05-22/demystifying-belt-and-road

21. Ashley Tellis, "Narendra Modi and US-India Relations," *Carnegie Endowment for International Peace* (November 2018).

22. Richard Verma, Discussion on "The United States and India: Forging an Indispensable Democratic Partnership," Centre for Policy Research, January 16, 2018.

23. Rahul Roy-Chaudhury and Kate Sullivan de Estrada, "India, the Indo-Pacific and the Quad," *Survival* 60, no. 3 (May 2018): 181–194.

24. Ram Madhav, BJP National General Secretary, Raisina Dialogue, New Delhi, India 2018.

25. Conversations with experts, National Institute for Defense Studies, Ministry of Defense, Japan, March 2019.

26. Akhilesh Pillalamarri, "Why India Should 'Look West' Instead," *The Diplomat*, March 7, 2016, https://thediplomat.com/2016/03/why-india-should-look-west-instead/.

27. Rajeswari Pillai Rajagopalan, "Minding the Gaps in India's Act East Policy," *The Diplomat*, September 17, 2018. https://thediplomat.com/2018/09/minding-the-gaps-in-indias-act-east-policy/

28. Swaminathan S. A. Aiyar, "Twenty-five Years of Indian Economic Reform," *Policy Analysis* no. 803, Cato Institute (October 26, 2016).

29. Elizabeth Roche, "India Is the World's Third-Largest Military Spender," Live Mint, April 28, 2020. https://www.livemint.com/news/india/indian-among-top-three-military-spenders-in-2019-sipri-11587957496033.html.

30. Manjari Chatterjee Miller, "China, India and Their Differing Conceptions of International Order," in *The China-India Rivalry in the Globalization Era*, ed. T. V. Paul (Washington, DC: Georgetown University Press, 2018), 87.

31. A version of this case was published in Manjari Chatterjee Miller, "The Role of Beliefs in Identifying Rising Powers," *The Chinese Journal of International Politics* 9, no. 2 (2016): 211–238.

32. Jurgen Forster, "Germany's Twisted Road to War, 1919–1939," in *The Origins of the Second World War: An International Perspective*, ed. Frank McDonough (London: Continuum International, 2011), 114.

33. Richard Overy, "Mis-judging Hitler: A.J.P. Taylor and the Third Reich," in *The Origins of the Second World War Reconsidered: A.J.P. Taylor and the Historians*, ed. George Martel (London: Routledge, 1999), 94.

34. Paul von Hindenburg's Testimony before the Parliamentary Investigatory Committee ["The Stab in the Back"], November 18, 1919, http://germanhistorydocs.ghi-dc.org/sub_document.cfm?document_id=3829.

35. Jurgen Forster, "Germany's Twisted Road to War, 1919–1939," in *The Origins of the Second World War: An International Perspective*, ed. Frank McDonough (London: Continuum International, 2011), 112.

36. Detlev Peukert, *The Weimar Republic: The Crisis of Classical Moderntity* (New York: Hill and Wang, 1992), 205.

37. Peukert, *The Weimar Republic*, 227.

38. Peukert, *The Weimar Republic*, 278.

39. Thomas Christensen, "A Modern Tragedy? COVID-19 and US-China Relations," The Brookings Institution, May 2020.

INDEX

For the benefit of digital users, indexed terms that span two pages (e.g., 52–53) may, on occasion, appear on only one of those pages.